Brain Dancing ™

Work smarter, learn faster and manage information more effectively

Patrick T. Magee

Published by BrainDance.com Inc, Bellevue, Washington
Copyright © 1996-1998 by Patrick T. Magee
All rights reserved including the right of reproduction
in whole or in part in any form

First Edition: 1996 Revised Edition: 1998
Printed in the United States of America **on recycled paper**.
10 9 8 7 6 5 4 3

Library of Congress Catalog Card Number: 96-094115
ISBN: 0-9646260-2-0

Editor: Caitilin Walsh
Copy Editors: Nancy Boatwright, Susan Lee, Loretta MacAllister
and Jan Schott
Dancing brain art on cover: Zoë Sideri, Debby Reger and Melody
Grieves at Image East
Cover designed by Image East
Cover photo of the author by Yuen Lui

Many of the designations used by manufacturers and sellers to
distinguish their products are claimed as trademarks. Where
those designations appear in this book, and the publisher was
aware of a trademark claim, the designations have been printed in
initial caps or all caps.

Mind Maps® and Mind Mapping® are registered trademarks of
the Buzan Organisation. Used with permission.

NLP™ and Neuro Linguistic Programming constitute an
intellectual property that is owned by Richard Bandler. Used
with permission.

THE POWER OF THE DREAM
By: David Foster, Linda Thompson and Babyface
Copyright © 1996 by One Four Three Music, Sony/ATV Songs
LLC, ECAF Music, Warner-Tamerlane Publishing Corp., and
Brandon Brody Music. Peermusic Ltd. administers on behalf of
One Four Three Music. International Copyright Secured. All
rights on behalf of Brandon Brody Music admistered by Warner-
Tamerlane Publishing Corp. All rights on behalf of Sony/ATV
Songs LLC and ECAF Music administered by Sony/ATV Music
Publishing, 8 Music Square West, Nashville, TN 37203

(continued on page 288)

To Mom

ACKNOWLEDGEMENTS

I am deeply grateful to the servicemen and women who risked their lives to create the freedom that made it possible for me to do the work and research required to write this book. I suspect that the toughest day at the office pales in comparison to the average day on the front line.

Brain Dancing was written while standing on the shoulders of intellectual giants who've gone before me. I am especially grateful to Richard Bandler, Tony Buzan, Stephen Covey, Anthony Robbins, and Peter Senge.

I also feel a deep sense of gratitude to the following individuals:

★ Nancy, Mike, Deb, Vernon, Ruth, Teresa, Irv, and Cherye. This book wouldn't exist if it weren't for you.

★ The members of my Toastmasters club, Premier Presenters. Somehow we made miracles happen in those meetings, and my life will never be the same. Thank you for demonstrating a commitment to excellence that inspired me to do my best.

★ Caitilin Walsh, for tireless and dedicated editing assistance.

★ Nancy Boatwright, Susan Lee, Loretta MacAllister and Jan Schott, for their copy editing assistance.

★ Zoë, Deb, and Melody, for the creation of the dancing brain.

★ Sheryn Hara of Hara Publishing for guiding me through the publishing process.

★ Brenda Davis, for helping ensure the accuracy of my notes from her nutrition seminar.

★ Faith Hamlin at Sanford J. Greenburger Associates, for book design coaching early on that helped shape the overall flow of ideas in throughout the book.

★ Professors Sailors and Savey at Western Washington University, for their dedication to teaching excellence and wise council of such lasting value.

★ Professor Robert Killingstad at Everett Community College. You made learning calculus fun and helped ignite my interest in learning.

★ Judy Roberts at Mountlake Terrace High School. I remember feeling that you believed in my potential, even though you didn't have much to base it on, except that which can be seen only by the most caring eyes.

CONTENTS

The ⚜ symbol has been placed in the left margin anytime a Web site is mentioned. An updated list of these links is available at **http://BrainDance.com/refdoc.htm.**

Warning-Disclaimer

This book is designed to provide information in regard to the subject matter covered. If expert assistance is required in any of the areas discussed herein, the services of a competent professional should be sought.

It is not the purpose of this book to cover all of the information that is otherwise available on the topics herein, but to complement, amplify and supplement other texts.

Every effort has been made to make this book as complete and as accurate as possible. However, there **may be mistakes** both typographical and in content. Therefore, this text should be used only as a general guide and not as the ultimate source of information on the topics covered.

The purpose of this book is to educate. The author and BrainDance.com Inc shall have neither liability nor responsibility to any person or entity with respect to any loss or damage caused, or alleged to be caused, directly or indirectly by the information contained in this book.

If you do not wish to be bound by the above, please return this book to the publisher for a full refund: BrainDance.com Inc, 1075 Bellevue Way NE, #161, Bellevue, WA 98004.

FOREWORD

When I was a student both at school and university, I was continually haunted by a vague and mysterious awareness that somewhere within my brain was a far greater capacity to learn, think, remember, organise, and create than I was in any way manifesting. Information poured in at me from all angles, and as time marched on and my academic career progressed (if that is the right word, which it probably isn't!) my frustrations grew.

One day I resolved to solve my growing and multiplicitous problems by confronting them face on. With both trepidation and expectation I marched into my university library, and asked the librarian for a book on how to use my brain. To my surprise and consternation, she pointed me to the medical section of the library. I explained that I did not wish to operate on or take out my brain, but rather to use it! Her somewhat casual reply was: "Oh, sir, there are no books on that."

Stunned, I left the library and determined to research the field myself. The rest, as they say, is Memory and Creativity!

While researching for and writing *Use Both Sides of Your Brain* and *The Mind Map Book* one of my fervent wishes was to find other Warriors of the Mind, who were similarly impassioned with the idea of creating a Mentally Literate Planet, and who had both the desire and ability to pass on the precious information about the human brain and its limitless capacity.

By now you will already realise my delight in having met the mind of Patrick Magee.

Few have shown the commitment and dedication to the brain, to life-long learning, and to the all important and joyful task of educating brains about their brains. The very title of his first and significant book *Brain Dancing* gives you an immediate insight into the energetic, rhythmical, expressive and playful nature of Patrick's mind.

This book is the delight it promises to be, and will take you on magical mystery tours of the most amazing organ in the known universe—Your Brain.

Tony Buzan
England

PREFACE

An ad in the Wall Street Journal in the mid-eighties showed the head of a Greek statue. Its nose had either fallen off or been broken off. The caption read: "Sometimes when you keep your nose to the grindstone, all you get is a flat nose." In the words of Dr. W. Edwards Deming, "Let's not talk about working harder. Everyone is already working their hardest. Work smarter." I hope that *Brain Dancing* will help you work smarter by optimizing strategic mental processes performed frequently in your work. Most of us are doing the best we can. The key is to learn how to improve what our best is.

The term "Brain Dancing" originated out of my efforts to describe the mental synergy that results from mobilizing right-brain thought processes, especially in those individuals who habitually favor the left side. Right-brain creativity gives the left side more and better ideas to analyze. The disciplined structure of the left provides a framework for organizing these ideas and coming up with questions that stimulate additional creativity. The result is a dynamic loop between the two hemispheres—a "brain dance." As you will discover, this metaphor has evolved over the past five years to include additional oscillations that are not necessarily between left and right-brain thinking.

Working on technical projects for dozens of companies has been my laboratory for testing the usefulness of various self-development techniques. These projects include the Boeing 777, multi-million dollar real estate deals for Weyerhaeuser and over three years of software-related projects at Microsoft.

While my goal was to write a book to help readers build technical capacity, the resulting ideas seem to be useful in a wide variety of contexts. Rapid technological change has forced people in all industries to become lifelong learners.

Patrick Magee
Bellevue, Washington

Quotes on the Importance of Thought

"The greatest discovery of my generation is that a human being can alter his life by altering his attitude of mind." William James

"I know of no more encouraging fact than the unquestionable ability of man to elevate his life by conscious endeavor." Henry David Thoreau

"For as he thinketh in his heart, so he is." Proverbs 23:7

"A man is what he thinks about all day long." Ralph Waldo Emerson

"If you think you can or if you think you can't, you're right." Henry Ford

"Change your thoughts and you change your world...You are not what you think you are; but what you think, you are." Norman Vincent Peale

"The thought is the ancestor of the deed." Thomas Carlyle

"You become what you think about." Earl Nightingale

"Our life is what our thoughts make it." Marcus Aurelius Antoninus

"Sow a thought, reap an action, sow an action, reap a habit, sow a habit, reap a character, sow a character, reap a destiny." Anonymous

"Go thy way, and as thou hast believed, so be it done unto thee." Matthew 8:13

"All that man achieves is the direct result of his own thoughts...A man can only rise, conquer and achieve by lifting up his thoughts." James Allen

CHAPTER 1

MENTAL LEVERAGE:

NOT ALL THOUGHTS ARE CREATED EQUAL

Wise teachers throughout the ages have emphasized the important role that our thoughts play in our lives. Given the infinite diversity of thought types available to us, the question becomes, "Which thoughts?"

We can concentrate our attention or let it wander where it will; think about the past, present, or future; ask questions or think of answers; make minor decisions or those with significant impact.

We can direct our attention to our feelings, internal dialogue, or mental images; flavor any thought with a positive or negative attitude; electrify any notion with passionate caring; or diffuse it with ambivalence.

We can amplify our awareness with the energy and attention of synergistic dialogue; think about detailed issues or high level concepts; or vary our minds' brain waves between beta, alpha, theta, and delta.

All of these thought types can occur at various levels of conscious awareness and be organized within the context of heart frequencies or mind frequencies.

abcdefghijklmnopqrstuvwxyz

If the hundreds of thousands of words in the English language can be formed from an alphabet of just 26 letters, imagine how many different thought combinations there must be. How are we to coordinate the mental dance between these various thoughts?

Scale	Range of Thought
Focus	Daydreaming←——————→Concentrating
Awareness	Subconscious←——————→Conscious
Time Orientation	Past←——→Present←——→Future
Decision	Minor←——————→Destiny Shaping
Inquiry	Questions←——————→Answers
Modality	Kinesthetic←→Auditory←→Visual
Attitude	Positive←——————→Negative
Emotion	Passionate←——————→Ambivalent
Brain Wave Frequency	Delta←→Theta←→Alpha←→Beta
Dialogue	None←——————→Many People
Detail Level	General←——————→Specific
Metaphor	Orientation↔Ontological↔Structural
Frequency Center	Heart←——————→Mind

Figure 1.1 Thought Spectrum Chart

Using willpower, we can decide to think in various combinations, yet it takes energy and other mental resources to make decisions. The prospect of decisional stress increases as "infoglut" expands and our choices multiply. In his classic book, *The Effective Executive*, Peter Drucker writes that effective executives don't make a great many decisions. They concentrate on the important ones. They think through what is strategic and generic, and focus on making a few important decisions at the highest level of conceptual understanding.

The idea is to focus our decision-making engines on thoughts that are likely to give us the most bang for our mental buck. In his book, *The Fifth Discipline*, Peter Senge describes the concept of leverage using a trim tab metaphor. A large ocean liner would require several tons of force on the bow to make it change direction. Instead, a rudder is used to swing the back end of the ship around, which causes the ship to turn. However, the rudder on an ocean liner is so large that tremendous force is required to turn it as well. So the technique is applied again by placing a trim tab on the rudder. When the captain turns the wheel, it turns the trim tab, which turns the rudder, which turns the ship. In this way a small action, properly focused, can have a much greater impact on the overall system.

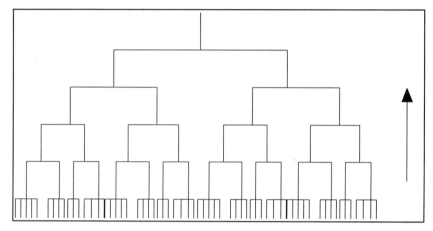

Figure 1.2 Layers of "Conceptual Understanding" at Which Decisions can be Made

Scattered throughout this book are strategies for achieving mental leverage. The overriding theme of *Brain Dancing* is to manage the mental dance between complementary opposite modes of thinking. Chapters 2 through 6 describe four pairs of complementary opposites:

Conscious ⟷ Subconscious

Individual Thought ⟷ Dialogue

Left-Brain Mode ⟷ Right-Brain Mode

Detailed Thought ⟷ High Level Thought

Chapters 2 and 3: The interplay between conscious and subconscious mental processes. The key to mobilizing our vast subconscious mental resources is learning to direct our brain with effective self-communication.

Chapter 4: Thinking alone vs. engaging in dialogue. Something special happens to our thinking whenever two or more people discuss an issue they care about.

Chapter 5: Right-brain vs. left-brain thinking modes. Each brain hemisphere is specialized and mental leverage can be obtained by overcoming the common tendency to favor one side.

Chapter 6: Detailed vs. "big picture" thinking. Just as information has structure, so do our thoughts. At the highest level, there are processes we use to perform key mental activities and they can be optimized.

These chapters lay down the foundation of the *Brain Dancing* strategy. Each chapter presents you with two types of information:

1. Underlying principles; and

2. What to do differently based on these distinctions.

Chapter 7 then describes how to apply all of these ideas toward learning software faster, which is becoming an increasingly high leverage use of our time. It takes energy both to learn and apply these ideas, so Chapter 8 discusses my favorite strategies for increasing personal energy. And lastly, Chapter 9 describes some lessons I've learned about maintaining balance while striving to mobilize untapped brain power.

Each chapter focuses on high level strategic decisions you can use to work smarter, learn faster and manage information more effectively.

WE ARE "IN-FORMATION"

Deepak Chopra points out that we are literally "information"—pronounced in-formation. Information has an impact on our decisions, decisions affect our actions, actions affect our habits, our habits determine our character, and our character determines our destiny. We are "information" because better information helps us make better decisions.

An extreme example of this occurred when I was twelve years old. My father died suddenly and unexpectedly of a heart attack at the age of 49. Dad died, at least in part, because we lacked the information that could have saved him: that his arteries were blocked by arteriosclerosis. This information could have led to some decisions that might have made a difference. I have no way of knowing for sure how much the "hand of fate" had to do with this.

Information literally shapes my life in countless ways: what and how I eat, when and how I exercise, how I carry myself, smile, think, communicate, etc. The most powerful information is "MetaInformation"—information that improves the processes we use to interact with information—which is what this book is about.

A WORD ON PERSONAL ECOLOGY

Your subconscious mind does a lot of remarkable things for you. One of its responsibilities is self-preservation—the ongoing process of keeping your life in balance. I refer to this process as "maintaining personal ecology." If a person learns a technique that increases their personal power and they do not have the discipline or strength of character to direct that increased power in disciplined ways, then using that technique could actually prove harmful to them. Fortunately, in most cases the subconscious mind has a clever way of filtering ideas out of our "awareness" when we are not ready for them.

For this reason, I encourage you to study the work of Stephen Covey (*The 7 Habits of Highly Effective People*[1]) and M. Scott Peck (*The Road Less Traveled*) in conjunction with this text. These books deal with the issue of character development and are written so brilliantly that it often astounds me to read them. They give specific instructions on how to build the mental and physical infrastructure that makes learning and applying *Brain Dancing* techniques "ecological." This gives your

---

[1] This book has now sold over fourteen million copies.

subconscious the go-ahead to open up your awareness to areas of new growth and learning.

> *"People who succeed in the computer industry tend to accumulate more and more power until they implode."*
>
> — *Esther Dyson*

You may already be beyond the need for these books, but I can tell you first hand that I've imploded a few times and it was not fun. Chapter 9 addresses this issue in depth.

POWERFUL QUESTIONS

> *"A powerful question can be vastly more useful than any answer."*
>
> — *Peter Senge*

It has been said that when one is truly ready for something, it will put in its appearance. This is similar to the Chinese proverb, "When a student is ready, a teacher appears." Ever wonder what you can do to increase the rate at which you are ready for new balanced growth and learning? This question is addressed in Chapter 2. While it is the most theoretical chapter in the book, it establishes the foundation for everything that follows.

CHAPTER 2

The Solutions Approach to Capacity Enhancement

"Capacities clamor to be used and cease their clamor only when they are well used."

— *Abraham Maslow*

In the movie *Apollo 13*, the character Jim Lovell states, "It wasn't a miracle that we went to the moon. We just decided to go." This decision created a context in which information about going to the moon could be understood and applied, a context that helped NASA identify which problems they had to solve in order to get to the moon and back. It also helped them distinguish between essential information and the merely interesting.

Our interaction with information is context driven.

Woven into this experience is a basic truth with broad application. If you want to use more of your brain, if you want to increase your understanding of something, then give yourself a reason to do so—a reason such as solving a problem or teaching others a better way of doing something. The following chapters present you with hundreds of ideas. Your understanding of these ideas will depend on the context you create in which to apply them.

Anthony Robbins teaches that clarity is power, and Stephen Covey encourages us to begin activities with the end in mind. This is great advice for the following reason:

Having a clear idea about where you want to end up forms the basis for communicating direction to your subconscious mind, which is the seat of action and the ultimate information filter.

If you study nature, you will notice that the amazing diversity of life on Earth is made possible by each species adapting itself to a particular niche in an ecosystem. Each species specializes in solving a particular problem upon which its life depends. Building such specialized capacity for effective action is also essential for success in business, and is the third key issue explored in this chapter.

"We operate in an economy that rewards specialization."

— Bill Gates

Solving problems builds capacity for effective action. When we change what we can do, we change what we notice and what we aspire to do. "When your only tool is a hammer, everything starts to look like a nail," wrote Abraham Maslow. When you expand your tool set of effective problem-solving capacities, you expand the scope and nature of problems that come into your awareness.

"People don't see the world as it is. They see it as they are."

— Stephen R. Covey

These are the basic ideas discussed in this chapter, and they form the foundation for the rest of the book.

THE ULTIMATE INFORMATION FILTER

We are immersed in a vast sea of information. We survive by directing our awareness to a small fraction of the total information available to us at any given moment. How do we determine which fraction to notice? Subconsciously. The subconscious mind is the ultimate information filter. Have you ever purchased a new car, and then begun to notice cars like it everywhere you went? When this happened, were you consciously looking for these cars, or did you just seem to notice them unexpectedly? That was your subconscious directing your awareness to information it thought you wanted to know based on recent events.

The following diagram shows up frequently in my self-development research:

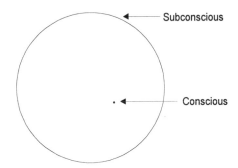

Figure 2.1 Relative mental capacities

The large circle supposedly represents the mental capacity of the subconscious mind, and the small dot the relative capacity of the conscious mind. The diagram is actually wrong because the dot representing the conscious mind is far too big.

"The conscious mind is brilliant and the unconscious mind is a hell of a lot smarter."

— *Milton Erickson*

I've never seen any proof that this diagram is true. This is probably because we are talking about something intangible. Just as there are two aspects to computers: hardware and software, there are two aspects to our thinking: brain and mind. The subconscious mind is part of the mental software that runs our brain. You can't point to it, but there are many common experiences, like the "new car" example mentioned earlier, that validate its role in our lives. Have you ever woken up in the middle of the night and noticed that your mind was cranking away on a work-related issue? This happened because the subconscious mind doesn't rest while we sleep: it continues to process or incubate issues it thinks we want resolved.

Why do Olympic athletes visualize their performances? They do it because:

The subconscious mind is the seat of action.

Subconscious mental processes govern every action we take. At this point in my seminars, I start juggling three tennis balls. While I consciously decide to juggle, subconscious mental processes govern the movement of my arms and hands. Timing, flow of blood and muscle contractions are all being regulated outside of conscious awareness. At the neuro-physiological level, every action is amazingly complex. How can you apply this distinction?

Use the conscious mind to define and clarify the target ("What") and the subconscious mind to guide your actions in order hit the target or carry out the action ("How").

I once heard a story of a photographer who understood this instinctively. He wanted to take a small number of photographs that depicted the essence of an unusual Indian horse race. Upon arriving at the scene, rather than just starting to take pictures, he spent a day surveying the situation. That evening, he listed the journalistic points he wanted to make, and the images that must appear in the pictures to accurately represent this culture. Then he imagined potential photographs that would contain as many of these elements as possible. He wanted to take photos that would do double or triple-duty, so that the reader would see a rather small set of photos that said it all. Over the next few days, he began taking photographs while keeping these images in his mind. While doing this, he remained completely open to whatever he might find along the way, including new dimensions to the story he'd missed on the first day. He didn't get all of the points or all of the photographs, but he got a lot of them. He also took and used photographs that he hadn't imagined.

By investing the time up front imagining photographs that would address multiple aspects of the culture, he had consciously primed his subconscious mind to be on the lookout for specific combinations of circumstances, and his actions were directed accordingly.

Another simple example occurred while visiting the Oregon Coast last summer. A friend and I were shooting a slingshot at a leaf on an embankment. After about ten tries each, I decided to try one of my *Brain Dancing* strategies. So I closed my eyes and visualized successfully hitting the leaf. I then opened my eyes, picked up a rock, and with almost no conscious effort, hit the leaf on the first try. "Oh wise master," my friend uttered.

In both examples, visualization (i.e., imagination) was used to send a directional message to the subconscious information filtering and action guidance mechanisms.

I call the process of directing the subconscious "self-communicating." You know you are self-communicating effectively when your actions are moving you closer to your desired outcome. Effective visualization produces effective action.

As you will read in the next chapter, visualization is just one of the strategies you can use to communicate direction to your subconscious.

How can we apply this towards working smarter? Any time you are entering an information-rich environment or a situation where you will be called upon to make many decisions, you can invest time up front clarifying your desired outcome. For example:

- Before going into a meeting, clarify exactly how you want the meeting to end up. Ask yourself, "When I walk out of this meeting, how will I know it was a success?"
- Before going grocery shopping, visualize you and your family experiencing vibrant health and energy.
- Before exercising, imagine how you want to look and feel as a result of this activity.
- Before visiting a bookstore, review your goals so your subconscious will have some basis for filtering information into your awareness and for directing you to the books and pages likely to help you reach those goals.

These up-front investments send directional messages to your subconscious. Your actions, decisions, and awareness of information will be directed accordingly.

When considering a potential project, the most important question I ask the project organizer is:

> At the end of this project, how will you
> know that I did an outstanding job?

I am asking for the evidence procedure that this person will use to evaluate my performance. It tells me how clearly the boundary conditions for the project have been determined. Without this clarity, I may end up with a "creeping request," where I am unable to clearly communicate direction to my subconscious because the direction is constantly changing. The situation is analogous to having your manager standing over your bowling lane blocking your view with a sheet. You throw the ball, and your manager tells you how many pins you knocked down. More importantly, if the project outcome has not been clearly defined, you don't even know which lane to use.

One of the best ways to evolve a clear definition of a project outcome is to write a specification document (or "spec"). Chapter 4 of *Microsoft Secrets*, by M. Cusumano and R. Selby, has a great explanation of how Microsoft writes specs to help them manage complex software development projects. As Microsoft manager Chris Peters puts it, "Remember, the problem is not lack of ideas; the problem is too many ideas. So what do you do to give you the discipline to find the essential ideas?" I believe one of the key things you do is create a well-written spec to help keep you and the team on track.

LESS THAN 10% OF OUR BRAIN?

What if you learned your car engine was running at less than 10% of its potential efficiency, and that this was probably true of most cars across the nation? Wouldn't that be a tragic waste?

Our willingness to act on this situation would likely depend on how much it would cost to correct. What if I told you that all it would take to double this percentage was some information about how to pop the hood and turn a lever? The great thing about information is that it doesn't get used up when one person applies it!

Now, it is often said that most people use less than 10% of their brainpower. Even if this statement were only partially true, this untapped brainpower would represent one of our nation's greatest underutilized resources. If we are going to make this statement a part of our culture, it makes sense to at least clarify exactly what is meant by it.

When you get home after a long day at the office, it's a tough pill to swallow that you used less than 10% of your brain. If there were any truth to this claim, clearly it wouldn't be resolved by working longer hours or rushing around in a panic all day: that would be working harder.

What is needed is information about how our brain works that will help us *work smarter.*

Do you think Bill Gates uses less than 10% of his brain? With his Microsoft stock now worth over $40 billion, he's obviously doing something right. But if he is using so much of his brain, why did he run out of gas in his ski boat out on Lake Washington and have to be towed in by my friends? Why did he forget to put oil in his Mercedes and burn up the engine?

The answer is that he chose to direct his attention to other matters he felt were more important. By using more brainpower, I'm not suggesting that it is possible to do every possible thing at any given moment.

If you are working on a computer and need to send someone e-mail, it won't do you much good to run the software that accesses your CD-ROM drive and plays multimedia. At any given point there are hundreds of things you can do with your computer. How you use its capabilities is determined by your objectives.

Software is to the computer what the mind is to our brain. The mental software we choose to run, the portion of our brain we choose to utilize, is determined by what we are trying to accomplish.

Would Microsoft be where it is today if Gates had the tendency to stand up in the middle of executive meetings and say things like, "Darn, I just realized that I'm not using the part of my brain that is accessed when I put oil in my car. Excuse me for a moment while I go put some in?"

"Focused action beats brilliance any day."

— Art Turock

Every moment offers virtually infinite choices about how we think and what we do. The goal should not be to use 100% of our brain, but to use our brain in a way that allows us to achieve our objectives as effectively and efficiently as possible.

Just as we don't use every feature of a computer at any given moment, it is unlikely that any single activity will allow us to use 100% of our brain. We should, however, pursue non-work activities that develop latent mental resources. This will help us respond more flexibly and ably to work challenges when they arise. This is why so many great programmers are also musicians. Left-brain programming is enriched with more input from the creative right brain, which is mobilized by developing musical skills.

USE PROJECTS TO BUILD PROBLEM-SOLVING CAPACITY

In Peter Senge's words, "First and foremost, the bedrock of what draws us into action is that we deeply care." Chapter 9 offers guidelines for "detecting" what you deeply care about. Placing this material in the last chapter allowed me to show how techniques and concepts described throughout the book can be applied during mission formulation and goal setting.

As you begin to clarify your mission—what you deeply care about—the next step is to identify the fundamental problem-solving capacities required to pursue this mission, and to take on projects that will help you develop these capacities for effective action.

What exactly is a project? I use the term to describe a chunk of work with a clear ending. It may be creating a new product, implementing a new system or creating a spreadsheet to help optimize a business process. It could be a sales project, a research project or a project to raise money for a charitable cause.

When you commit to a project, problems arise. In solving these problems you accomplish three things:

- you acquire specialized knowledge about solving these types of problems
- you develop specialized skills useful in solving these types of problems
- you increase your self-confidence in your ability to solve these types of problems

These three factors combine to increase your capacity to complete similar projects. My experience suggests that nature abhors unused capacity. This increased capacity tends to draw into your awareness opportunities to solve similar problems of increasing complexity. In this way, the problems you choose to solve will take you in a direction that can be destiny-shaping. In the words of Nobel Prize laureate Albert Szent-Gyorgyi:

"Ability brings with it the need to use that ability."

What a person desires to do is influenced by their existing capacity. This perspective was inspired by Ralph Waldo Emerson's statement: "There is nothing capricious in nature, and the implanting of a desire indicates that its gratification is in the constitution of the creature who feels it." A person is not likely to have a burning desire to do something beyond their ability. If, through the completion of a series of projects of increasing complexity, you enhance your capacity in a certain area, you can indirectly impact what you desire.

"Problems call forth our courage and our wisdom; indeed, they create our courage and our wisdom. It is only because of problems that we grow mentally or spiritually. When we desire to encourage the growth of the human spirit, we challenge and encourage the human capacity to solve problems."

— M. Scott Peck, M.D.

RIVER OF INCREASING SWIFTNESS

I started my career in public accounting. One day it dawned on me that the Government could come along at any moment and pull the rug out from under all my hard work. All they had to do was totally rearrange the tax laws that I was trying so hard to master. Switching fields to computer programming has not exactly been a safe haven from change. Beginning in 1982, I invested twelve months learning to program in COBOL and haven't used COBOL since. During the mid-80's I became proficient in four other DOS-based programming languages. I haven't used any of these languages for over three years. Over the last four years I've learned three Windows-based programming languages, any one of which is larger in scope than the four DOS-based languages combined! To top it off, I'm now beginning to learn a programming technology whose scope easily exceeds the material in the previous three Windows programming languages combined.

From my perspective, information is flowing through society like a river of increasing swiftness. It is becoming less important to be able to master the complete content of this river at any given moment, and more important to be able to interact with this river as it relates to your current project. In his book, *Unlimited Wealth*, Paul Zane Pilzer writes, "People who learn things the fastest will do much better than those who learn things the best." In an environment of rapid change, the ability to learn quickly may be the ultimate competitive advantage. Interacting with this "information river" means being able to quickly locate and use information related to completing your current project. Using your subconscious information filtering capacity is a great strategy for doing this.

> *"Two things seemed pretty apparent to me. One was, that in order to be a [Mississippi River] pilot a man had got to learn more than any one man ought to be allowed to know; and the other was, that he must learn it all over again in a different way every 24 hours."*
>
> — *Mark Twain*

DAILY SAW SHARPENING

If you make projects your only source of specialized knowledge, you risk limiting your career substantially.

The complementary opposite of highly-focused project learning is to invest at least one hour per day doing general non-project research in your field of study. When working on a project, pay particular attention to information related to that project as discussed above. During this hour, however, I suggest that you forget about the project and study topics related to your field that interest you. I am often amazed at how the two eventually overlap—what I learn while doing non-project research often plays a significant role in future projects.

"Specialized knowledge is the basis of all value added."

— *Tom Peters*

Sticking to this one hour a day (or some other fixed time limit) is critical for this non-project research. In this case, there is no customer with a clearly defined need to serve as a feedback loop on your progress. It is thus easy to lose track of time. You work on projects until they have been completed; you do non-project research only until the time limit is up.

I agree with Earl Nightingale's statement that if you consistently devote one hour per day accumulating specialized knowledge in your field, in five years, you will be a recognized leader in your field. Knowledge compounds much like interest in a savings account. Granted, some of that knowledge may become obsolete. Using a project orientation will help keep you grounded in what is useful.

The greatest wisdom not applied to action and behavior is meaningless data.

— *Peter Drucker*

CATCHING A TECHNOLOGY WAVE—GETTING STARTED

Acquiring specialized capacity is a Catch-22. Getting the opportunity to work on projects is where most specialized capacity is acquired. Yet it is often difficult to get a company to hire you for such projects until after you've acquired related experience. With the pace of technological change accelerating, an increasing number of opportunities are being created to solve problems that have never been solved before. Additionally, I agree with Paul Zane Pilzer in *Unlimited Wealth* when he writes that the technology gap—the difference between the best technology available and that actually in use—is greater today than at any time in our history.

Technology can be thought of as simply a better way of doing something. It doesn't have to involve electronics. Leverage existing industry expertise to create opportunities for applying new technologies within your current field. Bridging such technology gaps often requires an increase in your information metabolism, which is what this book is all about.

If possible, get a technical degree at the best learning institution available to you. Use it as a stepping-stone into a position at an established company in order to learn the ropes of that industry. Here are some additional things to consider for people already in the workforce:

1) "The value of information is in direct proportion to the number of people who know it," according to Harvey McKay, author of *How to Swim With the Sharks Without Getting Eaten Alive*. If you start out to learn a new technology and it proves difficult, consider adopting the attitude that this is a good sign. The rewards are likely to be higher because these barriers will keep out the weak of heart.

2) Align new projects with existing specialized capacity. Take on projects that require a combination of what you already know and new technology. Ask yourself how you can "informationalize" (i.e., enhance by incorporating information) traditional products and services, thereby delivering value in new ways. Technology is moving so rapidly that it is often difficult for schools to keep up to date. Incrementally transitioning yourself into new fields allows you to

use this cutting edge factor to your advantage. By choosing projects in new areas that leverage off existing skills and knowledge, you reduce the risk of biting off more than you can chew.

3) The Internet is expanding the opportunities for distance learning. Fierce competition has resulted in a flood of new Internet technologies that can be learned by anyone with access to the Web.

4) Participate in on-line communities and solve the problems people bring up there. CompuServe forums, Internet newsgroups and mailing lists provide such opportunities.

5) Build products that demonstrate what you know. I've always liked the saying: "When your work speaks for itself, don't interrupt." I used this approach in 1984 and was hired by Paul Brainerd to create the financial model he used in Aldus Corporation's early business plans as a result. After creating a cash flow spreadsheet using Lotus 1-2-3 that was fairly advanced at the time, I set up a PC on a table at the local IBM PC users group meeting and Paul just happened to walk by.

6) Start or participate in trade associations such as user groups, or create some other opportunity to teach what you want to master. I've started or helped start several software users groups. The "authority figure" approach works if you break things down into manageable chunks. Give presentations on narrow aspects of the field until you've covered enough of them to build some momentum with the technology. While this may sound contradictory, my experience has been that something special happens to our awareness when we definitely commit to a project or presentation. When you give yourself a reason to understand the material, it will make itself available to you.

7) Anticipate technology shifts. Attend COMDEX/Fall or the Consumer Electronics Show to see what is

coming. Almost every company is underutilizing new Internet/Intranet technologies in part because they are evolving so rapidly.

8) Form alliances with other businesses or individuals and combine areas of specialization to leapfrog into new areas. This might be tougher to pull off on an individual basis, yet there are possibilities here for determined people willing to be creative.

"Nobody has a money problem. Only an idea problem."

— *Robert Schuller*

NOT TO THINK UNLESS WE HAVE TO?

After investing 25 years writing *The Story of Civilization*, Will Durant writes: "Not to think unless we have to—there is much to be said for this as the summation of wisdom."

Does "Not to think" translate into, "Not to learn," "Not to decide," "Not to dream," "Not to explore," "Not to help someone," "Not *to go to the moon*," etc. unless we have to? Necessity is not only the mother of invention, it is often the mother of personal growth as well.

This is why competition can be such a powerful force for good. As Anthony Robbins points out in his *PowerTalk!* interview with Stephen Covey[1], the word "compete" comes from Latin roots meaning to "conspire together." From a broader perspective, competition is cooperation: it is people cooperating to help each other push themselves to new heights because they "have to."

How many organizations have you observed that don't discover new ways to cut costs, improve a product or refine a service until they "have to?" The U.S. auto industry is vastly more advanced today because Japanese auto makers came along and forced them to improve.

---

[1] *PowerTalk!*, Volume 20. This interview is a great overview of Covey's principles. Call RRI at (800) 898-8669.

The comet Hale-Bopp[2], twinkling in the twilight as I write, is a clear reminder that we may someday be called to think and act in ways only possible if we think and act now to prepare ourselves. Should one of the billions of comets orbiting our solar system beyond Pluto ever happen to target Earth, it could take the best of all of us to prevent it from blasting into our planet.

I have a poster that reads, "Only as far as we seek can we go...Only as much as we dream can we become." Yet dreams open up new possibilities often beyond those of the original dream. What dreams and aspirations are worthy of proactive thought? Which directions will best prepare us for the challenges ahead?

At a time of abundant knowledge and potential for contribution, *Brain Dancing* is a resource for lifelong learners in search of a better way of doing something they deeply care about. Committing to do a project related to

---

[2] Photo by "Zoë" Vortex Creations, 702-236-1750, zoevortex1@hotmail.com, www.geocities.com/~zoesvortex.

your mission stretches your capacity by putting you in a position where you "have to."

"You are much bigger, brighter, stronger, healthier; you've got more energy and more power than you are ever going to discover until you have to."

— *Anthony Robbins*

CONCLUSION

Conscious ⟷ **Subconscious**

Individual Thought ⟷ Dialogue

Left-Brain Mode ⟷ Right-Brain Mode

Detailed Thought ⟷ High Level Thought

This chapter introduced the first major pair of complementary modes of thinking—managing the interplay between conscious and subconscious thought. Learning and growth begins when we give ourselves a reason to do so. After consciously selecting a goal or project consistent with your mission, invest time, thought and energy clarifying the outcome. Then consciously self-communicate that specific outcome to your subconscious information-filtering action-guidance mechanisms, which leads us to Chapter 3.

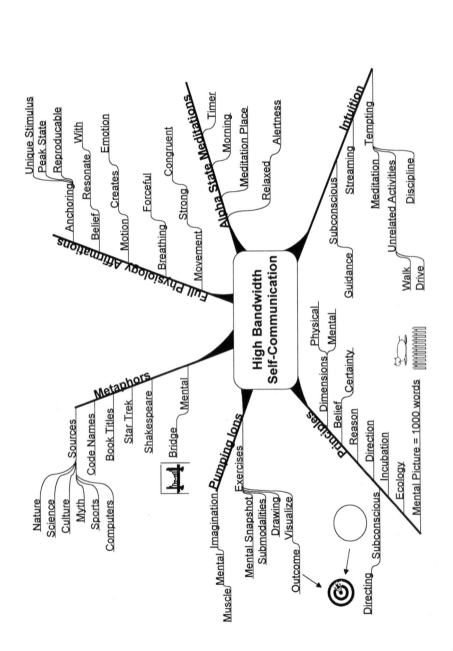

High Bandwidth Self-Communication

Full Physiology Affirmations
- Unique Stimulus
- Peak State
- Reproducable
- Anchoring
  - Resonate — With
  - Belief
  - Creates — Emotion
  - Motion
  - Breathing — Forceful
    - Congruent
    - Strong
  - Movement

Alpha State Meditations
- Timer
- Morning
- Meditation Place
- Relaxed
- Alertness

Intuition
- Subconscious
- Streaming
- Guidance
- Tempting
  - Meditation
  - Unrelated Activities
    - Walk
    - Drive
  - Discipline

Metaphors
- Sources
  - Nature
  - Science
  - Culture
  - Myth
  - Sports
  - Computers
- Code Names
- Book Titles
- Star Trek
- Shakespeare
- Bridge — Mental

Pumping Ions
- Muscle Mental
- Imagination
- Exercises
  - Mental Snapshot
  - Submodalities
  - Drawing
  - Visualize — Outcome
- Directing — Subconscious

Principles
- Dimensions — Physical
  - Mental
- Belief — Certainty
- Reason
- Direction
- Incubation
- Ecology
- Mental Picture = 1000 words

CHAPTER 3

HIGH BANDWIDTH
SELF-COMMUNICATION

"It's not what the vision is, it's what the vision does."

— *Alan Kay, The Walt Disney Company*

Your subconscious is an obedient and able servant once it knows which direction you want to go. Self-communication is the process of directing your subconscious mind. You know you are self-communicating effectively when your actions are moving you closer to your desired outcome.

"High bandwidth" describes communication in which a large volume of information is transferred very rapidly. Some methods of self-communicating are far more effective than others. After reviewing the basic principles involved, the following four strategies will be explained:

1) Visualization. Four exercises are presented for developing your imagination (mental snapshot, submodality, drawing, and ten-minute visualization).

2) Using metaphors to communicate meaning both to others and to your subconscious at higher bandwidths.

3) Full physiology affirmations that involve thinking about your desired outcome at moments when you have developed powerful physiologies.

4) Employing alpha brain waves by thinking about your desired outcome in a state of relaxed alertness.

Self-communication is a two-way street. The above strategies sow the seeds, yet you must also nurture the ability to "tune-in" to intuitive guidance as it blossoms from your subconscious. Thus I conclude the chapter with a brief discussion of intuition.

PRINCIPLES

The principles of self-communication are:

1) There are two dimensions to self-communication: physical and mental.

2) When you truly believe in the power of your subconscious, you won't hesitate to use high bandwidth self-communication techniques daily. You may even look forward to it.

3) Give yourself a reason to use the untapped mental capacity of your subconscious.

4) Your mind cannot focus on the opposite of an idea.

5) Your subconscious continues to process or "incubate" issues even when you are not consciously thinking about them.

6) The effectiveness of your self-communication is diminished to the extent it contradicts existing beliefs or behavior patterns that your subconscious believes are important to you. Your desired direction must be personally ecological.

7) A picture in your mind is worth a thousand words as well.

PRINCIPLE #1:
THE TWO DIMENSIONS OF SELF-COMMUNICATION

The way you use your physiology has a direct impact on how you feel. To quote William James: "Action seems to follow feeling, but really action and feeling go together; and by regulating the action, which is under the more direct control of the will, we can indirectly regulate the feeling, which is not."

In this sense, your physiology is a key part of self-communication. The section on affirmations later in this chapter describes how to combine this distinction with "mental" forms of self-communication for increased effectiveness. One of the basic challenges of self-communication is helping the subconscious cut through all the mental noise. If our subconscious mind didn't have some means of distinguishing true directional communication from mental chit-chat, our actions might be somewhat erratic. When you combine congruent physiology with emotionally charged affirmations, it says to your subconscious, "Pay attention!"

PRINCIPLE #2:
BELIEVE IN THE POWER OF YOUR SUBCONSCIOUS

If you truly believe in the awesome potential of directing your subconscious, you wouldn't hesitate to apply self-communication techniques such as visualization. There is so much conclusive evidence that it is no longer a question of *if* they work, it is only a question of *when*. Self-communication works when you have figured out how to do the right processes in your mind.

We do not have the ability to transfer mental software from one brain to another in the same way we transfer computer software today. You can't hand someone a disk and say, "Here, load this into your brain and give it a try." Consequently, one of the best ways to tell if you are truly running effective mental software is by the results you are getting. If, at the end of a day, week, or month, you can look back on your actions and see them taking you in the direction you want to go, then to that extent, you are self-communicating effectively.

When you consider how many decisions went into the writing of *Brain Dancing*, you'll understand why I believe that the quality of this book is directly proportionate to the degree to which I successfully communicated my desired outcome to my subconscious. In Alan Kay's words, "It's not what the vision is, it's what the vision does."

PRINCIPLE #3:
GIVE YOURSELF A REASON TO USE YOUR SUBCONSCIOUS

Your subconscious is a mental power reserve and the valve that opens the channel is this: you must give yourself a reason to use it. In his book, *The Power of Your Subconscious Mind*, Dr. Joseph Murphy tells the story of a young man who asked Socrates how he could obtain wisdom. Socrates took the lad to a river, pushed the boy's head under the water, and held it there until the boy was gasping for air. He then relaxed and released his head. When the boy regained his composure, he asked him what he desired most while under water.

"I wanted air," said the young man.

Socrates replied, "When you want wisdom as much as you wanted air when you were immersed in the water, you will receive it."

Having a problem to solve, somebody to help, something to create or something to teach to another—and wanting to do it as badly as that young man wanted air—that's what opens the gates to your subconscious mental power.

PRINCIPLE #4:
YOUR MIND CANNOT FOCUS ON THE OPPOSITE OF AN IDEA

It is more helpful to say to someone, "Drive safely" than to say, "Don't crash." The mind moves in directions. Telling your mind where you want to go is more precise than telling it where not to go. There is also the argument that each time you think a thought you increase the likelihood of bringing it into existence. In order to "not" think of something, you have to first think of the thing that you're not supposed to think about.

Wayne Dyer offers a corollary to this: "Everything you are for strengthens you, and everything you are against weakens you." Invest your mental energy into things you want to encourage. That gives you two choices: positive mental energy and neutral (i.e., no mental energy).

"What you pay attention to determines what you get. What you pay attention to determines what you miss."

— *Anonymous*

PRINCIPLE #5:
INCUBATION

As mentioned in Chapter 2, it is a common experience to wake in the middle of the night and notice that your mind is "processing" a work-related issue. This is what I refer to as "incubation." The subconscious mind seems to run on automatic pilot while we are off doing other things. My experience suggests that incubation occurs at a variety of levels on a variety of issues over time. I have no way of knowing whether my subconscious is working on multiple issues simultaneously or just doing a little here and there.

Many times I have listened to an educational audiotape series several times and felt overwhelmed by the material. Listening to the same tapes one year later often reveals that I've actually been applying some of the things that seemed confusing to me a year ago. In the words of William James, "We learn to swim in winter and skate in summer."

In his excellent book, *The Intuitive Edge*, Philip Goldberg writes that this "nonconscious synthesis" occurs while we are sleeping, walking in nature or doing our chores. In his words, "The factory of the mind continues to work while the manager is out, assembling diverse raw materials and putting them together in unusual ways to create new products."

You can apply this distinction any time you anticipate a need to learn a new skill or topic for a project. Get your subconscious working in this new area as soon as possible. In some cases, you can begin this incubation process by taking just five minutes twice a week to do a high level scan of the material—at least until your schedule permits more in-depth study.

When learning a new skill, begin doing the activity a couple of times a week for just five minutes. For example, in anticipation of the need to create audiotapes of this book, I did a couple of five-minute recording sessions at home using an inexpensive portable tape recorder. I did this several weeks in advance of actually needing to use the skill to get my mind/body accustomed to going through this new set of actions.

Incubation is one reason why it is often so helpful to finish each day by reviewing priorities for the next. Prime your mind for action when you arrive the next morning. In her superb autobiography, Mary Kay Ash (of Mary Kay Cosmetics) writes that one key to her success has been her habit of taking a few moments at the end of each day to write down the six most important things she must accomplish the following day.

If writing a list doesn't work for you, consider using a more right-brained approach, such as drawing a Mind Map (discussed in Chapter 5) as you visualize the following day going perfectly.

PRINCIPLE #6:
PERSONAL ECOLOGY

In their book, *Reframing*, Richard Bandler and John Grinder describe a technique called the "six-step reframe." This is a process where another person helps you establish a direct communication channel with your subconscious for the purpose of changing an unwanted behavior pattern. Your subconscious mind is asked to come up with three alternative behavior patterns. The final step involves asking your subconscious if there is any "part" that objects to any of the three new alternatives.

One time a friend was guiding me through a six-step reframe to help me stop picking at my fingernails. When she asked me the above question as an "ecology check," my entire body started trembling and I had no idea why! This experience made it absolutely clear how important it is that our "self-communication" not contradict existing beliefs or behavior patterns our subconscious believes are important to us.

PRINCIPLE #7:

A PICTURE IN YOUR MIND IS WORTH A THOUSAND WORDS AS WELL

Take a moment and "think" the following sentence:

"The dog jumped over the fence."

Now think the following picture:

Which thought was more efficient? To the degree that you can think the above picture almost instantaneously, you understand why mental pictures allow us to think at higher bandwidths. Most people can hold between five and nine ideas in their mind simultaneously. If pictures can be enriched to contain many objects or symbols, and each symbol can represent multiple ideas, then this distinction can be used to break this idea limitation.

Could Einstein have developed his theory of relativity without the ability to visualize himself hitching a ride on a beam of light emanating from the face of the clock? Could Nikola Tesla have invented his electrical generators without the ability to create mental images of the devices and run them for hours in his mind to see if they would work? I believe the ability to think in pictures played a key role in both cases and probably countless other inventions.

As Richard Bandler points out, a major benefit of the visual system is that you can easily see two different pictures simultaneously. It's much harder to pay attention to two voices at once.

The remainder of this chapter discusses what you can do differently to align your actions with the above principles.

PUMPING IONS: DEVELOPING YOUR VISUALIZATION MUSCLE

Developing the ability to create and manipulate images in our mind offers more potential for mental leverage than anything else I've studied. In Albert Einstein's words, "Imagination is more important than knowledge." By calling our imagination a visualization muscle, I hope to emphasize the fact that this aspect of our mind can be developed through exercise and practice.

Dharma Singh Khalsa, M.D., has just published a landmark book called, Brain Longevity *(www.brain-longevity.com)*. In it he describes research performed by the doctor who was chosen to dissect and study Einstein's brain. When compared to the brains of intellectually average men who had died near the same age (76), the only difference found was an enhanced Area 39, which researchers believe is the most highly evolved site in the brain. "When people have lesions in Area 39, they have great difficulty with abstract imagery, memory, attention and self-awareness," writes Dr. Khalsa. Einstein had an abundance of glial cells in Area 39, which serve as 'housekeeping' cells, as opposed to a measurable excess of 'thinking' cells. The job of the glial cell is to support the metabolism of the thinking neurons. The presence of these extra glial cells is what had enlarged Einstein's Area 39. Other experiments were performed that validated the hypothesis that Einstein had an enlarged Area 39 because he was in effect a "mental athlete" who had "trained hard" all his life. One of the ways he did this was via the extensive use of his imagination.

In addition to enhancing your creativity, developing this mental muscle can improve your memory, reading effectiveness and the speed at which you can think. Every memory course I've studied includes exercises for developing your imagination. The Evelyn Wood Speed Reading Method is based on a vertical-visual reading strategy. And when developing computer software, I find it much more efficient to think a series of screens than to think the paragraphs of words required to describe them.

When I did the visualization exercises in Kevin Trudeau's *Mega Memory* audiotape program, it wasn't clear how I was going to apply these techniques to my work. While I don't use peg lists or picture stories on a daily basis, I do think more visually now than before. For example, when designing a user interface, rather than thinking in words, I now think in "screens" more proficiently. I see the mouse pointer clicking a button and the next screen popping up. Instead of talking about these screens in my mind's ear, I am seeing them in my mind's eye.

In studying Evelyn Wood's reading program, I learned that a fundamental strategy for increasing reading speed is to silence subvocalization by "trusting my eyes" and thus reading visually. My mental reading process went from:

see→say→understand

to just:

see→understand

Building up my visualization muscle helped me do this more effectively. Admittedly, there are times when I still catch myself subvocalizing. Sometimes I want to read slowly, such as when reading conceptually dense material that is new. However, when I want to scan a lot of material very quickly, I am now able to cover more text in less time with greater efficiency. Developing my "visualization muscle" played a key role in helping me become a more flexible reader.

My memory seemed to improve even if I wasn't using the techniques. It became easier to take "mental snapshots" of images and to convert ideas I am thinking or reading about into pictures or symbols.

For knowledge workers, perhaps the highest leverage use of this visualization muscle is for beginning projects with the end in mind. Not all visualizations are created equal, and the best visualizations are the ones that generate the most effective actions toward project completion. If at the end of each day, you can reflect on the day's activities and honestly detect progress toward your goal, then you are on the right track. Over time, through additional trial and error, you may find that you can refine your visualizations to further enhance their effectiveness.

"The results you create depend on your clarity."

— Norm Levy

Some people are better at this than others. However, I know that it is a skill that can be developed because I have done so myself. The following four exercises have been helpful in developing my imagination.

Before continuing, I must emphasize that you should not do these exercises if you are prone to extreme mood swings or have problems with depression. See Chapter 9 for details.

VISUALIZATION EXERCISE #1:
MENTAL SNAPSHOT

Any time you have a free minute AND it is safe to briefly close your eyes, look at a nearby object, close your eyes, and notice if you can see its image in your mind's eye. If not, look at the object again, noticing more of the details, and close your eyes again. With your eyes closed, try to "zoom-in" on the image and notice the lines, colors, dimensions, etc.

If this seems a little mind-boggling, here is a slight variation: close your eyes and think about what your TV or computer monitor looks like. Sometimes when you turn a TV off, the picture shrinks down to a little white dot in the middle of the screen. Put a "white dot" in the center of your mental TV. Imagine that dot gradually getting larger until it fills the screen, and as it grows, imagine seeing the object you were trying to visualize earlier.

If you still don't "see" the mental image, try leaving your eyes open and defocusing. If you have ever looked out across the distance or at a blank wall and noticed that your mind wandered somewhere else where you weren't seeing the distant scenery or the wall, this "daydreaming" state is what I mean by defocusing. Try "daydreaming" the object.

Another variation is to use the telephoto lens technique. When you look at an object, notice that you can zoom-in on a particular aspect of the object, or zoom-out to see the scene in its entirety. When you close your eyes, try zooming in on various aspects of your mental image to see them more clearly, and then zoom back out again. Alternating between looking at the object and closing your eyes may help you refine your visualization incrementally.

Try starting with very simple objects like the letter 'A.' Write this letter on a piece of paper and then try to see it in your mind's eye.

Another way to break this learning process down into manageable chunks is to focus on a single color at a time.

For example, look at a tree, then close your eyes and try to mentally match the exact shade of green.

If this seems difficult, mark your calendar to try this exercise again tomorrow, in a week, or even a month. You may be surprised that taking mental snapshots is easier after your subconscious mind has had time to incubate the technique.

What I like best about this exercise is that it can be done during what would otherwise be wasted time. For example, I sometimes do it while waiting in a reception area with nothing to read or while standing in a line where it is safe to close my eyes for a few seconds.

VISUALIZATION EXERCISE #2:
SUBMODALITIES

Imagine that you are watching TV and suddenly the picture starts getting smaller and smaller until it's the size of a postage stamp. How motivated would you be to watch your program with the image that small? Then all of the sudden the picture starts getting larger, returning back to normal, but continues to "zoom-in" so that only a small portion of the normal image fills the screen. It's okay with you though, because it zoomed in on the face of your favorite character.

In the blink of an eye the picture zooms back to normal and then begins to blur. This makes it harder and harder to tell what is going on and again decreases your motivation to watch the program. Just when it's almost unbearable, the situation reverses itself and the focus returns. Not only that, but as it focuses, the colors and light seem to be getting brighter and brighter, adding a more cheerful atmosphere to the show.

Then a sad scene begins, but to your surprise, the scene suddenly converts to a cartoon and assumes a more playful tone. The sad scene ends in a way you don't like, so you play the cartoon backwards until it gets to the beginning. When it starts going forward again, you make things turn out much better. Finally, you decide to do something else, so you grab the mental image of the TV and throw it behind you in order to get it off your mind.

What I just described doing with a mental image of a TV program you can do with any mental image you can remember or create. This is another groundbreaking Neuro Linguistic Programming (NLP) technique taught by Richard Bandler and John Grinder in their book, *Frogs into Princes*, and in Richard Bandler's *Using Your Brain* book and audiotape. "Modalities" (visual, auditory, kinesthetic, olfactory and gustatory) are the major categories by which we represent the external world in our mind. We form mental maps of the external world using mental pictures, sounds, feelings, smells and tastes. In this way, we "re-present" external reality to our mind and take actions based upon this internal map or re-presentation. Everybody's internal map is different, primarily because the external world is so infinitely complex. We form mental models that approximate what our senses perceive, and these models drive our behavior.

Modalities are the major modes of mentally mapping external reality. Submodalities are the attributes used within each major mode of thinking. If you did the TV exercise above, then you adjusted the following visual submodalities: size of image, focus, brightness, location, speed at which the scenes were played and whether or not it was a cartoon or real-life. These are just a few of the submodalities you can vary. Others include viewpoint (the angle from which you are observing the picture), proximity (how close you are to the image), whether the image is framed or wrap-around, and whether or not you are in the picture or watching from a distance.

This exercise involved only visual submodalities. You can also change the attributes of the sounds you "hear" in your head and the feelings you sense internally. *Awaken the Giant Within* by Anthony Robbins contains an excellent one-page checklist of visual, auditory and kinesthetic submodalities. Richard Bandler's book and audiotape, *Using Your Brain,* are also excellent sources for further study.

The audiotape version of *Using Your Brain* gives extensive examples of how to expand your use of auditory submodalities. Bandler tells of a time when he fell asleep with the TV on. At four in the morning, a station came on playing a loud classical music concert. While most people would think that the TV came on and woke them up, Bandler just thought that he had woken up, because that is what his internal experience is like—frequently playing motivational, multi-instrument concerts in his head.

I believe that the techniques provided by Neuro Linguistic Programming (NLP) are so profound that even after twenty years of research and application, we are still just beginning to realize their full potential.

So many books have encouraged us to visualize what we want. Bandler and Grinder analyzed the structure of subjective experience and said, "here's how."

You may want to use "mastermind" energy discussed in the next chapter to accelerate your understanding and application of NLP distinctions.

In addition to being an excellent technique for developing your visualization muscle, there are many ways you can apply submodality skills at work. When visualizing how you want a project to end, experiment to discover which submodalities have the greatest impact on your motivation and energy levels. Think of your office at work. Do you have a dark, dingy picture of this place, or is it bright, large, highly focused and very close to your face? When you think of your workplace, what emotional response does it invoke? Does that emotional response contribute to or detract from your ability to deliver value to your customers? You may want to experiment with various submodalities in order to optimize this emotional response. What would happen if every time you walked in your office door, the song "Chariots of Fire" (or some other song that motivates you) began blasting at 70 decibels in your mind?

Stephen Covey encourages us to begin activities with the end in mind. Neuro Linguistic Programming teaches us to ask, "*How* can I represent this end in my mind in such a way that it inspires me to give my best performance on a moment by moment basis?"

"How many of you ever thought about the possibility of intentionally varying the brightness of an internal image in order to feel different? Most of you just let your brain randomly show you any picture it wants, and you feel good or bad in response."

— Richard Bandler

You may recall those attachments that fit on the end of a garden hose so that when the water is turned on, it starts whipping around wildly, spraying water every which way while the children run around trying to "avoid" getting sprayed. In some cases this is how people run their minds, waiting for external circumstances to occur that trigger certain thoughts, or just letting whatever thought that comes along occupy their consciousness. It's unpredictable and sometimes fun, but as a predominant way of thinking, this mental strategy can lead to disappointment. To take control of your submodalities is to grab that hose and focus the water like a laser beam in the direction you want to go!

VISUALIZATION EXERCISE #3:
DRAWING

As Betty Edwards teaches in her book, *Drawing on the Right Side of the Brain*, learning to draw involves learning to see things in a different way. I believe learning to draw can also help you improve visualization skills.

This exercise involves picking an object or a scene and looking at it until you see it clearly enough to draw it. The quality of the drawing becomes a feedback mechanism for the clarity of your vision. Here are some guidelines:

1) Initially, set a time limit such as ten minutes and stick to it. My experience has been that it is easy to lose track of time when I'm in a right-brain mode. As explained later in Chapter 5, each side of our brain specializes in certain activities. The left is usually more adept at dealing with linear issues such as time. Most people use the right brain for non-linear thinking such as drawing or perceiving dimension.

2) Use a thick leaded pencil. Drawing with a .5 mm mechanical pencil is more difficult.

3) Keep a large eraser handy and use it as much as needed to refine your drawing.

4) Alternate between focusing on the image and then defocusing. Each time, try to notice more and more details of the image.

5) Before starting to draw, make a few coordinate dots to mark the outer boundaries. For example, if you are drawing a tree, place a dot at the tree's highest point and a few dots to mark the perimeter and where the trunk begins. These coordinates provide a framework for guiding your drawing.

6) If light is reflecting off a certain portion of the object, draw it as if it wasn't and use an eraser to lighten the reflecting area.

7) Close your eyes and move your mental image of the object around in your internal visual sphere. Notice if it is easier to clarify the image in any of the positions. For example, if your visual screen is like a large white board, try moving the image to the upper left corner, upper right, straight ahead, to your left, etc. If your visual screen is like a wrap-around movie screen, try moving it to your direct left, right, or putting it above you. Finally, if your visual screen is like virtual reality, try walking through the image and looking at it from several different angles.

8) Give the exercise and drawing positive energy. Think about how grateful you are for the opportunity to explore a new skill with so many processional benefits in other areas of thinking. Think about the scene you are drawing with as much admiration and awe as you can generate. Appreciate what had to happen for the scene before you to exist. Let this positive energy flow into a brighter, fuller, more detailed internal image of the scene. Shift the frequency center of your attention from your mind to your heart by quieting your thoughts and amplifying these positive feelings. Then let this positive energy flow through your hand into your drawing. You can learn more about using positive energy in James Redfield's book, *The Celestine Prophecy*, and in Sara Paddison's book, *The Hidden Power of the Heart*.

9) Get a copy of Betty Edward's *Drawing on the Right Side of the Brain*, an excellent book on the subject.

VISUALIZATION EXERCISE #4:
TEN-MINUTE VISUALIZATION

While developing a software application, I occasionally use ten-minute visualization sessions that go something like this:

1) I look at my watch and create a mental image of what the clock will look like at the end of the ten-minute period. My watch is both digital and analog, so I prefer to use the stop watch feature to help ensure that I'm out of there exactly when my designated time limit is up.

2) I find an empty office or conference room where I won't be disturbed (how about designating a small office as a visualization room?). I find I need a comfortable temperature and the less noise the better. During summer months, I use the reclined passenger seat in my car.

3) I turn out the lights or I put something over my eyes to block the light.

4) I lay on the floor (only if it's clean and not heavily traveled—you may want to use a towel) or on a conference table.

5) I sometimes do a little light stretching of my lower back to help trigger a relaxation response.

6) I begin with a couple complete breaths as taught by yoga instructor Richard Hittleman. Begin a complete breath by exhaling completely. Without hesitation, begin filling your lower lungs with air. When your abdominal region won't expand any further, fill your chest with air. Hold for a few seconds, exhale completely, and then repeat without pausing at the point of full exhalation. Complete breathing generates *Prana* or "life force."

7) I then visualize the software working the way I want it to. I imagine somebody actually using the software: clicking the mouse, selecting menu options, and clicking buttons. Screens get repainted, new forms pop up, etc. If you work in a field other than software, then step into the future to the day after your project has been successfully completed. Imagine how life would be different for your customers as they use the results of your work. In as much detail as possible, see them using and benefiting from your work. If it seems difficult, first realize that it may be because you are working on a difficult project. Realize that this is the process of creating something new. All things are created twice: first in someone's mind and then in reality. Sometimes it takes several visualization sessions over time to evolve a clear mental picture.

8) I sometimes oscillate between focused visualization and letting my mind wander. In other words, I may invest a few minutes consciously working through the screens, and then let go of the mental steering wheel. I clear my mind with focused breathing and

just notice what related ideas drift into my consciousness. After a couple of minutes of this, I'll switch back into focused visualization in order to integrate the new ideas my subconscious mind has come up with during the pause.

While this may sound a bit weird, when I work on a project, what matters is successfully completing the project. This technique helps me do this—especially on the more difficult projects. It also gives my back a rest.

Win Wenger describes an excellent strategy for developing your visualization muscle in his book, *The Einstein Factor*. Check out **http://members.aol.com/einfactor/ein5.html** for more information. He calls it "image streaming."

"Some things you see with your eyes, others you must see with your heart."

— from the movie, *Land Before Time*

DEVELOP METAPHOR SKILLS

The second major strategy for effective self-communication involves metaphors. Metaphors are used extensively in this book to convey meaning—the essence of what I'm trying to say—very quickly. My aim is to use things you are already familiar with as a bridge to new ideas I'm presenting (river of increasing swiftness, brain dancing, etc.). This section describes how you can apply this same technique to communicate direction to your subconscious mind at higher bandwidths.

Many consider Milton Erickson to have been the greatest hypnotherapist who ever lived. Hypnotherapists are masters at communicating directly with the subconscious mind. Bandler and Grinder originated many of their breakthrough ideas from studying the work of Erickson and others. In his awesome book about Erickson called *Taproots: Underlying Principles of Milton Erickson's Therapy and Hypnosis*, William O'Hanlon writes that the word metaphor is derived from the

Greek roots *pherein* meaning 'to carry' and *meta*, which means 'beyond' or 'over.' "The function of metaphor is to carry knowledge across contexts, beyond its initial context into a new one."

According to O'Hanlon, Erickson believed that people already have the abilities needed to solve their problems. Erickson's task in therapy was to transfer this know-how across contexts, from the one(s) in which the patient currently has it to the context in which he does not. He accomplished this by using metaphor in its various forms. Erickson believed that analogy is one of the best ways to communicate directly with a patient's unconscious mind. Similarly, we can use metaphors to enhance the effectiveness of our "self-communication."

Thinking in metaphors is a skill, and I owe a lot to R.L. Wing, author of *The TAO of Power*, for accelerating my learning journey in this area. In this translation of Lao Tzu's classic, *Tao Te Ching*, Wing suggests that you identify an event, transaction, relationship or revelation that stands out on your path through life. Then "pull back your mind from the details of the situation," and describe it using a metaphor from nature. "For example," he writes, "a dead-end position that forced you to change careers might find an analogy in a river pouring into a box canyon and eventually overflowing to form a new waterway."

From this perspective, life is full of lessons. In 1992, I was standing barefoot on the shore of the Pacific Ocean. I knew that I wanted to make a major shift in my career direction by writing this book and doing related activities, yet it was proving difficult to imagine how I could pull off the transition. While standing ankle deep in the water, I noticed that about every third wave was larger and went much farther up the sand. What was happening was that a couple smaller waves would come in and form a base as they retreated. Then a third wave would come along and ride on top of what was left of the first two, in order to extend its reach up the beach. I realized that I could use a multiphase approach to make the transition, whereby each phase would provide a base for the "third wave" that would take me where I wanted to go.

The next time you get stuck on a project, think of a metaphor from nature or some other aspect if life that enriches your perspective. The metaphor collage in Figure 3.1 was excerpted from the Brain Dancing Coach software module for helping you come up with metaphors. Scanning this collage may trigger some ideas.

Project code names are another potential use of metaphors. A well-designed code name can do more than just serve as temporary name. I've observed several cases where code names were based on a metaphor that encapsulated key elements of the project vision, and thus served to inspire and guide team members. How do you identify a good metaphor? To paraphrase Alan Kay:

It's not what the metaphor is. It's what the metaphor does.

Good metaphors inspire innovative thinking or more focused action.

Bill Gates uses metaphors occasionally to convey his vision for the future of the computer industry. He is currently using the phrase "Digital Nervous System" to convey the potential for properly networked PCs to help companies increase their overall information metabolism.

The best way I've discovered for developing metaphor skills is to start an idea collection (IC) sheet for gathering metaphors as they drift into your awareness from time to time. IC sheets are discussed in Chapter 5. For now, just think of it as a blank piece of non-lined paper turned sideways where you to jot ideas in an abbreviated fashion. As you read *Brain Dancing* and other books, note any metaphors you come across. Soon you may find metaphors popping into your awareness from daily life experiences and conversations. You may be surprised how often this linguistic tool is used.

Shakespeare's writings are loaded with metaphors. Here are a few examples from *Hamlet, King Richard II, Measure for Measure,* and *Romeo and Juliet:*

Brevity is the soul of wit.

There's a divinity that shapes our ends,
Rough-hew them how we will.

Truth hath a quiet breast.

Our doubts are traitors,
And make us lose the good we oft might win,
By fearing to attempt.

Adversity's sweet milk, philosophy.

As an exercise, scan the excerpts of Shakespeare's plays at the Bartlett Quotations Web site.

http://www.columbia.edu/acis/bartleby/bartlett/

Identify five insightful uses of metaphor and jot them in the space below. You are more likely to do this exercise if you set a time limit of ten minutes. You can always go back. This exercise is just to "tip the first domino"—get you started with metaphors.

_____

_____

_____

_____

_____

I like Marvin Minsky's definition put forth in his book, *Society of Mind,* "A metaphor is that which allows us to replace one thought with another." Metaphors are a tool for traversing mental compartments; for taking ourselves and others from what we know to what we don't know. For example, metaphors created to describe the Internet have helped large numbers of people understand this new phenomena more rapidly. The World Wide Web is a an ever-expanding collection of interconnected linkages.

Newsgroups are *electronic gathering places* for creating *virtual communities* irrespective of the participant's physical location. Esther Dyson's company, EDventure Holding, has set up the following Web page dedicated to exploring how metaphors have shaped the Internet and our interaction with it.

★ **http://www.edventure.com/pods/**

Some of the most useful and successful books of our time are rooted in insightful metaphors: *Men are from Mars, Women are from Venus; Awaken the Giant Within; The Road Less Traveled; How to Swim with the Sharks Without Getting Eaten Alive.* Stephen Covey's book, *The 7 Habits of Highly Effective People*, is loaded with great metaphors: Emotional Bank Account®, True North™ principles, Goose and the Golden Egg®, to name a few.

Metaphors are often culturally based. This point was emphasized in the Star Trek: The Next Generation episode, *Darmok.* The Enterprise meets an alien race that speaks entirely in metaphors. "Shaka, when the walls fell"—signified an ending of some kind; "...with sails unfurled"—to depart, "In Winter"—silence, and "Sokath, His eyes uncovered"—he understands. Each statement references past events that shaped their culture. The first word references the cultural icon, followed by a brief statement describing some event involving that icon. It was a great exploration of the world of metaphors.

The more I think about it, the more truth I see in Minsky's statement that, "Every thought is to some degree a metaphor." Think of your metaphor idea collection sheet as an idea bucket for gathering the more insightful and inspiring metaphors you come across. This will train your subconscious mind to be on the lookout for metaphors and will help propel you to the point where you are creating new metaphors.

Metaphors We Live By, by George Lakoff and Mark Johnson, is a good book for exploring this high leverage topic in more depth.

Figure 3.1

DEVELOP FULL PHYSIOLOGY
AFFIRMATION SKILLS

The third major strategy for effective self-communication involves affirmations. Earlier I wrote that there were two dimensions to self-communication: what you are thinking and how you are using your physiology. This section summarizes the basic rules for doing affirmations and emphasizes a related distinction pioneered by Anthony Robbins that is not as well known.

In his book, *The Power of Your Subconscious Mind*, Dr. Joseph Murphy states that "Motion and emotion must balance." What Anthony Robbins did was apply this to the *nth* degree. While this is just one of Anthony Robbins' optimum performance strategies, I believe it has played a significant role in his considerable success.

So what does he do differently? Robbins uses affirmations during moments where he has generated powerful physiologies. For example, he describes how he used to run along the beach in California saying his affirmations over and over again. As he ran, he said his affirmations with all of the intensity that he could muster. Robbins also uses this distinction to achieve a peak state before going on stage to speak. The following is an adaptation of one of Robbins' affirmations that has worked well for me:

I now command my subconscious mind to direct me in helping as many people as possible today, by giving me the STRENGTH! POWER! BREVITY! HUMOR! EMOTION! whatever it takes, to motivate these people to take action that will improve their lives NOW!

Say this with increasing emphasis and intensity as you progress through the affirmation. This emotional charge can be significantly amplified with powerful physiology. Some of the components of this physiology are strong breathing, strong congruent posture, physical gestures that encourage a sense of resourcefulness, and the use of your 80 facial muscles. Your whole physiology should encourage feelings of highly focused determination.

"Emotion is created by motion."

— *Anthony Robbins*

Emotionalized thoughts are more likely to have an action influence on the subconscious mind. Why? Because most people are constantly talking to themselves. Your subconscious must have some way of distinguishing between mental chit-chat and the really important stuff. Emotionally charging your affirmations is one such way of signaling to your subconscious to pay attention. And because emotion can be created by motion, powerful congruent physiologies are one "lever" you can use to get the attention of your subconscious mind.

The only way you can truly appreciate the effectiveness with which Robbins "peaks" himself is to actually watch him in action. Robbins is by far the most effective public speaker I've ever observed. I highly recommend that you attend one of his seminars both for its content, which is consistently first rate, and to observe his public speaking abilities, which set a new standard for us all.

In her book, *Creative Visualization*, Shakti Gawain states: "In general, the shorter and simpler the affirmation, the more effective." It should be a clear statement that conveys a strong feeling—the more feeling it conveys, the stronger the impression it will make on your mind. Long, wordy, and theoretical affirmations lose their emotional impact. She encourages you to choose affirmations that come from your heart, not your head.

Shakti Gawain also suggests that you only use affirmations that feel right to you. "When using affirmations, try as much as possible to create a feeling of belief, an experience that they can be true." The implied message I get from Anthony Robbins is that he is able to create and associate to feelings of strong belief more easily when he is in his most powerful and resourceful physiologies.

Chloe Wordsworth has developed a new technology for personal change called Holographic Repatterning (HR). In an introductory video (available for $17 by calling 520-204-9960), she teaches that in order for an affirmation to be effective, you must "resonate" with it. You resonate with an affirmation when it is consistent with frequencies of thought dominating your awareness and energy field.

HR uses muscle testing to establish a direct communication channel with your energy field (i.e., subconscious mind with a twist) in order to identify the most efficient means of altering the beliefs that you resonate with. She has cataloged dozens of techniques for doing this which have proven helpful in various circumstances. Muscle testing is used to identify which one to use, exactly how to apply it, who should do it and for how long. I must emphasize that HR deals with much more than affirmations. It is an all-encompassing methodology for personal change. Until more information on HR becomes readily available, full physiology affirmations can be used as one approach to change what you "resonate" with.

Two affirmations I used frequently while writing *Brain Dancing* are: "*Brain Dancing* inspires effective mental action now!" and "*Brain Dancing* mobilizes untapped intellectual resources of knowledge workers!" While running along the shores of Lake Washington, I repeated these two affirmations with all the intensity that I could muster. Sometimes I would say them just in my mind. However, saying them out loud in a strong voice involves more physiology and is more effective, even though you may get a strange look or two.

I have conditioned myself such that each time I turn a certain corner to where I can first see the rippling water of the lake, the affirmations begin in my mind automatically. In Neuro Linguistic Programming, this is referred to as "anchoring." You may know a song or two that remind you of certain people, places or events. Those songs are auditory anchors. At the time you first heard them (or heard them several times), you were probably experiencing some strong emotions. The important thing to notice is that you are reminded of these experiences without even having to try. Thinking about them is automatic.

I like to think of this process of building resourceful anchors as if I'm climbing a mountain. Each time I use this powerful running physiology to generate strong emotions and then anchor it, it is like pounding a spike into the rock face. When I engage that anchor next time, it propels me back to that spot on the mountain. From there I can climb a little higher by intensifying the emotional state while seeing the visual stimulus (Lake Washington), thus pounding in another spike a little higher up the mountainside.

Anchoring offers you the opportunity to leverage your will power by creating "push button" emotions. The above example is just one of the many types of anchors you can create. Here are the basic rules for creating effective anchors:

- You need a unique stimulus, which can be visual, auditory, kinesthetic, olfactory or gustatory.
- You must be in a peak state when you see the sight, hear the sound, feel the touch, taste the flavor or smell the odor.
- You must be able to reproduce the stimulus precisely in order to engage the anchor.

To apply this distinction, pick a spot on your running path where you turn a corner and see something unique. (If you are not a runner, you could try walking strongly and directly.) It should be a point where you are in peak physiology (i.e., running strongly). As soon as you turn the corner, begin saying your affirmation with all of the intensity you can muster. Say the affirmations out loud if it helps. Sometimes I shout them in my mind. If you invest the conscious energy the first time or two, you won't have to consciously remember to make your affirmations while you run in the future. They will begin in your mind automatically when you see that particular scene.

Anchors have many applications beyond affirmations. For example, on the Bill Moyers' PBS television show *Healing and the Mind*, a young girl had a serious illness for which the only medication was a drug known to have serious side effects. In order to get her off this medication as soon as possible, she smelled rose perfume and sipped cod liver oil each time she took it. The message to her body was: "When you smell this and taste this, do this." While there is no way to know for sure, it appears that this conditioning helped the doctors reduce and eventually eliminate the need for both the medicine and the sensory stimuli. The strong taste and smell appears to have established a communication channel with the girls' immune system that triggered her body's memory of the healing response.

To recap then, repeat affirmations while in a peak physiology, and use anchors to make each affirmation an investment in your future resources.

USE ALPHA STATE MEDITATIONS

The last major strategy for effective self-communication involves thinking about your desired outcome while in a meditative state conducive to alpha brain waves. As explained in Chapter 1, one of the many spectrums of thought involves brain wave frequencies. The brain produces electrochemical impulses that travel three to four hundred feet per second as shown in Figure 3.2.

States conducive to alpha brain waves open up the communication channels between conscious and subconscious thought. This self-communication is a two-way street: alpha states are helpful both when communicating a desired outcome to your subconscious, and when tuning into subconscious guidance (i.e., intuition). In either case, the process of generating alpha brain waves is the same. The difference is what you do once you have reached this state.

Type	Cycles/ Second	Typical Mental Activity
Delta	.5 - 3	Large and slow. Deep, dreamless sleep.
Theta	4 - 7	Seem to be involved in emotionality, creative imagery and computation on a deep level. They rarely occur while awake.
Alpha	8 - 13	Associated with an alert but relaxed state of mind. Most people produce alpha waves when they close their eyes or when their brain is scanning for a pattern. Typical waking, eyes-open EEG shows alpha waves mixed with other patterns. However, steady alpha waves are uncommon in one whose eyes are open.
Beta	14 - 30	Fast, tight pattern occurs during logical thought, analysis, action and normal conversation.

Figure 3.2 Brain wave frequencies as described by Marilyn Ferguson in her book, *The Brain Revolution.*

Generating alpha brain waves is a skill that can be developed by progressing through the four stages involved in learning any new skill:

1) Unconscious incompetence
2) Conscious incompetence
3) Conscious competence
4) Unconscious competence

Unconscious incompetence is where you don't know what you don't know. Conscious incompetence is where you become aware that you don't know how to do something that you have a desire to learn. Conscious competence is where you can do the task, but only by devoting all of your attention to it. The fourth stage, unconscious competence, is the stage where you can do the task without having to think about it much, if at all.

Just as you learned to drive a car, you can learn to drive your subconscious mind with alpha brain waves.

"Therapy is often a matter of tipping the first domino."

— *Milton Erickson[1]*

Over one million people have graduated from the Silva Mind Control Training course developed by José Silva. While I haven't taken this course, I have experienced good results from applying the techniques described in his book, *The Silva Mind Control Method.* Silva suggests using the alpha state to do "dynamic meditation." After reaching an alpha state, Silva recommends going beyond traditional meditation (which he acknowledges is significant in and of itself). He suggests that this state is also an excellent opportunity to develop visualization skills. You do this by placing a simple image on your "mental screen." This image can be an apple or a desired outcome in vivid detail. Silva believes that your results will be significantly influenced by the degree to which you desire the outcome, believe that the event can take place, and expect that it will occur.

However, in her book, *The Brain Revolution,* Marilyn Ferguson wrote, "Mentally visualizing an object in minute detail usually blocks alpha production, for example, just as actual visual observation does." She also points out that some individuals can perform tasks such as speed reading and mathematical computation without reducing alpha wave production. Visualizing while staying in an alpha state may be a skill we can develop. Perhaps your own experiments will help shed some light on this potentially high leverage mental activity.

If you are new to meditating, Dr. Andrew Weil recommends that you begin by taking five minutes a day to just sit and observe your breathing. I find it helpful to use a digital kitchen timer made by Component Design (Time Check, Model PT1A, $20). It allows me to totally forget

---

[1] As quoted in *Taproots*, by William O'Hanlon.

about time with the comfort of knowing that I won't go into a loop and sit there too long. This timer doesn't tick, and the four programmable time settings make it convenient to use. I just press two buttons and I'm ready to start. If you can't find one at a kitchen supply store near you, try calling the manufacturer at (503) 297-5944.

Think of consciousness as a beautiful mountain lake. When you meditate, calm the waters until they reflect the surrounding beauty. It sometimes helps to imagine a single candle flame burning before you. If your mind wanders, the flame disappears. Just bring the flame back. Watch the flame move towards you as you inhale, and lean away slightly as you exhale. When finished, Dr. Khalsa recommends sitting quietly for a minute or two. During this time, try to merge your calm state of mind with your normal, non-meditative outlook.

I have found it helpful to create a "meditation place" in my home. Using the same place conditions your mind/body to go into meditation mode whenever you sit there. My meditation place is at the foot of my bed next to a plant. The only thing I do there is meditate.

The state of mind and body conducive to alpha brain waves is common just after waking. Therefore morning is the best time to meditate. I prefer right before bedtime.

Alpha state meditation is the complementary opposite of the "full physiology affirmation" approach discussed in the previous section. Whereas that approach involved whipping yourself into an emotional frenzy, this strategy involves visualizing your desired outcome in a state of relaxed alertness. Quieting your mind reduces interference, and the messages you send your subconscious are better understood. There is less background noise for your subconscious to filter out.

Silva encourages you to be consistent from day one as to how you go in and come out of an alpha state. This will help you condition yourself to go in and out of the desired state more rapidly. Eventually, you can develop the ability to go into this alpha state anytime during the day.

The more I learn about meditating, the more respect I gain for the process and the important role it plays in maintaining personal ecology. While the above ideas were intended to help you get started with meditation, I encourage you to explore this practice further. A great book for doing this is *Meditation,* by Eknath Easwazan. It will teach you how to avoid common difficulties with meditation by doing it right from the beginning.

Self-communication is a two-way street, yet everything in this chapter so far has dealt with communicating *to* your subconscious mind. One of the many uses of more traditional meditation is receiving guidance *from* your subconscious. The final section in this chapter addresses the issue of intuition.

INTUITION:
LISTENING TO SUBCONSCIOUS GUIDANCE

I think of intuition as the process by which our subconscious mind sends us messages, some of which are in response to the directional information we have self-communicated to our subconscious. The best book I've found on intuition is called *The Intuitive Edge*, by Philip Goldberg. Shakti Gawain's writings touch on many related themes as well, such as her book, *Creative Visualization.*

In multimedia technology, there is a concept known as "streaming," whereby video images are transferred directly from the CD-ROM to the video driver, bypassing the computer's CPU (Central Processing Unit). To do otherwise would slow the computer down considerably. The process of managing the interplay between the conscious and subconscious is similar. You use the various techniques presented in this chapter to create a "multimedia" program in your subconscious mind. As you go about the day, your subconscious plays back this program in the form of actions that bypass conscious processing to varying degrees. Your actions are guided to take you in the direction defined in your subconscious multimedia program.

During this process, interpreting the signals that our subconscious sends us can be challenging. For example, life is full of temptations pulling us every which way. Determining which signals are intuitive guidance and which are influenced by environmental circumstances can be difficult. Traditional forms of meditation can help a person be more "tuned-in" to their intuition. Goldberg recommends Transcendental Meditation, as does Deepak Chopra, author of *Quantum Healing* and promoter of Ayurvedic health principles. Transcendental Meditation classes cost several hundred dollars, so I've chosen to develop my meditation skills through books, audiotapes and by interviewing people who meditate regularly.

"Intuition is to be tempted, not pursued."

— *Philip Goldberg*

Goldberg notes that without exception, the people he interviewed have their most significant intuitive experiences while away from work. For Mozart, this occurred while traveling, going for walks or during the night when he couldn't sleep. "*Whence* and *how* they come, I know not; nor can I force them," wrote Mozart. Goldberg concludes, "...a well-timed incubation period seems to be good bait for intuition."

This idea forms one of the major underlying themes of Chapter 5, Synergistic Oscillation. When I am away from work on boat trips, I am so far removed from my work that I can't recall this time being a major source of business-related ideas. My work, often highly technical and detail-oriented, requires a great deal of concentration. While boating, I defocus my mind, relax my concentration muscle, and go with the flow of the experience—very much the opposite of my mindset at work. I do get high-level ideas while on these trips. These periods of mental rest also recharge my mental batteries. This allows me to deal with technical issues with more proficiency and mental clarity when I return to work.

I also get a surprising number of ideas while stretching after a workout or doing some other disciplined act, such as turning down a particularly tempting sweet. Stretching is the part of my workout that requires the most discipline.

Intuition is a broad subject and difficult to pin down. Readers interested in pursuing this topic further should consult the books mentioned above. I sum up my strategy for using intuition as follows:

- Clearly communicate your desired project outcome to your subconscious using the strategies discussed in this chapter. This is "sowing the seeds."

- Develop the mental flexibility and discipline required to quiet your mind into a meditative state. This is one of the fundamental skills for "tempting" intuition and for developing your ability to tune-in to intuitive guidance.

- Use synergistic dialogue as discussed in the next chapter to reap the rewards of your self-communication efforts. One of my greatest sources of useful ideas has been discussion with project team members. I am not saying that the ideas come from them, rather, they come from the process of discussing issues with them. There have been many times when I've received useful ideas from discussions where the other person never even said a word.

Chapter 4 Overview

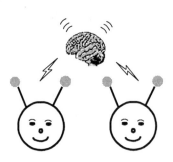

Principles

* Mastermind
* Character Ethic
* Sending Positive Energy

Alliances

* Strategic
* Personal Development
* Technology
* Public Speaking
* Project Teams

Project Team Interaction

* Rapport
* Building Positive Energy
* Dialog vs. "Chit chat"
* Precision Communication
* Six Thinking Hats
* Sowing and Reaping Ideas
* Intrapersonal Synergy

SYNERGISTIC DIALOGUE

"Human beings have an extraordinary capacity to think together."

— *Peter Senge*

Something special happens to our thinking whenever two or more people discuss an issue they care about, something special that increases our access to a pool of intelligence not readily available when thinking alone. Many people seem to underestimate the true potential of this distinction.

"Idea flow management" is an invaluable interpersonal communication skill. My goal with this chapter is to help you reach the point where you can brainstorm on the fly in virtually any conversation. This is the second major strategy for using complementary opposites to achieve mental leverage.

$$\text{Conscious} \longleftrightarrow \text{Subconscious}$$

Individual Thought $\longleftrightarrow$ **Dialogue**

$$\text{Left-Brain Mode} \longleftrightarrow \text{Right-Brain Mode}$$

$$\text{Detailed Thought} \longleftrightarrow \text{High Level Thought}$$

After giving you an overview of the best teachings I've found on this subject, the five main ways I use synergistic dialogue in business are summarized. The majority of this chapter covers suggestions for applying this idea within project teams.

PRINCIPLES

NAPOLEON HILL'S MASTERMIND PRINCIPLE

In *Think and Grow Rich*, one of the all-time best-selling business books, Napoleon Hill states that, "No two minds ever come together without thereby creating a third, invisible, intangible force which may be likened to a third mind." Hill discovered that using mastermind groups was a key strategy of several highly successful business leaders including Andrew Carnegie, Henry Ford and Thomas Edison. His basic message was to form alliances with individuals who have knowledge and mental capacities that complement your own. The more brainpower and the more they care about the issue, the better. Once you've located such individuals, arrange to meet with them on a regular basis for the purpose of developing and refining strategic plans.

Hill believed that each person's brain is both a broadcasting and receiving station. Thought vibrations released by one brain may be picked up and interpreted by all other brains that are 'in tune' with the broadcasting brain. While discussing issues with your mastermind group, the rate of thinking of group members is "stepped up" in a way that increases the degree to which they can tune in to thoughts released by other brains.

When I first read this, I began searching for people interested in forming such alliances. What took me a little longer to realize was that every conversation could benefit from this distinction to some degree. That last sentence is worth reading again, because it has played a critical role in every project I've worked on. Being able to form mini-mastermind groups on the fly is one of the most important interpersonal communications skills you can develop.

You know you are applying the mastermind principle correctly when your "rate of thinking" is stepped up such that ideas begin to flow into your mind during conversation. When you verbalize these ideas to the group, it fuels further conversation that evolves into useful knowledge. I refer to this stepped up rate of thinking as "nuclear beta" because it feels very different from both alpha and normal beta. What is needed to confirm this pattern is a way to monitor brain waves while a person is giving a speech. This is when the phenomenon seems most pronounced.

Oftentimes we can increase our awareness of certain ideas by experiencing their opposite. You can experience the opposite of the mastermind effect by delivering a speech to a blank wall. One reason this requires so much discipline is that the energizing and amplifying dynamic of the audience is missing.

As an exercise, the next time you have the opportunity to speak to a group, pause for a moment before you begin to speak and notice if ideas seem to "present themselves" to you. The ideas may not seem related to what you are going to say, but they usually turn out to be brilliantly related. You must exercise faith when doing this. You must believe that ideas will come to you as necessary for effective communication. This experience, even if you only speak for one minute, is a microcosm representing the essence of one of the most profound lessons a person can learn.

One way to experiment with "nuclear beta" is to attend a Toastmasters meeting and volunteer to participate in "Table Topics." This is the part of the meetings where members practice impromptu speaking. The designated "Table Topics Master" arrives at each meeting with a list of prepared subjects or questions. After the main speeches for the meeting have been delivered, there is a break while the evaluators prepare their responses. During this time, the Table Topics Master calls on individuals at random who must stand up and give a 30 to 90 second talk on the assigned subject off the top of their head.

Now this is truly faith in action. The more you are willing to trust that ideas will come to you, the more they seem to flow in abundance. Rather than sitting and fretting about what you might say in such situations, you can look forward to the "idea burst" that occurs and for the opportunity to develop your "faith muscle." Non-members are given the option to decline the invitation to speak in case they would just like to observe the process. At the time of this writing, there are over 8,000 clubs worldwide. To locate the Toastmasters group nearest you, or for information on how to start your own club, call (800) 993-7732.

Peter Senge, Director of the Systems Thinking and Organizational Learning Program at MIT's Sloan School of Management, sums it up beautifully with the words, "Human beings have an extraordinary capacity to think together." In his landmark book, *The Fifth Discipline*, Senge describes this phenomenon as dialogue—a type of conversation whereby the group "becomes open to the flow of a larger intelligence." He quotes the physicist, Werner Heisenberg (formulator of the famous "Uncertainty Principle" in modern physics) as saying, "Science is rooted in conversations. The cooperation of different people may culminate in scientific results of the utmost importance." In his book *Physics and Beyond: Encounters and Conversations*, Heisenberg recalls how conversations with Pauli, Einstein, Bohr and others had a lasting effect on his thinking and literally gave birth to many of the theories for which these men eventually became famous. Senge's *Fifth Discipline* audiotape series also contains excellent ideas on the subject of dialogue.

"There is this idea factory to which I subscribe."

— *Isaac Asimov*

We don't know for sure where ideas come from when engaged in dialogue. Are we immersed in a sea of infinite intelligence to which the extra energy provided in synergistic dialogue helps us tune in? Or is it that our mind simply has access to more internal resources when provided with this energy? For knowledge workers, knowing where the ideas come from is not as important as knowing how to lure them into consciousness. It is to this end that I direct the majority of this chapter. How can we best prepare ourselves for the mental leverage that can come from applying the mastermind principle? What can we do to encourage the flow of ideas to others in conversation? To answer these questions we must turn to Stephen Covey and James Redfield.

CHARACTER ETHIC: PREPARING YOURSELF FOR SYNERGY

You can enhance your ability to receive ideas in conversation and help others do the same by nurturing the habits Stephen Covey describes in his book, *The 7 Habits of Highly Effective People.* Covey teaches that synergistic dialogue occurs between two or more individuals when there is a high degree of trust and cooperation. Rather than aiming for synergy, Covey believes it is more likely to occur as you master the first five habits.

You are more likely to benefit from dialogue when you are not threatened by the ideas of others. This can be minimized by centering your personal security on the degree to which you have aligned your habits with fundamental principles. Being able to generate ideas in the presence of others is nurtured by abolishing the fear of appearing stupid. I am constantly tossing out "off the wall" ideas; some of them are useful, many aren't so great. Oftentimes it is a variation of these rejected ideas that ends up solving the problem. Covey's habits present a road map for building a sense of worth based on your alignment with principles, as opposed to what others might think.

"SENDING POSITIVE ENERGY" IN DIALOGUE

Napoleon Hill introduced us to the "mastermind principle," Stephen Covey gave us a strategy to prepare ourselves for synergistic dialogue by developing our character, and recently James Redfield took us another step forward on this journey by explaining the energy dynamics of conversation itself. In his book, *The Celestine*

Prophecy, Redfield describes the process by which you can support or send energy to other meeting participants. He describes how this energy can flow from person to person as a conversation evolves. If you have ever spoken to a group and felt like someone in the audience was throwing mental darts at you, then you have experienced the opposite of "sending positive energy." On the other hand, if you've experienced a surge of ideas and mental clarity while speaking, then you have experienced the potential of "sending positive energy" to others.

Before you can send it to others, you must first cultivate energy within yourself. I am not referring to adrenaline, but rather to a type of energy that is most noticeable by the presence of heightened mental clarity among group participants. Personally, sending positive energy involves concentrating my attention on a person's strengths, coupled with faith in their abilities. Most people can tell at a gut level when someone has faith in them. Redfield believes that loving and energizing others is one of the best things we can do for ourselves—the more support we give others, the more energy flows into us.

The topic of employing positive energy will be expanded upon later in this chapter.

APPLICATIONS

The five primary ways I use dialogue to produce synergy in knowledge work are strategic alliances, technology alliances, professional development alliances, public speaking and multifunctional project teams.

STRATEGIC ALLIANCES

Leaders use strategic alliances to formulate overall direction and guide project selection. A board of directors is an obvious example of a strategic alliance. I've also seen CEOs of similar sized businesses in non-competing industries meet monthly to review each other's operations.

Each month the focus is placed on just one business, which is a great way of pooling executive knowledge. Startup companies can mastermind with their investors or other partners. Participants in this type of alliance should be selected with extreme care. Additionally, it is usually not wise to discuss strategies developed by this alliance with people outside the alliance.

TECHNOLOGY ALLIANCES

Your effectiveness at implementing technology can be enhanced by building a network of individuals who have developed specialized capacity in areas complementary to your own. Developing a high degree of specialized knowledge and skill in your own niche allows you to offer value back to your developing network. Local trade associations, national trade shows and people you meet while working on projects are all good sources of technology contacts.

Anyone you want to talk to is usually no more than five layers of contacts away.

PROFESSIONAL DEVELOPMENT ALLIANCES

You can accelerate your self-development by finding one or more people who share your love of learning and meet with them periodically for collaboration. Toastmasters International provides a great opportunity to do this. There are thousands of Toastmasters groups worldwide which meet weekly to help people develop public speaking and communication skills. In Toastmasters, you can give short speeches about the self-development topics you most want to learn. This way, you are developing a valuable skill at the same time you are helping others, acquiring knowledge about interesting new topics and meeting high quality people who share your love of learning.

I've also found executive tape-sharing clubs highly useful. This is where you locate a group of people willing to contribute a certain amount of money for the purchase of educational audiotapes from companies such as Nightengale-Conant (800-323-3938). There is a substantial discount when purchasing ten cassette albums at a time, which can then be circulated among club members.

It was through one of these clubs that I first learned of Anthony Robbins, who opened the doors to so much of the material presented in this book. The process went something like this: listen to tapes, buy book, buy books referred to in book, buy books referenced in those books, attend related seminars, meet people who refer me to other quality books, tapes and seminars, which then lead to further sources of useful information.

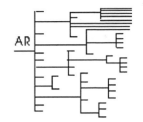

PUBLIC SPEAKING OPPORTUNITIES

When speaking before a group, we often receive positive energy from a lot of people simultaneously. As mentioned earlier, public speaking is a great opportunity to observe the impact this energy has on your thinking. This increased awareness can help you utilize mastermind energy on various levels during other types of dialogue.

MULTIFUNCTIONAL PROJECT TEAMS

Most of this chapter discusses how to apply synergistic dialogue within multifunctional project teams. While not an authority on the design of multifunction project teams, I have been a participant in such teams over the past fifteen years at dozens of companies in a variety of industries. After giving you an overview of team formation guidelines recommended in other literature, I devote the last half of the chapter towards helping individuals participate in such teams more effectively.

"If there is a single visible element that distinguishes [Fast Cycle Time] competitors from others, it is their extensive use of multifunctional teams."

— *Christopher Meyer*

In his book, *Fast Cycle Time: How to Align Purpose, Strategy, and Structure for Speed,* Christopher Meyer states that multifunctional teams "...establish the structure that brings the necessary people, regardless of technical expertise or functional base, into real-time contact to accelerate the speed of learning."

One of the most surprising lessons I learned from consulting with all these businesses is the degree of diversity between companies and even departments. By diversity, I mean not only the type of problems, but the way even common problems are addressed. While the specific requirements of project teams can vary widely, the following guidelines on project team formation seem fairly generic:

- Balance "What" and "How" Specialties. One or more people, including the project leader, must understand exactly what the customer needs. Additionally, they must know exactly how the project fits into the larger scheme of things in their business and to some extent, the industry. The other half of the team addresses the "how" part of the equation. Their job is to understand available technology and figure out the best way to apply it within agreed-upon time frames to successfully complete the project. "How" people usually must be very detail oriented, especially when dealing with technology. "What" people must be adept at seeing the big picture.

- Give each person a stake in the success of the project. Give them a sense of "ownership" of their piece.

- Structure the work to minimize the extent to which each individual must rely on someone else for the success of their contribution.

- The ideal team culture is one that supports the efforts of individual team members to make their unique strengths productive.

- Use small, cohesive teams staffed with self-motivated, highly experienced and technically knowledgeable leaders. Limiting the size of each team to between three and seven people helps maintain focus.

- Weekly status meetings lay the groundwork for more focused brainstorming later on. They do this by keeping team members informed and building a sense of team—an awareness of how each person is contributing their particular skills and knowledge to the project. Consistency is a plus: same day of the week, same time, place and structure. The quicker the better. Concentrate on getting the issues out on the table and making it clear who "owns" them. Beginning each meeting with an individual "check-in" is a great way to build team synergy. This is where each member gives a brief verbal status report on his or her area of the project.

TEAM SELECTION GUIDELINES

Notice individuals with whom ideas seem to flow best. Napoleon Hill observed that some minds clash the moment they come in contact with each other, while others show a natural affinity. Some people just take more time to build rapport with. Then there are people with whom dialogue was just not meant to be, at least in their present state. In his book, *Liberation Management,* Tom Peters writes, "Jack walks into a room and 5, 55, or 555 people tense up instantly. Gloom and doom follow in his wake. Then there's Maria. She walks in, under exactly the same conditions (good or bad), and people lighten up a bit, feel a little more energetic. Look for 'Marias.' Avoid 'Jacks' like the plague."

On his *Five Keys to Wealth and Happiness* audiotape[1], Anthony Robbins shares a related story. A speaker asks a group of children what would happen to him if his worst enemy came along and dropped two lumps of sugar in his coffee. "Nothing" responded the children. The speaker then asked what would happen if his best friend accidentally dropped a single drop of strychnine in his coffee. "You're dead," the children replied. "That's right," continued the teacher, "In life, your mind is like your coffee. You need to be very careful about who dumps what inside of it."

Two more points to consider:

- Fast-paced dialogue is usually more productive. Visually oriented people talk faster, and this allows for higher bandwidth conversations. Anybody can develop the ability, or flexibility, to switch into a visual mode for such a conversation.
- The more team members that understand the principle of dialogue and are open to the potential for synergistic dialogue, the better. Companies who can work this material into employee orientation training will be at an advantage.

For more information on how to design a company to make use of project teams and how to design the teams themselves, refer to the following sources.

- *Fast Cycle Time: How to Align Purpose, Strategy, and Structure for Speed*, by Christopher Meyer, is loaded with useful information on structuring an organization to make maximum use of project teams.

---

[1] This audiotape is available from Robbins Research International at (800) 898-8669. It is included along with the *Unleash the Power Within: An Owners Manual to the Brain* videotape program.

- Chapters 11-14 of Tom Peters' book, *Liberation Management*, discuss the dynamics of project teams within professional service firms.

- For guidelines on structuring software development project teams, refer to Chapter 4 of the *Building Client/Server Applications with Visual Basic* manual included in the Enterprise Edition of Microsoft Visual Basic 4.0.

- For information on how Microsoft uses project teams, see *Microsoft Secrets,* by Michael Cusumano and Richard Selby.

The remainder of this chapter is designed to help individuals obtain maximum benefit from their participation in project teams.

GUIDELINES FOR PROJECT TEAM INTERACTION

You don't need a roomful of people to create synergistic dialogue. I derive most of the benefits of this distinction from one-on-one hallway or "stand-up" meetings. Such meetings are initiated by asking a project team member if they have time to "brainstorm an issue." Another useful phrase for creating the proper frame of mind for the meeting is, "Can I bounce some ideas off you?"

These meetings can be done in person or over the phone. I begin the conversation by stating the issue, and then describe the challenges I am facing or the options I am considering. Oftentimes, ideas will pop into my mind without the other person even saying a word. I sometimes blurt out bizarre ideas that end up being totally useless. It's not that I get a kick out of making crazy suggestions, but at a gut level, they just seem appropriate to the flow of meaning in the conversation. Off the wall ideas are often the stepping stones to useful ones.

I don't participate in these sessions with any conscious strategy for structuring the conversation. My focus is entirely on the successful resolution of the issue. I am not trying to impress anybody, nor am I concerned about being judged incompetent by what I say. I define a "win" on a larger scale: successful completion of the project. I know if that is accomplished, appearing foolish a time or two along the way can be forgiven.

During hallway meetings, I use verbal and nonverbal reactions as sources of input. My sensory acuity is tuned in to the flow of ideas into my head and whether or not they resolve the issue being addressed. Brainstorming effectiveness is enhanced by asking thought-provoking questions or by starting to talk about partial answers that seem promising. By talking out a partial answer, the flow of ideas evolves dynamically.

I'm not claiming to have a unique gift in this area. The key is just being aware of the potential and remaining open to it. I've been in meetings with two client representatives where one of them will ask me to "stand by" for just a moment. The next thing I know they are having a conversation in what sounds like English—the individual words don't even seem that complicated—but I haven't the foggiest idea what they are saying. It's like I'm not tuned in to their wavelength. They might as well be speaking Chinese.

When two or more people work on a project for a while, the project itself develops its own language based upon key terminology, acronyms and metaphors. Shared experiences or previously discussed issues can be referenced by a simple word or two, and this "project language" allows team members to communicate at higher bandwidths. Oftentimes, team members don't even have to complete their sentences once they realize that others have anticipated what they are going to say.

Some of the great results I've realized from these stand-up meetings stem from the fact that I've had the good fortune to work with a lot of bright people over the years. After working with hundreds of team members on dozens of projects, it is my opinion that this one-to-one or many-to-many synergy is something anyone can achieve. The process works better with some people than others. Here are some of the factors that I think contribute to synergistic dialogue:

- Intelligence: Some people are inherently brighter than others. Some are just better at expressing their intelligence in conversation.

- Rapport: Sometimes I don't get along with people—they can be the brightest person in the world, but if they don't like me to the point where they won't engage in the conversation, the ideas just don't flow. See discussion on "rapport" later in this section.

- Emotional Commitment: The degree to which the team members care about successfully completing the project has a huge impact on dialogue effectiveness. You can buy a person's back, but not his or her heart.

- Shared Knowledge: This is where groupware such as electronic mail (e-mail) can play a significant role. The better informed the participants are, the stronger the underlying foundation for high-bandwidth conversations. E-mail increases the information metabolism of the team by reducing the overhead of an information exchange event. In other words, the less time and effort it takes to exchange information, the more likely you are to do it. E-mail is discussed further in Chapter 7.

A similar phenomenon occurs with larger groups, but there are some disadvantages:

- The brainstorming sessions I'm talking about usually last between one and five minutes. If you try to include more people, it will take longer than that just to get them all together.

- One-on-one conversations can occur at higher bandwidths because there is only one other communication style to match. The more people involved, the greater the chances that you will have to stop and explain an issue to someone who may be working on multiple projects and thus isn't quite up to speed. You may be asking, "But don't you have access to more ideas if more people are involved?" Sometimes. Yet I seem to be able to resolve most issues just by talking things out with one individual. In some cases, I'll do multiple stand-up meetings, which are often preferable to coordinating a large formal meeting. On the other hand, if the issue impacts multiple areas "owned" by multiple people, then they should have the chance to offer their two cents worth. Sometimes this can be handled by firing off an e-mail that lets them know which direction you are going, so they can respond if they disapprove.

"Don't you interrupt people a lot with this method?" I try to minimize the number of these meetings by:

- Saving up the issues for a later conversation. Sometimes I'll figure things out after my unconscious has cranked on it a while.

- Making extra effort to resolve the issue on my own. Dialogue is not an excuse to avoid having to think through an issue. I balance dialogue with individual analysis and reasoning.

- I use e-mail as much as possible. However, I do not experience the "stepped-up" rate of thinking phenomenon (nuclear beta) when writing or reading e-mail. Some issues need the energy and dynamics of interpersonal conversation. If I can reduce the issue to a single, clear-cut question, then I use e-mail. The importance of the issue is also a factor. Deciding between e-mail and dialogue is sometimes a tough call.

- When I do ask to do a stand-up hallway meeting, I show respect for their time by keeping the conversation as short as possible.

In knowledge work, where one is often dealing in the realm of thought, pursuing a wrong direction can be costly in terms of both time and money. So when I sense that I'm at a critical juncture in my decision-making processes, it is usually a good time for a quick discussion. Other times, I will concentrate on an issue until I get to the point where I feel stuck, lost in the details and in need of fresh perspectives. Just as new ideas often appear when I begin writing—as if my hand knew it all along, I can gain new insights on an issue by using that part of my mind involved in a conversation.

The effectiveness of dialogue is further evidence that knowledge is distributed throughout the body and in some ways "compartmentalized." Dialogue is one way to tap into multiple compartments or lines of thinking.

Sometimes I am credited with coming up with great ideas when I am sure they were more a result of the process I was using (dialogue), than a product of any brilliance. There are many cases where the other person never even gets a word out! I walk in, start talking, and 30 seconds later the idea I need hits me right between the eyes. I thank them for "all their help," and walk out. They often respond, "But I didn't do anything!" After over ten years of this, I can say with a high level of certainty that they *did* a great deal. These great ideas were not my ideas. They were *our* ideas!

RAPPORT

My favorite strategy for building rapport is to consistently demonstrate a strong commitment to successfully completing the project. There are two dimensions to commitment: creating the appearance of commitment and the real thing—truly being committed (i.e., consistently doing the things that someone with a strong commitment would do). I try to focus on the "doing" and not worry about the appearance issue.

"To be, not to seem."

— Anonymous

When things aren't going so well, I try to remember that every disagreement or challenging relationship is a chance to learn something. I start by trying to understand them more completely, as described in Stephen Covey's *Seven Habits* teachings. While listening, I send them positive energy to help them verbalize their issues. The "control drama" distinctions in *The Celestine Prophecy* are sometimes helpful in my attempts to understand them. Also helpful are the ideas in Chapters 13-15 of Anthony Robbins' book, *Unlimited Power*. These chapters are a great overview of how Neuro Linguistic Programming (NLP) distinctions can be applied to relationships. Dale Carnegie's perennial favorite, *How to Win Friends & Influence People*, is also worth a look.

As much as possible, I emotionally disconnect from ideas presented by others, or myself, since they are the means. Instead I focus on the end—resolving the issue in a way that contributes to a successful project. It is usually obvious to all participants when this has been achieved. If not, then it's time to apply Stephen Covey's rule: "Value the differences," and work together to create a third alternative that satisfies all.

"When your work speaks for itself, don't interrupt."

— Henry J. Kaiser

BUILDING POSITIVE ENERGY

When I picked up James Redfield's book, *The Celestine Prophecy*, I didn't expect to learn a distinction that would positively impact almost every discussion with another person from that point on, but that is exactly what happened. The idea was this:

People have the ability to project energy consciously during a conversation.

Redfield describes the phenomenon as a "conscious conversation," whereby each person speaks when the energy moves to him or her. He states that during a discussion, only one person will have the most powerful idea at any given moment. Alert participants can feel who is about to speak and consciously focus their energy on this person, helping to bring out his or her idea with the greatest clarity. Redfield states, "The key to this process is to speak up only when it is your moment and to project energy when it is someone else's time." According to Peter Senge, Quakers apply this distinction by remaining silent until they "quake" from the need to express an idea.

This process can be disrupted if a participant experiences ego inflation when in a group. This occurs when an individual gets caught up in the power of an idea. Because the burst of energy feels so good when the idea is expressed, they keep on talking long after the energy should have shifted to someone else. These individuals try to monopolize the group, causing others to pull back to the point where they won't risk expressing themselves when they feel the power of an idea. The group fragments and members don't get the benefit of all the messages. Redfield states that the same thing happens when some participants are not accepted by other members. These rejected individuals don't receive supporting energy, increasing the likelihood that the group will miss the benefit of their ideas.

This is not codependency, according to Redfield, because real projection of energy has no attachment or intention, each person is just waiting for messages.

Others do not have to be aware of this principle in order to benefit from the energy you are sending them. You build positive energy within yourself by appreciating beauty and abundance in nature or life, and you project it to others by seeing them in their most positive light.

Sending positive energy is the opposite of throwing mental darts, or listening with a cynical attitude.

DIALOGUE CONTRASTED WITH "CHIT-CHAT"

Not all conversations are created equal. The synergistic dialogue I'm referring to is directed at solving a specific problem or resolving an issue as effectively and efficiently as possible. Ben Franklin lived his life by forming the habitude of thirteen virtues. The second virtue was to avoid trifling conversation by only speaking words that may benefit others or himself. To quote from his autobiography: "...my desire being to gain Knowledge at the same time that I improved in Virtue, and considering that in Conversation it was obtain'd rather by the Use of the Ears than of the Tongue, & therefore wishing to break a Habit I was getting into of Prattling, Punning and Joking, which only made me acceptable to trifling Company, I gave *Silence* the second Place."

FLUFF-BUSTING LANGUAGE

In their first NLP book, *The Structure of Magic*, Bandler and Grinder describe a "meta model" for reducing language to a highly specific, sensory-based description of what another person has said. It is based on the fact that people use three basic mechanisms for creating mental models or maps of external reality. When you run out of options in a discussion, it may be time to scrub off your mental models with the following set of distinctions:

- **Generalization**: "If something is true in one case, it is probably true in other cases." The words "always" and "never" indicate that a person is generalizing. Bandler and Grinder point out that the ability to generalize is an essential coping skill. However, each generalization must be evaluated in its context. We limit ourselves when we transfer generalizations used in one area of our lives to other areas where they don't apply. Sometimes it is useful to reply to such generalizations with questions such as "always?" or "never?"

- **Deletion**: External reality presents us with so much sensory information that we delete or ignore parts of it in order to maintain our sanity. The problem comes in when we delete information that could be used to expand our options—our behavioral flexibility. If you feel that you have run out of options in a conversation, try asking some innovative questions. When you hear the words "can't," "have to," or "should," try responding with questions such as "What would happen if...?" or, "What has to happen in order for...?" Questions are a great way to open up our awareness to information we have been deleting. In his book, *Awaken the Giant Within*, Anthony Robbins teaches that asking better questions often leads to better answers. He writes that we can tear down barriers in our life by questioning our limitations—that all human progress is preceded by new questions.

- **Distortion**: Another way people distort reality is by seeing a process as an event. The statement: "That person is intelligent," is *event* language, whereas: "That person does intelligent things," is *process* language. The statement: "I don't know how to do that," is *event* language, whereas "I don't know how to do that yet," is *process* language. Once you are aware that something is a process rather than an event, you can ask the question, "How can that process be optimized in order to better meet our objectives?"

THE SIX THINKING HATS

In his book, *The Six Thinking Hats*, Edward de Bono has developed a communication strategy based on the use of six different colored hats to represent various complementary modes of thinking. It allows you to ask for someone's response in a particular mode of thinking just by referring to the hat color. This strategy makes it more efficient to refer to the structural aspects of the conversation, which frees up your attention for content issues. The six thinking hats help unscramble mental activity by using only one thinking mode at a time. De Bono uses the four-color printing analogy: colors are printed separately in layers. When the process is complete, they all come together.

He has divided these six thinking modes into three pairs of opposites:

White and Red: White is neutral and objective (just the facts please), while red is emotional (gut reactions).

Black and Yellow: While wearing the black hat, one plays the devil's advocate, looking for what's wrong. This is complemented by yellow hat thinking, which is optimistic, positive, and focuses on the potential of the ideas.

Green and Blue: The green hat is for being creative and generating new ideas, while the blue hat is concerned with control and organization—making sure that the other hats are used effectively.

If you invest the effort ahead of time to explain the simple metaphor to your teammates, then you are much better prepared to deal with an individual who is being overly pessimistic or emotional. This allows you to say things like: "How about if we set down our red hats for a moment and emphasize what we know to be true before getting into gut reactions?"

Dr. de Bono believes that the six thinking hats can eventually develop into anchors for triggering specific chemical backgrounds in the brain which support the different modes of thinking.

SOWING AND REAPING IDEAS

Your efforts at communicating your desired end to your subconscious mind (as described in Chapter 3) are analogous to sowing seeds. Dialogue is one of the main places where you reap the idea harvest. The more you have primed your subconscious idea "pump" by clearly self-communicating your desired project outcome, the more likely you are to come up with related ideas on the fly while involved in synergistic dialogue. The following factors also enhance dialogue effectiveness and are discussed in later chapters:

- Mobilizing right-brain mental processes to increase mental flexibility in conversations (Chapter 5).
- Increasing the amount of related information your mind has access to at various levels of consciousness by doing high-speed scans over volumes of related information. Reviewing key terminology and concepts periodically enables faster conscious recall of these items in fast-paced conversations (Chapter 6).
- Using groupware such as e-mail to optimize the process of information sharing (Chapter 7).
- Doing things that optimize your mental clarity to increase your energy level, thus giving you access to more of your brainpower (Chapter 8).

CHAPTER 5

SYNERGISTIC OSCILLATION:
OPTIMIZING THE CREATIVE PROCESS

"Fully involve the right brain and you don't just double your brain power, you increase it many times over."
— *Colin Rose*

"The more complex the activities of the mind, the greater the need for play."
— *Star Trek*

Where and how do you get your best ideas? What process do you use to maximize the quantity and quality of the ideas you have to work with? What is known about the brain/mind that can be used to optimize this process?

Chapter 2 described how to obtain ideas and information from the external environment by directing our subconscious information filtering mechanisms. Chapter 4 suggested ways to increase the effectiveness of brainstorming sessions with others. This chapter discusses strategies for optimizing the individual brainstorming process. Dialogue was discussed first because forming project teams that balance complementary "what" and "how" expertise establishes the optimum infrastructure for supporting creative thought by individual team members.

Just as we have two legs, we have two brain hemispheres that specialize in complementary opposite modes of thinking. Just as we can run more than twice as fast as our top hopping speed, we can more than double our brain power by overcoming the tendency to use one side most of the time—by learning to use both sides of our brain synergistically.

Mobilizing the creative right brain gives the logical left brain more ideas to analyze. The disciplined structure of the left provides a context within which creative ideas can be organized and applied, often resulting in new questions for the right side to brainstorm. The result is a dynamic loop between the hemispheres, which I call a "brain dance."

The notion of using complementary opposite modes of thinking goes beyond left-brain right-brain synergy, however, so I expanded the brain dancing metaphor to include other sets of opposites:

Conscious ⟷ Subconscious
Individual Thought ⟷ Dialogue
Left-Brain Mode ⟷ **Right-Brain Mode**
Detailed Thought ⟷ High Level Thought

In his book, *Use Both Sides of Your Brain,* Tony Buzan writes that developing a mental area previously considered weak, rather than detracting from other areas, seems to produce a synergistic effect in which other areas of mental performance are improved. When I find a worthwhile activity that requires a huge amount of discipline to perform or even attempt, that is often a sign that I'm about to create some "intrapersonal" synergy.

To some extent, the idea of oscillating between left and right hemispheric mental processes is more of a metaphor than a hard and fast rule. Much work remains to figure out exactly which part of the brain is doing what. As a knowledge worker, the important question is not *which* part of the brain is involved, but rather, which thinking styles are complementary opposites and which areas have been neglected that offer the potential for mental leverage. Figure 5.1 summarizes the difference between left and right-brain mental processes.

Left-brain Mode	Right-brain Mode
Thinking in words, analyzing something in a linear, step-by-step fashion; Reducing a problem to smaller chunks; Using symbols such as 1, 2, 3 or +, -, /, and * as in mathematics; Remaining aware of time while you are doing something; Using reason and logic to make decisions based on facts.	Being aware of something without labeling it or using words to describe the experience; Seeing the big picture, how parts or ideas relate to each other and the overall context; Awareness of high level structure; Synthesizing; Operating without an awareness of time; Going with the flow; Thinking in metaphors to transfer meaning from one context to another; Rhythm and spatial awareness.

Figure 5.1 Left-Brain vs. Right-Brain Thought Processes.[1]

Brain dancing involves using the strengths of both modes in complementary ways. This could mean using the right brain as the idea factory and the left to provide a context in which those ideas can be applied; using left-brain mode to come up with questions and right-brain mode to provide possible answers for the left brain to analyze; using the left brain to make a decision and the intuitive, holistic right brain to do an ecology check. You can think of it as a sort of mental ping-pong.

While testing complex interactive software for clients, I found it helpful to combine both left and right-brain tests. Using left-brain analysis, I created a detailed test plan covering every situation I could think of. The software was so complex, however, that there was no way it could cover every possibility. To compensate, I used right-brain intuitive hunches to "sniff out" bugs by trying unusual test

---

[1] Adapted from material in Betty Edwards book, *Drawing on the Right Side of the Brain*, and *The Brain Book*, by Peter Russell.

combinations that "came to mind" as I was performing the left-brain tests.

Western society and educational systems tend to favor left-brain usage, yet the right brain is capable of equally valuable but different mental processes. Mobilizing these latent capacities often has a synergistic impact on left-brain mental processes.

Hemispheric specialization pioneer Robert Ornstein writes in his book, *The Psychology of Consciousness*, that "It is the polarity and the integration of these two modes of consciousness, the complementary workings of the intellect and the intuitive, which underlie our highest achievements." He points out that some people have a tendency to habitually prefer one mode. Verbal, logical scientists sometimes forget or even deny that they possess another side. In such a case, they might find it difficult to do right-brain activities such as art, crafts, dance, or sports. According to Ornstein, Einstein used the phrase "combinatory play" to describe the impact these activities had on his creative thinking.

It takes discipline to override this tendency to habitually prefer one mode. Is it worth it? Consider the lives of two great thinkers in history: Albert Einstein and Leonardo da Vinci. Einstein complemented his left brain efforts in mathematics and science with violin playing, art, sailing and imagination games. Da Vinci excelled in art, sculpture, athletics, architecture, mechanics, anatomy, physics, geology and engineering. The synergistic benefits of these various activities were evident in his paintings. According to Tony Buzan in *Use Both Sides of Your Brain*, da Vinci's plans for his paintings often looked like architectural drawings.

Did these two men accomplish great things because they were geniuses, and thus had the mental capacity to do these complementary activities? Or did performing these complementary activities help them accomplish great things? Probably some combination of both. However, it is more useful to emphasize the latter. Smart is as smart does.

"Not all birds can fly. What separates the flyers from the walkers is the ability to take off."

— *Carl Sagan, Cosmos*

TIPPING THE FIRST DOMINO

So how does one "tip the first domino" in breaking this tendency to involve only one brain hemisphere? Here are four overall strategies:

1) **Give yourself a reason to do so.** Set a goal for yourself or take on a project that demands the use of your latent capacities. To activate subdominant visual and perceptual right-brain processes, present your mind with a task that the analytical and verbal left-brain processes will reject. The tendency for most people is not to think in new ways unless they have to. Truly committing to a challenging project that demands the use of right-brain thinking can be a booster rocket on your mental journey from "Can't" to "Must!"

2) **Decide to teach this material to others.** This shifts your paradigm in a way that increases how much you pay attention. It forces you to crystallize your thoughts—to organize, simplify and fine tune them. Tony Robbins makes a key point when he states that most people will do far more to help others than they'll ever do for themselves.

3) **Act "as if."** Begin doing an activity that requires right-brain activity, acting as if you already know how to do it. As discussed later in this chapter, Mind Mapping is an excellent opportunity to apply this strategy.

4) **Model someone.** Find creative people and observe them. It is one thing to use complementary opposites and quite another to do it effectively.

THE CREATIVE PROCESS

Edison took short naps, Einstein played the violin and da Vinci engineered his paintings. The Japanese inventor, Yoshiro NakaMats, uses a three-step mental process, Walt Disney used three modes of thinking that he called dreamer, realist and critic,[2] creativity consultant Roger von Oech suggests alternating between four complementary roles, and, as discussed in Chapter 4, Dr. Edward de Bono teaches six "Thinking Hats" which correspond to three pairs of opposite thinking styles. This section explores strategies used by some highly creative people involving complementary opposite styles of thinking.

THE BEST OF THE BEST

Have you ever wondered who invented the floppy disk and digital watch? According to Charles Thompson, author of *What a Great Idea: The Key Steps Creative People Take*, the answer is Dr. Yoshiro NakaMats, a Japanese inventor who holds over 3,000 patents (Edison had 1,093). Thompson's excellent book includes an interview with Dr. NakaMats that details many of the secrets to his extraordinary success.[3] The following is a brief summary of the interview. Each of the three steps in Dr. NakaMats' creative process is done in a separate room:

- Static Room: In this room, Dr. NakaMats calms himself as much as possible by surrounding himself with natural things such as a rock garden, natural running water and plants. He uses this room to free-associate and let his mind "wander where it will." Before focusing on one thing in the next room, the static room is used to churn out volumes of ideas.

---

[2] For more information on Walt Disney's creative process, refer to *Skills for the Future* by Robert Dilts.

[3] The complete text of this interview is available online at: **http://www.whatagreatidea.com/main/naka.html**.

- Dynamic Room: The décor in this room is the opposite of the Static room. This may serve as an environmental anchor for conditioning his thinking to switch modes as he moves between rooms. In this room he listens to a variety of music as he focuses his mind on a specific issue.
- Creative Swimming Room: The final step involves swimming underwater with a Plexiglas writing pad. It is here that he comes up with his best ideas. According to Lynn Schroeder and Sheila Ostrander in their book, *Superlearning 2000*, Dr. NakaMats sits cross-legged on the bottom in five feet of water in four to five minute stretches. "The water pressure forces blood and oxygen into my brain, making it work at peak performance," NakaMats explains.

Schroeder and Ostrander report that Dr. NakaMats is now a billionaire. The following material elaborates on some of the distinctions applied by Dr. NakaMats in his creative process.

OUR THINKING IS STATE BOUND

Renowned creativity consultant Roger von Oech believes one of the reasons we forget is that our memory is state bound. Changing our state changes the associations we "notice" in our mind. The most obvious example of this phenomenon goes something like this: while sitting on the couch in the living room, you realize that you need something from the bedroom. When you get to the bedroom, you have no idea what you went in there for, so you head back. As soon as your rear hits the couch, you remember what it was. If these situations were caused simply by a declining memory, why do we remember the idea so consistently when we sit back down on the couch? Because when we returned to the same location and physiology where we had the original idea, it triggers the same synaptic storm in our mind and we remember instantly. One woman told me that when this happens to her, she starts walking backwards until she remembers.

Not only is our memory state bound, but so is our thinking. The lesson is this: when involved in creative problem solving, vary your physiology and think about the issue in different locations. Dr. NakaMats seems to apply this principle to the *nth* degree. If the need to generate new ideas arises while working on site, I sometimes walk up a hill where I can look out over a distance. Other times I take a pad or pencil to the cafeteria, library, or even a conference room. These changes of scenery seem to trigger different "modes of thinking" and broaden my access to ideas.

Several books have mentioned Bill Gates' practice of scheduling management retreats for evaluating strategic issues in an environment unencumbered by reminders of daily responsibilities. Our usual surroundings can become anchors that limit our thinking to a few well-worn paths.

This link between state and idea flow may also explain why we get so many ideas while taking showers. Next time you shower, notice all of the unique movements involved in scrubbing down. If you get ideas while showering, and you need more ideas, Roger von Oech suggests taking more showers. I guess a person could apply this at work by standing up in their office and begin moving around as if they were taking a shower. Imagine having to explain *that* to your boss: "Well, uh, I was just doing a brain dance in an attempt to create a shower of innovative ideas into my mind." I've tried this and for some reason these "virtual showers" don't work for me. The water in the shower seems to play a key role in turning up the "flow" of ideas.

THE LINK BETWEEN WATER AND CREATIVITY

Using a swimming pool gives NakaMats great freedom of movement, which may account for his creative effectiveness in this room. However, another possible explanation for NakaMats getting his best ideas in this pool, and for so many people getting ideas when showering, is that water has an amazing ability to store and transfer information. Is it a coincidence that creativity master Roger von Oech is a competitive swimmer? In *Whack on the Side of the Head*, von Oech writes that Atari founder, Nolan Bushnell, invented the game *Breakout* while running his fingers through the sand on a beach.

We live in an ocean of air. Spaceships returning to Earth will bounce off the atmosphere if they come in at too steep an angle. The air may be able to store information as well. Alexander Graham Bell believed that various thoughts are bouncing around in the ether along with radio waves. Many people, including myself, get ideas while driving, especially on roads out of my normal routine. Wolfgang Amadeus Mozart claimed that many of his best musical ideas came while he was walking or riding in a carriage.

At a recent seminar, Deepak Chopra held up his hand with the ends of his thumb and index fingers touching to form a circle. He pointed out that within that small circle exists the information necessary to reproduce all of the local TV and radio station broadcasts, hundreds of cellular phone transmissions, satellite transmissions, marine band, and amateur radio broadcasts—I think you get the point. We are immersed in a sea of literally infinite information. Our body, more specifically, our brain, is a tuning device. You may have heard of some individuals picking up radio stations in their fillings. Is it possible that the various minerals in our body are tuning into thoughts at various levels of awareness?

Hold up a battery-powered radio and adjust the tuner to scan the various channels. Notice that there are no wires connecting that radio to those stations. We often overlook just what a miracle this is.

Just as radios can pick up different stations from different locations and when directed at different angles, our body/mind may be able to tune into different thoughts as we travel. The increased diversity of sensory input when traveling to new places probably opens up new synaptic pathways, which can translate into more flexible thinking.

In most cases, we don't need to know exactly why an idea helps us be more creative in order to apply it effectively.

THE LINK BETWEEN MUSIC AND CREATIVITY

Thompson reports that NakaMats uses various types of music (jazz, easy listening, and classical) in his Dynamic Room. Everybody is different, and we each work on different problems in different ways, so I recommend that you experiment to see which music works best for you. Studies indicate that listening to Mozart can increase brain function. I believe this happens because the music stimulates a variety of neurons in precise sequence and with precise timing—something like a brain massage. True listening requires that you invest attention noticing the details of the music, as opposed to merely bouncing sound waves off your eardrums.

THE LINK BETWEEN MENTAL CLARITY AND CREATIVITY

As Dr. NakaMats explains in his interview with Charles Thompson, we can improve the flow of ideas into our mind by eating only the best foods and avoiding alcohol. Food can have a dramatic impact on our thinking, a topic explored in depth in Chapter 8—Optimizing Mental Clarity. You can't take the chips out of a computer, drop them in mud, and expect them to run the same software with equal grace. Our brain is the hardware, the vehicle through which ideas flow and are processed.

"A pessimist sees the difficulty in every opportunity; an optimist sees the opportunity in every difficulty."

— *Sir Winston Churchill*

FRACTALS: CLASSICAL MUSIC FOR THE EYES

Jollean McFarlen, based in Vancouver, B.C., teaches vibrant seminars about the specific impact various colors have on our thinking. Not long after attending her seminar, I watched a PBS special called *The Colours of Infinity*, hosted by Arthur C. Clarke. The show featured computer-generated art derived from fractal mathematics. Two sections of this program can be used to stimulate creative thinking, although they were not intended for this purpose. The first, called "Cycling Colors," is where a single fractal image is shown, but the number used to derive color is varied continuously. The result is an image that appears to be moving and flowing in wondrously precise and beautiful ways.

The second section of this program with potential to enhance creativity is what I call "Infinite Zoom." This is where the camera appears to zoom in on a portion of the fractal image continuously. Because the fractal set has virtually infinite depth, the zooming process just goes on and on. It is like traveling through a fractal wonderland of mathematically precise, yet incredibly varied colors and images. After watching this program for the first time, I noticed that I had a significant surge of creativity. I've since discovered other ways of using fractals to promote creativity.

To give you a rough idea what they look like, I've included black and white versions of a couple fractals in Figure 5.2. Color versions of these and several others are available at **BrainDance.com**.

You can create fractals similar to these using the Mandelbrot Explorer at the following Web site sponsored by the National Technical University of Athens in Greece:

http://www.softlab.ntua.gr/mandel

You can do a rough approximation of the "cycling colors" effect mentioned above, by downloading a copy of the FractInt software from **Shareware.com**. The filename is frain192.zip.

I also keep a poster of fractal images on the wall by my desk to occasionally bathe my eyes in creative color. You can order "Fractal Collage" from the Pacific Science Center in Seattle, Washington for $6.95 (plus shipping) by calling (206) 443-2870. Ask for poster #5091.

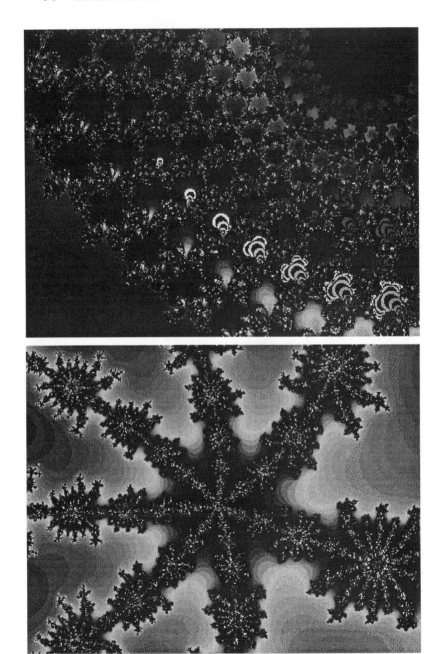

☗ Figure 5.2 Black and White Screen Shots of Multi-Colored Fractals. See refdoc.htm for Color Versions.

ROGER VON OECH'S FOUR ROLES FOR HIGHLY CREATIVE PERFORMANCE

In his book, *A Kick in the Seat of the Pants*, Roger von Oech recommends alternating between four roles for highly creative performance—Explorer, Artist, Judge and Warrior. This approach looks at the overall creative process on a larger time scale. The following discussion explains how these four roles can be applied to capacity enhancing projects.

Explorer: This mode involves gathering the raw materials from which ideas can be made. This includes ideas such as facts, theories, rules, concepts, feelings and impressions. In this role, the high speed scanning skills discussed in the next chapter are invaluable. When exploring, von Oech suggests that you do whatever it takes to break out of your mental ruts and routines. He recommends that you temporarily set aside your need to specialize—to be a master of a narrow field that is often so valuable to businesses. I believe that the principle of "personal ecology" plays a significant role in buying yourself this flexibility. If you are going to abandon your structure, you had better do it in a structured way—by setting specific time limits on your unstructured time. I use Explorer mode by periodically visiting bookstores, libraries, trade shows or surfing the Internet. These sources provide so much information that if I don't set specific time limits, I might get carried away and end up spending more time than I can afford. The price for giving myself the freedom to explore these vast information storehouses is the discipline it takes to set a specific time limit for this exploration, and then sticking to it.

Artist: After you broaden your idea pool on a given subject, von Oech suggests that you perform a variety of mental gymnastics to do something to the information. He suggests asking yourself which patterns you can change and how you can alter the way you think about an issue.

Von Oech gives several suggestions for using imagination to transform raw information into useful ideas while in this mode. Mind Maps, discussed in the next section, are a useful tool for operating in this mode.

Judge: Evaluate an idea and decide what to do with it: implement, modify or discard it. According to von Oech, this is the role people are most likely to get stuck in. The Judge neither creates nor implements, so if you spend too much time in this role you risk not getting much accomplished. I use this mode when converting Mind Mapped ideas into linear plans for action, whether that plan be the precise order to deliver a speech, write a paper or accomplish a task.

Warrior: In this role, you carry your ideas from the world of "what if" into the world of action. Von Oech suggests that the creative process is not a series of linear steps, but an ongoing cycle. The warrior completes the loop, providing feedback to the other roles. Schedule your most productive time for warrior mode activities.

What does the life cycle of an idea look like in your life? What do you do with ideas that drift into your awareness? Do you incorporate them into conversations periodically to explore them verbally, write about them, incorporate them into products, or log them into a knowledge base or journal for future reference? Do you incorporate them into speeches, Mind Map them, or extrapolate them into areas of thinking other than the one in which they originated? Do you have a "Potential Project/Product" folder for filing related notes? Have you created a "Spec" directory on your hard drive where you can quickly create a new specification without loosing track of it and begin to flesh out the outline of a product or service based on the idea?

If your cup runneth over, there may not be room for new ideas. Being good stewards of the ideas we do get may help to encourage their inflow.

There are times when we need to shut off this flow, as in warrior mode—the "just get it done" phase. When ideas get in their way, people often find ways of indirectly (unconsciously) disrupting the flow.

Input → System → Output

Where's the bottleneck for new ideas in your life, if any? Do you need better ideas (input)? Better processes for acting on the ideas you are already getting (system)? Or just better strategies for formulating more useful outcomes—one of our primary means of opening up the faucet of new input?

As in many areas of life, it is usually a combination of things (habits, actions and decisions) that result in creative productivity.

The next three sections will give you three specific techniques to bridge the gap between oscillation theory and practical application:

- Mind Maps: Outlines a three-step process for using Mind Mapping and related techniques for optimizing the creative writing process.

- Two to ten minute breaks: Sometimes the most productive thing you can do when performing a challenging task is to take a short break. This section suggests some of the most effective break activities I've discovered.

- Mental Rest: On a larger scale, the mind needs to rest just as the body does, yet the mind does not rest while we sleep. This section discusses the principle and strategies for achieving effective mental rest.

MIND MAPS®

Tony Buzan invented Mind Maps in the 1960's while he was serving as editor for the *International MENSA Journal.* Buzan introduced this technique in his book, *Use Both Sides of Your Brain,* and recently published an update called *The Mind Map Book,* which is now the definitive work on the subject (**www.buzan.co.uk**).

Mind Maps give you a new way to represent ideas on paper that more closely resembles how ideas are stored in your mind. The technique is so different from established norms that it has met some cultural resistance. However, Mind Maps are beginning to make inroads into mainstream business. For example, Buzan's latest book mentions that Boeing condensed an engineering manual into a 25-foot long Mind Map. This enabled a team of 100 senior aeronautical engineers to learn in a few weeks what had previously taken a few years. The result was an estimated savings of $11,000,000.

Figure 5.3 is a Mind Map of the content of this chapter. Notice how concisely it conveys the structure of the ideas. When I list the rules for Mind Map creation later in this chapter, you will notice that I don't always follow them. For myself, Mind Maps usually serve as a means to an end, not as an end in themselves, and I adapt them accordingly.

Four years passed between the time I first learned of Mind Maps and when I actually started using them. I remember being sort of proud that I even knew what they were. Taking so long to bridge the gap between "knowing" and "doing" was a mistake. The following material is designed to help shorten your journey from awareness to actual use.

What I've discovered is that Mind Maps are much more than another note-taking method. In addition to increasing my understanding of how my mind works, they have improved my memory, creative thinking and writing skills, and reading effectiveness. The process of learning to draw is a great way to learn how your brain handles information.

This image of an oak tree offers a great metaphor for understanding how ideas are organized in the brain: associatively, with many overlapping branches of knowledge. Mind Maps often resemble trees. Each large branch signifies a central issue, with related ideas branching off to represent related sub-issues.

Many accelerated learning strategies involve techniques that mobilize both hemispheres of the mind in a synergistic fashion. Mind Mapping does this by helping you think at "meta" levels—dealing with the structure of information and seeing how the ideas relate to each other, which is a right-brain mental process. Sometimes the essence is in the pattern of relationships. The concise representation of a topic's structural organization encourages perspectives and connections not always obvious when the ideas are viewed in a linear fashion.

The easiest way to get started using Mind Maps is to just start doing them as if you already know how. Set short time limits on your initial efforts (five to ten minutes) so you don't get carried away. Periodically refer to the rules in order to gradually refine your technique. As mentioned earlier, most Mind Maps I create are a means, not an end—they are just a step in the process of getting the work done, and are often discarded when the task is done.

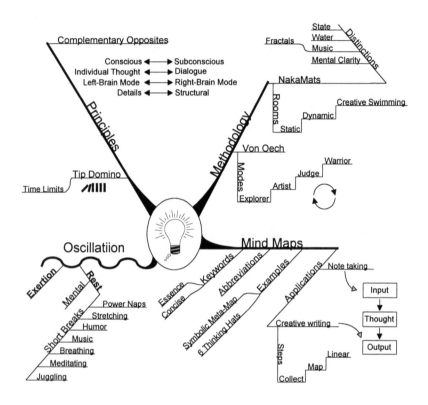

Figure 5.3 Mind Map of this Chapter.

While Mind Maps involve using pictures, I normally don't consider it a wise investment of my time to make them works of art. Quick sketches usually serve just fine unless I plan to publish them. Tony Buzan's latest book presents truly awesome examples of Mind Maps that really are works of art. While this may be an excellent way to mobilize right-brain capacity, I create so many Mind Maps that to make each one a work of art would make their use impractical.

I rarely use Mind Maps in "Warrior" mode; this is a time for action, not tossing ideas around as in the "Artist" phase of a project.

KEYWORDS

The concept of keywords is fundamental in Mind Mapping and has broad implications for other mental processes. Consider the following sentence:

> While computers have come a long way and had a dramatic impact on society, the potential of multimedia and the Internet offer strong evidence that the computer revolution has really just begun.

The keywords in this sentence, the words that are most memorable and contain the essence of the sentence, are *computers, impact society, multimedia, Internet* and *revolution begun.* The remaining words are there for grammatical purposes and are not necessary for recall. Take one of the following paragraphs and highlight the keywords. Select keywords that represent the essence of the meaning to you—the ones that will help you recall its content. These are the words to use on Mind Maps.

Keywords are highly personal. Some words carry different meaning for different people. Secondly, the keywords you want to emphasize depend heavily on your specific objectives at the time. Substantive text often addresses issues from a variety of angles. Life is multidimensional; written text is linear. The keyword distinction can help you bridge this mental gap in a way that is appropriate to your circumstances.

Chapters 6 and 9 of this book include modified Mind Maps of their content. The Mind Maps you draw of these chapters may be completely different. Material you have already mastered will need little attention. Other ideas may be so new that you'll want to Mind Map them in much more detail. When creating a Mind Map, it helps to be clear on whether you are creating it for your own review or to convey information to others. My primary objective in using Mind Maps in this book is to convey *Gestalt,* or overall structural information, about each chapter. I felt this objective could best be met by including a few extra words that wouldn't be there if these Mind Maps were only for my own reference.

TWO MAIN WAYS OF USING MIND MAPS

The way you use Mind Maps depends on whether you are taking in information (Explorer mode) or doing something with the information (Artist and Judge modes). Since the emphasis of this chapter is on creative thinking, I will emphasize the "output" side of the Mind Mapping equation. The next chapter covers the "input" side.

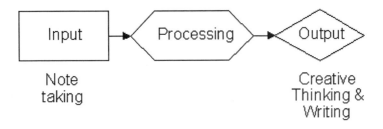

Figure 5.4 Two Basic Uses of Mind Maps.

THREE-STEP CREATIVE WRITING PROCESS

Whether you are writing a speech, technical white paper, specification, strategic plan or chapter in a book, the following three-step process can be applied:

1) **Idea Collection**: Use various brainstorming techniques to gather your thoughts on a specific topic.
2) **Idea Mapping**: Create Mind Maps that organize your thoughts structurally.
3) **Conversion to Linear Form**: When writing or speaking, ideas must be presented one word after another. The challenge is to present the material in a way that the associations and structure of the material are not lost.

These are general guidelines to be adapted to specific circumstances. For example, when doing presentations, I'll sometimes do step three on the fly trusting my subconscious to pull ideas off the Mind Map spontaneously.

IDEA COLLECTION SHEETS

Idea collection sheets serve as a bridge across the space and time that separate the great ideas you are capable of coming up with on any specific topic. The steps are:

1) Use unlined paper. Lined paper shuts down the right brain. I use 11x17 or larger paper when tackling major issues.

2) Try turning the paper sideways. "Landscape" mode seems to work better for me in part because it helps me see more of the page at one time.

3) Write the topic in the center and circle it, or quickly sketch a symbol representing the essence or theme of what you plan to write.

4) Set your stopwatch for 5-7 minutes, or just jot the ending time in the upper left corner as a reminder.

5) As quickly as possible, write as many ideas related to this topic as you can. Use personalized abbreviations, symbols, or any other method you have for writing at higher bandwidths. This is not a steadfast rule. To evolve an idea, I sometimes choose to write a short sentence. Collecting ideas is an art, not a science. Your success is measured by the quality of the ideas you come up with, not by how many of the rules you followed in coming up with them. Use whatever writing instrument allows you to write the fastest in the most comfortable manner. Avoid pens that drag across the paper unless held at a certain angle.

Many of the aspects of Mind Mapping disrupt the rapid flow of ideas during the collection phase. The idea collection phase differs from the Mind Mapping phase in the following ways:

- Use the same writing instrument throughout. Don't take time to switch pens to write or draw in a different color.

- Write down your ideas as they flow without judging whether the idea is related to the topic. Some ideas are "mental bridges" to other useful and more directly related ideas.

- Write your ideas in the first place that comes to mind. Don't take the time to position the idea in the optimal place. Placement is a Mind Mapping step.

After completing the initial mental burst, take a short break to incubate related ideas. The Two to Ten Minute Break Ideas section later in this chapter offers some ideas. After your break, take 30-40 minutes to pull related ideas from various reference materials. Follow this session with another short break or just move on to another project. Some topics require multiple passes.

If possible, place the idea collection sheet in a place where it will be handy over the next day or two. When related ideas come to you, write them on this sheet or jot them in your calendar and transfer them to the idea collection sheet when convenient. I usually carry a portfolio around which contains a few sheets of unlined paper for this purpose. I slide the unlined paper behind the pad of lined paper until needed. Idea collection sheets in progress are often stored here as well. Carrying idea collection sheets around with me allows me to round them out from the perspective of a variety of mental states or compartments.

The quicker I can access these idea buckets, the more likely I am to use them, so I carry a small stack of Post-it™ notes in my DAY-TIMER®. Before putting an idea collection sheet away for the first time, I'll attach a labeled Post-it tab on the right side so that it sticks out a little.

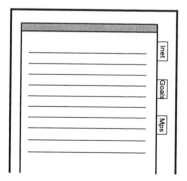

CATEGORIZING IDEAS

Using idea collection sheets as a precursor to Mind Mapping was inspired in part by material in Charles Thompson's book, *What a Great Idea!* Thompson suggests using various symbols such as circles, squares and triangles to help categorize the points on the idea collection sheet before organizing them into a map. For example, in reviewing an idea collection sheet, you might notice that there are four main themes to the ideas. You could place a circle around all ideas related to theme one, a triangle for ideas related to theme two, etc. These symbols make it apparent how many ideas relate to each theme, which helps you decide how to organize them in the Mind Map. In some cases, I find it easier to just put small symbols next to each idea rather than take the time to draw all the way around the text.

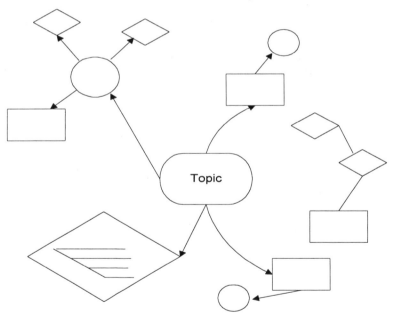

Figure 5.5 Using Symbols to Categorize Items on Idea Collection Sheets. Ideas are placed on the sheet quickly without much concern for neatness or organization.

Now that you have gathered your thoughts, you are ready to organize them into a structure based on how they relate to each other. This leads us to Mind Maps.

CONVERTING TO MIND MAP FORM

The rules for converting your ideas into a Mind Map are as follows:

1) Use unlined paper or a whiteboard. Sometimes bigger paper allows for "bigger thinking." I know one individual who made an entire wall into a whiteboard for strategic thinking and planning.

2) Start by drawing a color symbol in the middle of the page. This encourages right-brain activity from the outset. If an image doesn't come to me in 10-15 seconds, I use keywords and circle them with a border. Sometimes the border is simply a geometric shape such as a square or circle. Other times I use shapes like a 3-D book or computer monitor. At any rate, the best way to get it done is quickly!

3) Branch lines for the main ideas off this central image.

4) Use one keyword or symbol per branch line. Avoiding clutter permits more ideas to be represented and encourages your mind to see how they relate to each other.

5) Print the words on top of the lines. Printed words are easier to read than cursive.

6) Use color throughout. This can be especially useful in grouping related ideas.

7) Use images throughout your Mind Map. In practice, I usually include a few quick sketches and symbols. But I don't think "on the job" is the best place to create a drawing masterpiece unless they are to be used by others. Most of my Mind Maps are used as a means, not an end.

Mind Maps are versatile tools that can be applied in as many ways as there are people to apply them. To expand your understanding of what is possible with Mind Mapping, refer to *The Mind Map Book* and *Use Both Sides of Your Brain* by Tony Buzan, *Get Ahead!* by Vanda North, and *Mindmapping* by Joyce Wycoff.

At this point in the three-step process you know *what* you want to communicate—the substance. You still have to figure out the *how*—the sequence. Whether you are writing a paper or delivering a speech, these are linear forms of communication where the material must be presented one word after another.

CONVERSION TO LINEAR FORM

In the case of a speech, you have three possibilities: writing it out word for word (extreme left-brained approach), winging it from your Mind Map (extreme right-brained approach), or something in-between. One technique is to write numbers next to each major section of the Mind Map to indicate the order of delivery. Sometimes I write out the speech based on my Mind Map simply as a mental exercise, then use new distinctions gained from this writing to evolve a new more sequential Mind Map organized something like Figure 5.6.

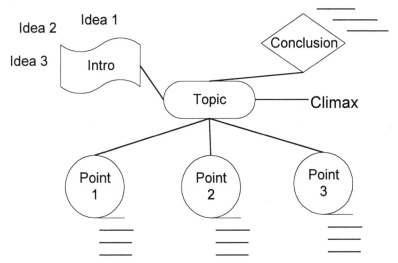

Figure 5.6 "Sequential" Mind Map for Speech Delivery.

The more right-brain deliveries you rehearse from Mind Maps, the better your chances of successfully speaking extemporaneously in front of an audience.

DEVELOP A PERSONALIZED ABBREVIATION SYSTEM

Developing a personalized abbreviation system can help you write at higher bandwidths. It can help you express ideas more rapidly in written form when brainstorming an idea collection sheet or recording an idea in your journal. Writing faster allows you to think faster, and when ideas come in rapid bursts, you are able to capture more of them. I have found it helpful to accumulate abbreviations and symbols for commonly used words on an idea collection sheet. This allows you to easily add new words near related terms. Periodically reviewing this sheet will help transfer these ideas to long term memory to ensure consistency. A further advantage is that when creating Mind Maps, the symbols and abbreviations help reduce clutter. This in turn helps you fit more ideas on a single page. Here are the symbols I used to represent the chapters of my book:

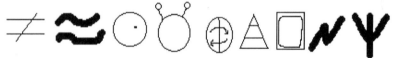

The first one is a "not equals" symbol, because the first chapter was originally called, "Not All Thoughts Are Created Equal." The second symbolizes a river, because the second chapter addresses the issue of interacting with the "river of increasing swiftness." The third is a miniature version of the figure illustrating the relative capacities of the conscious and subconscious minds, as Chapter 3 is about directing the subconscious. The fourth symbol is a pair of antennae being raised since having a mastermind discussion with others somehow increases our access to a broader pool of ideas. The fifth symbolizes the synergistic loop between the two brain hemispheres when we are engaged in activities such as Mind Mapping, which mobilizes both hemispheres. The sixth symbolizes the structure of information, with the small triangle at the top representing high level structural information. The seventh is a small computer monitor, since that chapter is about learning software faster. The eighth is a bolt of lightning representing the chapter on energy. The last symbol is a miniature version of one of the Mind Maps in that chapter.

The table below summarizes many of the abbreviations I use frequently in Mind Maps and when writing.

bus-business	i/s-income statement
co-company	stmt-statement
ee-employee	acct-account
e-entrepreneur	acctg-accounting
er-employer	app-application
mktg-marketing	diff-difference or differentiate
mo-month	auto-automatic(ally)
mp-metaphor	inet-internet
yr-year	mstr-master
pship-partnership	/-and or
exec-executive	loc-line of credit
mm-mindmap	cust-customer
uc-unconscious/subconscious	ics-idea collection sheet
bd-brain dancing	lm-life mgmt
ey-energy	sys-system
ptnr-partner	fin-finance
- pause in speech	sched-schedule
bplan-business plan	perf-performance
info-information	otl-outline
tech-technology, or techniques	#-number
ef-effectiveness	hr-hour
ey-efficiency	dy-day
admin-administrative	min-minute
dev-develop	lit-literature
char-character	req-required
w/-with	comm-communicate
w/o-without	
w/i-within	**Meeting Notes**
s/b-should be	A-action item
res-resource	?-question
gen-generate	N-note and file
c/f-cashflow	->postpone issue

SYMBOLIC META-MAPS

While writing this book, I found it useful to create what I call a Symbolic Meta-Map (SMM). This involved placing nine pieces of 33" x 27" flip chart paper on a wall as represented in Figure 5.7. Each sheet represented one chapter.

My objective with the SMM was to represent as much information as possible as efficiently as possible. I wanted to symbolize ideas to the point where I could mentally traverse the content of the entire book in just a few minutes. The SMM became a tool for thinking about how the ideas would flow from chapter to chapter.

Why didn't I use software for this? Speed. If I had all of this on the computer, I would have been loading files, pressing keys and clicking the mouse in order to move around. All of these steps would have distracted my thinking while trying to make new connections. Someday when I have a wall size monitor, I'll reconsider my approach. Again, the medium influenced the message. I used the PC for many things in writing this book. Designing high-level idea flow wasn't one of them.

The purpose of each section of the SMM was as follows:

- **Objectives**: In the lower right-hand corner of each sheet, I wrote my specific objectives for the chapter. Only ideas that contributed to these ends made it on the sheets. These objectives also helped me determine when I was "done" with a chapter.

- **Chapter Symbols**: A simple symbol was selected for each chapter and placed in the upper left corner of the corresponding sheet. These symbols were used to classify lists of ideas, DAY-TIMER journal entries, and Post-it tabs placed in books that I wanted to reference. When working on a chapter, I could pick up lots of books on the subject and quickly locate sections related to that chapter. I could also easily flip through my journal and reference just the ideas related to the chapter I was working on.

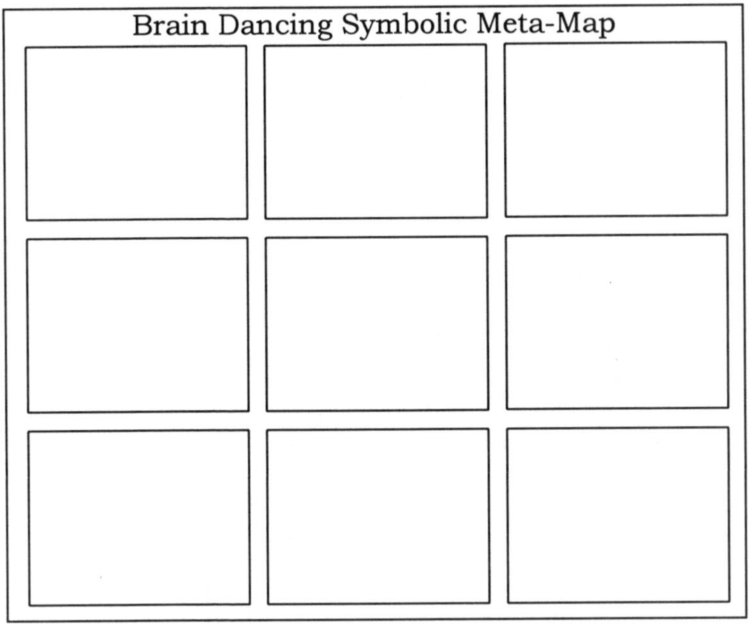

Figure 5.7. Symbolic Meta-Map Covering Entire Wall.

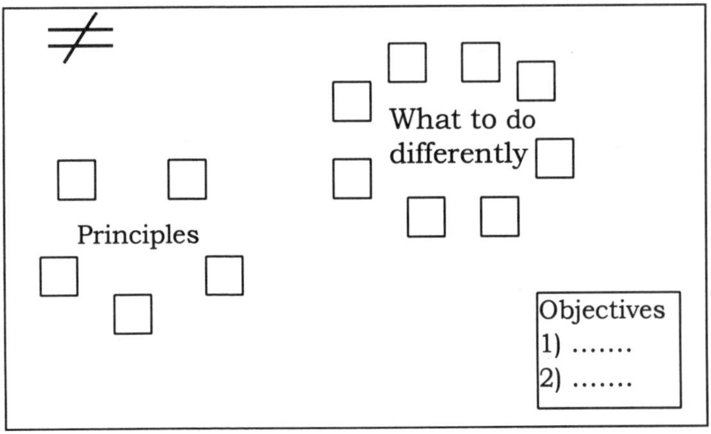

Figure 5.8 One Chapter in Symbolic Meta-Map.

- **Sticky notes**: All ideas were placed on Post-it notes of various sizes and colors (sometimes I used normal paper with a little tape). This allowed me to easily move the ideas around, on and between sheets. Different sizes and colors were used for different categories of ideas (beliefs, principles, quotes, metaphors, examples, action items, etc.).

- **Placement**: Initially, the ideas were just pasted randomly on the sheet corresponding to the chapter in which I thought they belonged. The ideas were then divided according to whether they described a principle or instructed the reader on what to do differently. Related ideas were stacked on top of each other. For example, this chapter's "What to do differently" section had a sticky note entitled "2-10 Minute Breaks" (discussed in the next section). Behind this note I had stacked several notes representing different types of short breaks a person can take.

- **Cross-references**: I developed symbols for referencing material in other places. For example, "DT 4/5/94" meant "see related material in my DAY-TIMER on April 5, 1994." "REE 64" meant "see page 64 in the book *Re-engineering the Corporation.*"

In addition to helping me organize this book, this SMM was very helpful when it came to writing each chapter. Large, complex projects are ideal candidates for using this variation of Mind Mapping.

OTHER MIND MAP APPLICATIONS

Mind Mapping is new territory and the last word has not been written. You may even discover a new, more useful way to do them. As an example, Jeff B.R. Gaspersz, Ph.D., Associate Professor of Human Resource Management at Nijenrode University in the Netherlands, suggests the following: Write the idea you are working on in the middle of the page and then draw six lines, one for each thinking mode represented by Dr. de Bono's six hats. Think about the issue from each perspective to see what ideas flow onto the page. Then examine them as a whole.

If you are just beginning to learn how to access the Internet, you may want to create an ongoing Mind Map of what you learn. Each time you pick up a new distinction, you can add it to this sheet and see how it relates to other ideas you have discovered. The larger the body of information surrounding what you are learning, the more helpful it will be to create an ongoing Mind Map.

Mind Maps play a key role in multiple areas of my life. In the next chapter, you will see how they help optimize reading effectiveness. I also use them when learning new computer software, as discussed in Chapter 7. Chapter 9 describes how I use Mind Maps to evolve and "detect" my mission statement, values, and goals. I also use them in time management and journal writing.

TWO TO TEN MINUTE BREAKS

Oscillating between focus and rest is just as important as oscillating between right-brain and left-brain modes of thinking. One of the most valuable things I learned in college was to take a ten-minute break every two hours. It worked so well that I began to ask: "What is the most rejuvenating thing I can do during this ten-minute break?" This is when I discovered power naps discussed below.

Since then, I've learned that it also helps to take short breaks every 30-40 minutes. This, along with new distinctions about mobilizing right-brain mental capacity, encouraged me to develop additional turbo-charging short break ideas. This section summarizes activities that can be done quickly in an office setting to complement the intense concentration required to perform challenging knowledge work.

TEN-MINUTE POWER NAPS

When others hear that I take ten-minute naps during the day, they often respond with: "I could never do that. I'd sleep for hours or feel groggy afterwards." I'll bet at some point they couldn't ride a bicycle either. Like riding bicycles, taking power naps is a skill that can be learned. Countless times in my life, I have awakened ten minutes to the second after laying down and felt *more* refreshed than I feel after a full night's sleep!

John D. Rockefeller, who lived to be ninety-eight, took a half-hour nap every day at noon. Edison attributed his enormous energy and endurance to his habit of sleeping whenever he wanted to. Dale Carnegie suggested that you could add one hour per day to your waking life by sleeping six hours at night instead of eight, then taking a one-hour nap before the evening meal. He felt that this would do you more good than eight hours of unbroken sleep. As described in Charles Thompson's book, *What a Great Idea*, Dr. NakaMats sleeps only four hours a night, and then takes two 30-minute naps during the day in a "Cerebrex" chair that he designed.

Until your company purchases a Cerebrex chair, Bio-Battery, Voyager, Mindscope or other device for getting compressed rest, here are some guidelines that might help you get started with ten-minute power naps.

1) Find a place with a comfortable temperature and very little or no noise. Noisy computer fans in the same room make effective napping impossible for me. Try to give your ears a break from the sounds they hear throughout the working day.

2) Nap on a flat hard surface and lay flat on your back. Conference room floors work well in the winter, or outside on a bench in warmer weather. Lying on a grass lawn also works well. The surface must be as close to level as possible. Laying flat removes the

burden of gravity from your internal organs while equalizing and redistributing body fluids.

3) Look at your watch before closing your eyes and decide exactly when you want to wake up. I usually use the digital stopwatch component of my watch, which removes any doubt about when I need to wake.

4) Cover your eyes or turn off the lights. Coat sleeves do just fine.

5) Relax your entire body as much as possible and settle in a comfortable position. I sometimes do light stretching or a couple of "complete breaths," as taught by yoga instructor Richard Hittleman, to help me relax. A complete breath begins by slowly inhaling through the nose to fill your lower lungs completely, then inhaling further to fill your upper lungs, holding for a few seconds and then exhaling slowly. When you exhale, you want to completely empty the lungs and begin the next breath without pausing. Complete breaths should be done comfortably without straining yourself.

6) Take naps when you need them. For me, this is usually right after lunch or right before dinner. Some people reach for caffeine when their eyes get heavy. I take a nap.

Some authors caution against taking naps because it can disrupt sleep at night. This risk can be minimized by limiting the duration. For myself, power naps are most helpful during busy times when I am only getting four and a half to six hours sleep at night.

A friend interested in learning this technique studied me while I napped on several occasions. She noted that I go completely unconscious. I seem to slow my breathing and heart rate significantly, but not consciously. I just try to relax as much as possible and my body takes over from there.

STRETCHING: FLEXIBLE BODY → FLEXIBLE MIND

Stretching improves circulation and energy flow by releasing body tension. A flexible body contributes to a flexible mind. Chapter 8 discusses several techniques and references for refining your stretching skills and discipline. The important thing to note is that stretching is best done after warming up a bit, either by going for a walk or doing some jumping jacks. I've hurt my neck twice while doing a rather intense stretch (the plough) without adequate warm-up. The second time I misjudged how much warm-up I needed.

HUMOR

In their *Mental Toughness* audiotape, Dr. James E. Loehr and Peter J. McLaughlin state that humor can lower your blood pressure and pulse rate, increase the flow of blood to your brain, increase your energy level and encourage you to take fuller breaths. Humor helps us be more creative.

Humor is all around us if we would only tune in. You might want to set up a joke file so that when you hear a good joke you can save it away for the next time you need a good laugh.

"You can always tell an intelligent person—they have the same views as you do."

— Walt Evans

If you have e-mail at work, consider setting up a humor alias. Over time, build up an electronic network of associates who value humor. When one of you discovers a humorous line or story, e-mail it to the alias coordinator. The coordinator maintains a personal group in their e-mail software containing a list of people in the humor alias. If they deem it worthy, they will forward the humorous text on to everyone in the group.

Here are some ideas for locating humorous material:

- Dilbert's Web site, **www.dilbert.com**, is worth a look.
- Check out the following books in the humor section of your favorite bookstore: Gary Larson's *The Far Side*, Jerry Seinfeld's *Seinlanguage*, Scott Adam's *Dilbert,* and Gene Perret's (Bob Hope's head comedy writer) *Classic One Liners.*
- I've posted some of my favorite clean humor at **BrainDance.com/humor.htm**.

"Lord, help my words be gracious and tender today, because I may have to eat them tomorrow."

— *Walt Evans*

BREATHING

The brain consists of 3% of our body mass yet it consumes 20% or more of the oxygen we take in. That's a sentence worth reading again. Breathing smarter will help you think smarter. Not all breaths are created equal. If you work in an office building, try walking outside in the fresh, unprocessed, uncooked air and take a few complete breaths or alternate nostril breaths (discussed in Chapter 8). The movement of breath is said to be the movement of consciousness. It alters our physiology by altering the flow of oxygen in our bloodstream. As discussed in Chapter 8, the most important breathing distinction is learning how to fill your lower lungs with air on a habitual basis.

"Remember also that, in most instances, diversion from one activity to another is more relaxing than complete rest...the body is not built to take too much stress always on the same part."

— *Hans Selye*

OTHER IDEAS FOR TWO TO TEN MINUTE BREAKS

- **The Brain Dancing Coach**™: Software for people who work on computers for long hours at a time. It makes it practical to take a variety of short breaks by minimizing the number of decisions you need to make. See Appendix A for information on how to download the free trial version.

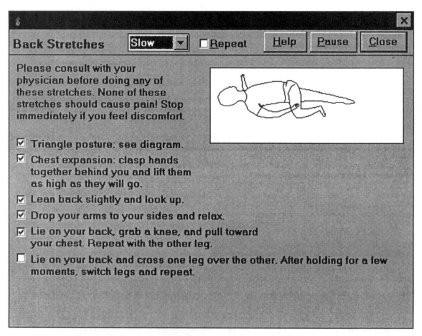

Figure 5.9 Brain Dancing Coach Stretching Routine.

- **Meditation**: Meditation increases alpha brain waves and improves relaxation. A study performed by Dr. Bernard Glueck at the Institute for Living in Hartford, Connecticut, found that men and women practicing meditation showed an increased synchronicity between the right and left sides of the brain. One study does not a principle make, but my experience suggests that this is an excellent two to ten minute break idea.

- **Visualization**: As mentioned in Chapter 3, I sometimes lie down on the floor somewhere in a very relaxed state with the intention of visualizing software I'm developing. While visualizing, I remain awake and perform various mental gymnastics. I "see" the screens in my mind, and as the user makes selections, the software responds appropriately. I also use this time to mentally walk through the strategy I'm using to develop the software and search for possible refinements. There is usually a point of diminishing returns with this process, so I try to set specific time limits to prevent losing track of time. If you don't do these breaks ecologically, you'll tend to avoid them over time.

- **Mini-tramping**: This great ten-minute workout on a mini-trampoline is discussed in Chapter 8.

- **Juggling**: I keep a can of tennis balls in my office for this purpose. This involves coordination, timing and dimension.

- **Drawing**: Purchase a copy of Betty Edwards' book, *Drawing on the Right Side of the Brain* and begin chipping away at developing this valuable skill.

- **Listening to music**: I use a portable CD player to listen to variety of music depending on which mode or mood I'm in. I have inspirational music such as *Chariots of Fire* or *Theme from Rocky*, creative music such as baroque music and Mozart, high energy music such as Bryan Adams' *Summer of 69* or Boston's *I Think I Like it,* and relaxing music such as Kenny G's *Live* album or Stephen Halpern's *Crystal Suite.*

- **Creating music**: I use a Miracle Keyboard by The Software Toolworks, Inc., which is a 48-key piano keyboard with full size keys, great sound (digitized recordings) and pressure-sensitive keys. It also comes with an integrated software learning system.

- **Nerf hoops**: This is where you hang a small plastic hoop on a door and play basketball with a soft spongy ball. These components are available at discount stores for $5-10. Nerf basketball involves dimensional thinking, which is handled by the right brain.

MENTAL REST

Your mind continues to work even while you sleep. This is one reason why it's a good idea to finish the day by writing down the six most important things that you want to accomplish tomorrow. Your subconscious mind starts to work on them immediately and helps prepare you for action when you arrive at work the next day.

Sleep rests the body, but what is the best way to rest your mind? I learned this idea from Vernon Bowlby over ten years ago. He suggests doing an activity that completely rips you out of your mental ruts, something you absolutely love to do. I seem to get my best mental rest from snow skiing, water skiing and boating. These things require 100% of my attention and they get me out in nature where the air is fresh and the scenery beautiful. Connecting with the beauty and magnificence of nature is a powerfully rejuvenating experience. Most importantly, they give me a chance to spend quality time with my family and friends.

It is sometimes difficult to realize just how much I need mental rest until after returning, so scheduling such trips on a regular basis is wise. The difference in my knowledge work productivity is so pronounced after one of these trips that, at least for me, violating this one rule is enough to compromise the benefits gained from every other technique suggested in this book. Nolan Bushnell, inventor of Pong and founder of Atari, gets the majority of his most profitable new ideas when he's doing things out of his normal routine. While away from his usual surroundings in "play" mode, he believes that he allows a different part of his brain to be activated. As mentioned earlier, he invented the game *Breakout* while running his fingers through the sand on a beach. He claims that his life oscillates between being a morning person and an evening person. Evening mode promotes creativity while morning mode is more conducive to getting things done.[4]

If you have ever studied weight lifting principles, you know that our best understanding to date is that you should use a one-day-on, one-day-off cycle. During exertion, muscles are strained and, to some degree, torn. During the day off they repair themselves and build themselves into a stronger state than before the workout. Mental rest is this same idea applied to your mind. In his classic book, *The Road Less Traveled*, M. Scott Peck calls this "balancing," or disciplining discipline.

PERCEIVING TIME IN A NON-LINEAR FASHION

One way I know if an activity is giving me effective mental rest is by how I perceive time passage during the trip. If an activity is restful, time seems to slow down. Four hours cruising on the boat often feels like two whole days. Time isn't dragging along; it just feels like we've packed two days of life into those four hours. Not that we rush around on these trips. In fact, it's just the opposite. Activities are scheduled very loosely and we just "go with the flow." If you doubt the possibility of perceiving time in such a nonlinear fashion, consider the words of Paul Harvey when he asked, "How long is a minute?" After a brief pause he replied, "I guess that depends which side of the bathroom door you're on."

ANCHORS

You can leverage your mental rest activity by selecting a single tape of favorite music that seems in harmony with the mood of your vacation. By listening to this music periodically throughout the vacation, it will "anchor" the experience. Whenever you hear songs from this tape in the future, it will remind you of the state of mental rest you achieved on the vacation.

---

[4] Adapted from Roger von Oech's book, *A Kick in the Seat of the Pants*.

A formula for burnout in knowledge work is focus, focus, focus. By oscillating—focus, rest, focus, rest—we increase our ability to focus and to rest effectively. You might find it helpful to plan such oscillations on a daily, weekly and per-project basis.

CONCLUSION

Conscious ⟷ Subconscious
Individual Thought ⟷ Dialogue
Left-Brain Mode ⟷ **Right-Brain Mode**
Detailed Thought ⟷ High Level Thought

This chapter addressed the third major strategy for using complementary opposite modes of thinking to achieve mental leverage. Hemispheric specialization is a fact, and oscillating between right and left-brain thinking is a useful way to apply this distinction. However, the principle of mental oscillation extends beyond the left/right analogy. While the above diagram summarizes the four main types of oscillation emphasized in Chapters 2-6, you will find other oscillation strategies woven throughout *Brain Dancing*.

The mental flexibility required to employ complementary opposite styles of thinking requires discipline. It often requires us to suspend previous training, habits and mental structures. One strategy for maintaining ecology during such dismantling is to set specific time limits for activities involving new modes of thinking.

Mind Maps help shift our thinking to "meta" or structural levels; this is a right-brain mental process that helps get creative juices flowing. The next chapter shows how such structural thinking can be applied towards optimizing other mental processes frequently performed by knowledge workers.

EXERCISE 1

1) Pick the topic in this book that you would most like to learn.

2) Find someone to teach it to. This could be one or two people who you think could benefit from it. Or, you may want to give a five-minute speech on the subject. A third alternative is to write a one or two page article for a newsletter.

3) Take out a blank sheet of unlined white paper. Turn the sheet sideways and, in the middle, either draw a small picture, symbol or a few keywords that represent the essence of the topic.

4) (Optional step) Set a timer for two to five minutes. A kitchen oven timer works well because the bell interrupts your pattern when it goes off. At the office, you can use the stopwatch feature of a digital watch or just write the ending time in the upper right corner of the page as a reminder. During this time, act as if you have mastered Aldous Huxley's "Profound Relaxation" technique: Relax yourself as deeply as possible and then focus on a single thought. Ask your subconscious mind to make available to you all possible knowledge on the topic you are going to brainstorm. Ask that it flow through your hand and on to the page abundantly. Stop when the timer goes off.

5) Set a timer for five minutes. This time, write as many ideas as you can think of on the subject. Use symbols, shorthand, keywords or any other technique you can think of to get the ideas on the page as quickly as possible.

6) Take a five-minute break.

7) Scan this book for additional ideas on the subject, adding them to the idea collection sheet where you think it appropriate.

8) Take out a second sheet of paper and organize the ideas into a Mind Map according to the structure of the information. This is the content of your presentation.

9) Decide on the order in which the content will be presented using one of the techniques described in this chapter.

10) Practice the delivery a couple of times and then give the presentation. Just do it and trust that whatever resources you need to pull this off will come to you. Developing faith in this process is a "meta-lesson" of far-reaching potential.

"When [Kepler] found that his long-cherished beliefs did not agree with the most precise observations, he accepted the uncomfortable facts. He preferred the hard truth to his dearest illusions. That is the heart of science."

— Carl Sagan, Cosmos

CHAPTER 6

GOING META

"I think it is an extremely valuable thing to train our mind to stand apart and examine its own program."
— *Stephen R. Covey*

"In a time of rapid change, it is the learners who inherit the future. The learned find themselves equipped to live in a world that no longer exists."
— *Eric Hoffer*

"People who learn things the fastest will do much better than those who learn things the best."
— *Paul Zane Pilzer*

"Meta" means above, so I use the phrase "going meta" to describe the process of rising above. There are two main ways of applying this distinction to knowledge work:

- Traversing the structure of information, facilitated by tools such as Mind Maps.
- Traversing the structure of your thoughts in order to optimize key mental processes.

The emphasis in this chapter is on training your mind to stand apart and examine its own "program." Specifically, this chapter is about fine tuning the mental software you use to learn and interact with information.

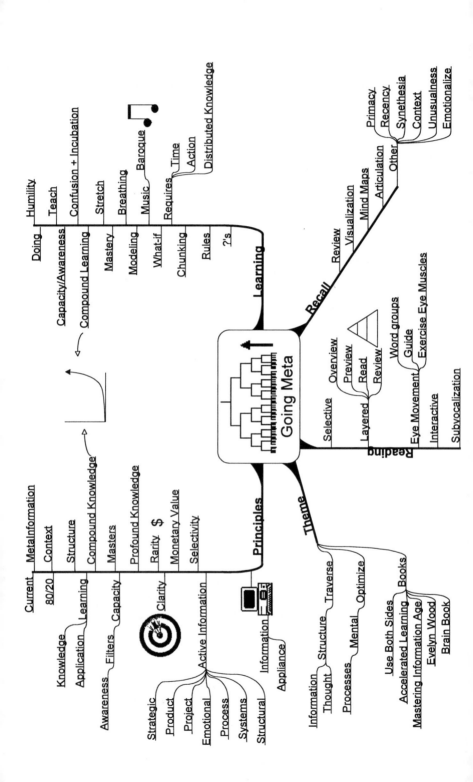

Going Meta

Learning
- Doing
- Humility
- Teach
- Confusion + Incubation
- Capacity/Awareness
- Compound Learning
- Stretch
- Breathing
- Mastery
- Music — Baroque
- Modeling
- What-if
- Requires — Time
  - Action
- Chunking — Distributed Knowledge
- Rules
- ?'s

Recall
- Review
- Visualization
- Mind Maps
- Articulation
- Other
  - Primacy
  - Recency
  - Synesthesia
  - Context
  - Unusualness
  - Emotionalize

Reading
- Selective
- Layered
  - Overview
  - Preview
  - Read
  - Review
- Eye Movement
  - Word groups
  - Guide
  - Exercise Eye Muscles
- Interactive
- Subvocalization

Principles
- Current
- MetaInformation
  - 80/20
  - Context
  - Structure
  - Compound Knowledge
  - Knowledge
  - Application — Learning
  - Masters
  - Profound Knowledge
  - Awareness — Filters — Capacity
  - Rarity — $
  - Monetary Value
  - Selectivity
  - Clarity
- Active Information
  - Strategic
  - Product
  - Project
  - Emotional
  - Process
  - Systems
  - Structural
- Information Appliance

Theme
- Information
- Thought
- Structure — Traverse
- Processes — Mental — Optimize
- Books
  - Use Both Sides
  - Accelerated Learning
  - Mastering Information Age
  - Evelyn Wood
  - Brain Book

If you find yourself doing something repeatedly, it may be worthwhile to periodically examine the process you use. I once read a study that calculated the number of hours the average person spends tying their shoes over the course of their lifetime. The amount of time was so huge that I became determined to figure out how to reduce this number. I explored ways of tying my shoes faster, then eventually started wearing shoes that just slip on and off so I don't have to tie my shoes at all. In addition to optimizing a mental process, sometimes there are ways of organizing yourself so that certain activities are no longer necessary.

The amount of information that knowledge workers must interact with has increased significantly throughout my career and this trend is likely to continue. This chapter presents a number of distinctions you can use to optimize frequently performed processes while interacting with information in ways such as reading, remembering and learning.

These ideas, and indeed this entire book, were inspired by Tony Buzan's book, *Use Both Sides of Your Brain.* Buzan taught me that it is one thing to read a book about a specific topic such as science or math, and quite another to read a book that improves the way I read every book from that point forward. Buzan's ideas took me from reading fifty books every couple of years, to extracting useful information from fifty books every couple of months. This increase in my information metabolism led me to four other metalearning books:

- *Accelerated Learning,* by Colin Rose
- *Mastering the Information Age,* by Michael J. McCarthy
- *Remember Everything You Read: The 7 Day Evelyn Wood Speed Reading Program,* by Stanley D. Frank
- *The Brain Book,* by Peter Russell

This chapter explains just a few of their ideas that I've found valuable in my work.

Before diving in, I want to emphasize that the notion of "going meta" can be applied to more than just mental process optimization. For example, you may want to have an occasional "metadiscussion." This is a discussion about the structure or format of the conversation you are having with someone. It goes something like this:

> "I'd just like to take a moment to make sure that there isn't anything about the way I'm communicating with you that is abrasive. I know my attempts to do things creatively sometimes cut across established boundaries, and I want to make sure that you feel comfortable openly expressing any concerns you have about my methods."

Be on the lookout for any activity that you perform repeatedly. It may be worth your while to invest some thought and/or practice into optimizing such activities. And, by considering the context in which that process is performed, you may even discover ways of achieving the same benefit without having to tie your shoes at all.

OPTIMIZING THE READING PROCESS

One of my favorite scenes from the TV sitcom "Taxi" was when Alex was rapidly flipping through the pages of a book in traditional speed reading style. Elaine walks up and says, "Alex, so you're taking that speed reading course—what are you reading?" Alex responds, "I haven't the foggiest idea."

I took a speed reading class in high school and was left with pretty much the same impression—a belief that speed reading had no substance to it. This perception changed when I read *Use Both Sides of Your Brain* by Tony Buzan. This book increased my information metabolism by teaching me both how to tie my shoes faster and pointing out cases where I didn't need to tie them at all. Rather than learning to become a speed reader, he taught me how to become a "speed understander." In summary, he teaches how to:

- Read more selectively,
- Optimize the way you use your eyes, and
- Optimize the process you use to remember key ideas.

The following discussion elaborates on the above themes by synthesizing ideas from several related books.

READING MORE SELECTIVELY

The underlying principle is this:

> As the amount of information in a given area increases, there is an increasing need for the ability to scan that information at a high level and be highly selective of the areas you choose to study in detail.

When I read anything, my objective is not to look at every word and picture as fast as I can. Rather, it is to identify and understand useful ideas as efficiently as possible, and then to either transfer this information to long-term memory or note it for future reference.

Imagine arriving at a large lake and being told that somewhere in the water there is a buried treasure. To find that treasure, you could either put on your trunks and go for a swim, or jump in a high-speed boat with radar programmed to detect the presence of anything resembling treasure. This would allow you to do a fairly quick pass over the entire lake, noting areas that look promising, and then go back to each promising location, drop anchor, and go for a dive. You are much more likely to find the treasure because you will have eliminated huge portions of the lake very quickly.

When it comes to reading, your subconscious mind is your radar, and it is "programmed" when you self-communicate the outcome you are trying to create.

When using this strategy, the most important thing is to make sure you are swimming in the right lake. Any time I'm presented with an information-rich environment, such as a bookstore or a trade convention like COMDEX, I invest time up front clarifying my goals, and then do some high-speed scans over the entire terrain before diving into a single book or booth. It often takes discipline to finish the complete scan before stopping at an extremely promising location. Ray Dolby, inventor of Dolby noise reduction, encourages would-be inventors not to jump at the first solution because sometimes the perfect solution is right around the corner.

I have just described a rather left-brain approach to reading. Its complementary opposite is to allocate some time looking for the unexpected. The key to this strategy is to set a specific time limit, since we tend to ignore time when operating in right-brain mode. My experience suggests that without the discipline of setting specific time limits for right-brain mode activities, there is a tendency to avoid them in order to maintain personal ecology (i.e., we tend to avoid activities likely to prohibit us from managing our overall set of responsibilities in a balanced manner).

LAYERED READING

In addition to using your subconscious mental radar, you can read books more selectively by using a layered reading or multi-pass approach. Here are four phases that commonly show up in layered reading strategies:

- **Overview**: Look over the entire book at the rate of one second per page to determine its organization, structure and tone. Try to finish the overview in five minutes.

- **Preview**: Should you decide to read further, preview the first chapter at the rate of four seconds per page. Pay particular attention to beginnings and endings such as the introduction and conclusion, and the first sentences of paragraphs and sections. Mark key sections with Post-it tabs or a highlight marker.

- **Read**: If any part of the chapter warrants closer attention, go back and read it at whatever speed seems appropriate.
- **Review**: As discussed in the following section on memory, doing short reviews periodically after reading new ideas can significantly increase the amount of detailed information that makes it into long-term memory.

There are several advantages to having seen every page of a document. It partially eliminates the intimidation of the unknown. It is also much easier to comprehend material at rapid speeds when your eyes have already seen the material twice, even if only briefly. And lastly, your right brain is a lot happier about the whole situation because it has at least some idea of the context or overall picture in which the material is being presented.

Think of this figure as a birds-eye view of the pages in a book. The dark squares represent the pages with the ideas most relevant to your particular circumstances. Your task when reading the book is to identify those useful pages as quickly as possible and prioritize your time accordingly. In some cases, the only way you will fully understand these relevant ideas is to read some or all of the material leading up to them. Having identified them 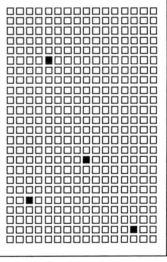 up front can speed your reading by giving you a context in which to read the preceding text. How many books do you have sitting around that you haven't finished reading? Many of us have far more to read than we have time for. In such cases, this prioritization is essential.

As useful as this approach has been to me, I must acknowledge that it doesn't apply in all situations. It has proven especially helpful in situations where I want to significantly broaden the scope and variety of ideas available in planning and problem solving situations. However, it doesn't work well with books written in a story format, where the deeper messages are developed continuously throughout the text.

Saying that someone has one reading speed is like having a car that only goes one speed. Different material calls for different speeds. Layered reading is about being flexible in the strategy you use to extract useful ideas from written material.

Exercise

Step up to a large magazine stand with the objective of scanning ten magazines in thirty minutes. The idea is to develop the discipline to not dive-in to the first interesting article you find. Just put a Post-it tab on the page and continue scanning. It may become less interesting after you've gone through the rest of the magazines. When you finish scanning, you are in a much better position to prioritize your reading efforts.

Progressively Rendered Consciousness

A useful metaphor for understanding the benefits of layered reading comes from the way interlaced graphic images are downloaded from the World Wide Web. When you visit a Web site that has interlaced graphic images, you don't have to wait until the entire image has been downloaded before beginning to see the image. Interlaced images are downloaded in layers. When the first layer is downloaded, you see a fuzzy outline of the entire image. With each of the succeeding four layers, the image gets clearer and clearer. Unlike non-interlaced images, you don't have to wait for the entire image to be drawn one pixel at a time in order to see the overall picture. If you judge the fuzzy image irrelevant, you don't have to wait to move on.

When you use layered reading techniques, you are progressively rendering your understanding of the material. Oftentimes, the fuzzy outline is enough to determine the material's relevance to your priorities. Sequential readers on the other hand, who read text one word at a time from start to finish, may never get to page 233 containing the most valuable idea in the book relative to their needs.

The exciting thing about layered reading is the potential for increasing the sheer number of truly great ideas you come across. The more productive your reading, the more likely you are to invest time doing it. You have only to walk into any great bookstore or library and open your eyes to realize that dozens of great ideas await your discovery. Layered reading makes it practical to discover them.

Here are some additional suggestions for reading more selectively:

- Focus on key words and ignore filler words. As discussed in the previous chapter, most of the meaning in sentences is transferred by a few key words. Many times it is unnecessary to read all the "is's" and "the's."

- Skip what you already know. As you transfer more and more knowledge from an area into long-term memory, the sections you can skip will become larger and thus accelerate your journey along the compound learning curve.

- Skip material that doesn't apply to you.

- Skip material that seems particularly confusing and come back to it if necessary after reading other sections. Books are linear while their subject matter is often multi-dimensional. As Hannah Arendt put it, "Nothing we use or hear or touch can be expressed in words that equal what we are given by the senses."[1] It may be far easier to understand

---

[1] As quoted in *Mastering the Information Age*, by Michael J. McCarthy.

the material in light of information that follows. Giving your subconscious time to incubate the material might help as well.

OPTIMIZING EYE MOVEMENT

Given that we use our eyes a great deal when we read, it makes sense, in the interest of optimization, to examine the processes involved. This section discusses three aspects of eye involvement: reading groups of words, exercising your eye muscles and using a guide.

READING GROUPS OF WORDS

It turns out that our eyes can only take in information when they are stopped. What feels like continuous motion is actually move-stop-read-move-stop-read, etc. You can easily verify this by sitting face to face with a partner, holding up a book and watching their eyes as they read. The key is to minimize the number of stops by maximizing the number of words you see at each stop.

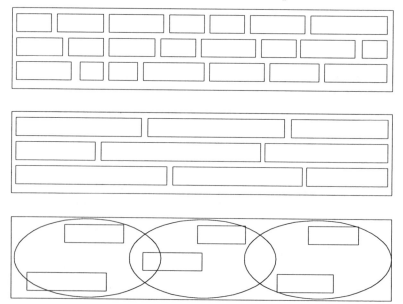

Figure 6.1 Three Eye Movement Patterns.

Three different patterns are shown in Figure 6.1. The person who uses the first eye movement pattern is looking at every word, one at a time. The person who uses the second is still looking at every word, but in groups. The person who uses the third eye movement pattern "notices" only a few key words and does so by reading both horizontally and vertically simultaneously.

"But," you may be thinking, "the first reader is going to comprehend the material much better than the third!" Possibly. However, if the third reader actually uses all three eye movement patterns, using the slower patterns very selectively, then he has a better chance of investing his mental energies on the material of most relevance to him.

"The art of becoming wise is the art of knowing what to overlook."

— *William James*

The third reader is much more likely to find the treasure chest in the information lake than the first reader who just wades in with no flippers. The smart reader is the one who uses the third technique to scan the entire book (overview) or chapter (preview), and then comes back and uses some combination of the first two techniques to further explore the sections of greatest relevance.

Getting to both the second and third levels requires a visual reading strategy. You must silence subvocalization (the tendency to talk the words in our mind as we read) and learn to trust your eyes. This involves shifting your mental reading process from:

see→say→understand

to just:

see→understand

A recent newsgroup post asked for suggestions on how to eliminate subvocalization in order to increase reading speed. One man responded that repeating a single word in his mind while he read for six months did the trick for him. I couldn't help but wonder if there was a quicker way to achieve this, so the next time I found myself subvocalizing, I observed what I did to stop: I increased the rate at which my eyes moved across the page to the point where it was impossible to subvocalize. I switched into the reading mode whereby I noticed gulps of words at each eye resting point. I was still understanding what I was reading, but in a different way. I caught myself thinking, "But now I'm not really reading." In other words, part of my mind still believed that the definition of reading was to look at every word and sound it out in my mind. A better way to look at this issue is that you are wise to develop multiple reading strategies, some of which may include subvocalization and some that do not.

How can you make the leap to reading gulps of words at a time? One way is to adjust the focus of your eyes (or attention). Look at any nearby image and zoom in on a particular aspect, like the button on a shirt. Then adjust the focus of your eyes so you can see the entire shirt. That's the process you can use to increase your reading speed by increasing the number of words you take in at each eye stop.

Here's an exercise that will help you do this. Try looking at the following sentence in three ways:

Success leaves clues.

First, focus your attention/eyes on the first 'S' in success. Next, adjust your focus/attention so you can see the entire word. And finally, adjust your focus so you see all three words at the same time.

Because you can't say three words at the same time, you can't subvocalize when you read three words at a time.

273	_____	11454	_____	17 44 34	_____
545	_____	87879	_____	86 32 77	_____
142	_____	12342	_____	65 41 28	_____
275	_____	45411	_____	27 33 11	_____
848	_____	78989	_____	66 32 97	_____
109	_____	21314	_____	32 45 81	_____
2763	_____	56548	_____	44 18 72	_____
5478	_____	09711	_____	31 73 90	_____
4452	_____	33442	_____	27 11 88	_____
1127	_____	83219	_____	72 61 49	_____
9956	_____	76675	_____	16 64 34	_____
3313	_____	33228	_____	26 89 55	_____

Figure 6.2 Grouping Exercise.

The exercise shown in Figure 6.2 was adapted from material in *Speed Reading* by Tony Buzan. It will help you train your eyes to take in words in larger gulps. Begin by covering the numbers with a sheet of paper. Then uncover one at a time for a fraction of a second. From memory, write the number you saw to the right. The idea is to increase the amount of information taken in with each glance. To make it more challenging, try uncovering two numbers at once.

Our brains are capable of receiving and processing information hundreds of times faster than we ordinarily read. Slow reading may keep the brain challenged, but reading faster forces the brain to pay attention and keeps it interested.

Periodically read as if you could read three to five times your best speed. Stay relaxed, breathing fully and rhythmically while you do this. When you settle back to your "normal" speed, you may find that it has increased.

Several of these ideas are based on the "visual-vertical" strategy taught in the Evelyn Wood program. For the upcoming class schedules, call (800) 447-7323. This strategy is also covered by Stanley Frank in his book, *Remember Everything You Read: The Evelyn Wood 7 Day Speed Reading and Learning Program.*

EXERCISING EYE MUSCLES

In Richard Hittleman's yoga teachings, he recommends the following exercise for strengthening your eye muscles:

1) Close your eyes for a moment, then open them.
2) Without moving your head, look up as high as you can go without straining.
3) That's twelve o'clock. Now move your eyes around the numbers of the clock, pausing briefly at each number.
4) Go around twice counter-clockwise and twice clockwise, pausing for a moment after each circle.

USING A GUIDE

Question: How do you know when someone is "speed reading?" Answer: They're running their fingers up and down each page. Evelyn Wood discovered the idea of using a guide to improve reading speed and comprehension. After studying the fastest readers she could find, one day she dropped a book in the dirt. She picked up the book and brushed off each page only to discover that she had basically read the book. Using a guide does four things: it keeps your mind from wandering; it keeps your eyes focused on the right part of the page; it limits the number of fixations per page which encourages bigger "gulps" of information; and, by deliberately speeding up your guide, it helps your eyes move faster. When reading material on a computer screen, you can use the mouse pointer as your guide instead of your fingers.

This 'S' pattern works well for the preview and reading phases, but I use a different method for doing high-speed overviews. In an effort to minimize hand movement and maximize speed, I hold the left page with the left hand and the 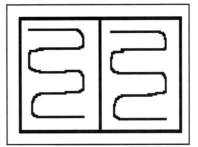 right page with the right hand. The left hand starts at the top of the left page. As the left hand moves down the left page, the right hand moves to the top of the right page and prepares to turn it. When the left hand reaches the bottom of the left page, I begin moving it back up the page as my gaze moves to the top of the right page. My right hand begins moving down the right page with only my thumb on the side of the page that I'm reading. In effect, I'm scanning the right page as I turn it. When my right thumb reaches the bottom of the right page, I finish turning the page and begin moving my right hand up into position to scan and turn the next page.

In summary, the key variables that determine how fast you read are:

- How long you stop at each place.
- How many words or how much area on the page you take in at each stop.
- How long it takes you to move your eyes to the next stopping point.
- The degree to which you minimize backskipping.
- The extent to which you mentally bypass your internal dialogue system as you read.
- Your state of mind and body at the time you are reading. This includes factors such as alpha brain wave activity, energy level, breathing technique, level of interest in the material, clarity about why

you are reading the material and beliefs regarding the potential benefits.

- The percentage of the material you already know, which to some extent depends upon how much you remember of material you've read in the past.

OPTIMIZING THE PROCESS OF REMEMBERING

The more information about a topic that you have transferred into long-term memory, the faster you can take in new material on that subject. Long-term memory is where your Social Security number is stored. The key question becomes "What is the most efficient method of transferring information from short term into long-term memory?" There are several memory tricks available, but the four that have given me the most benefit are:

- Using short periodic review sessions
- Developing my mental "visualization" muscle
- Drawing Mind Maps
- Articulation

The following sections explore these themes in greater detail.

USING SHORT PERIODIC REVIEW SESSIONS

Performing two to three minute reviews of material ten minutes, 24 hours, one week and one month after initial learning helps transfer more of the ideas into long-term memory in a way that they can be recalled quickly. This strategy comes from *Use Both Sides of Your Brain* by Tony Buzan. While the idea is useful, trying to follow it exactly creates something of a scheduling nightmare. I am learning so many things from so many sources that it is virtually impossible to overlap review sessions for all ideas into my schedule.

In practice, the ten-minute review session is the easiest for me to perform. I just set the material down for a few minutes and do something else. Then I come back and review the ideas for a couple of minutes before completely moving on to the next topic. The 24-hour review usually ends up being some time the next day, if I get a chance to review it at all. I like to read in the evening before going to bed, so I just scan the highlighted material from the previous night before moving on to the next section.

I am hit with new ideas via e-mail and other sources throughout the day. Scheduling review sessions for this material is more difficult. If an e-mail is important, I may leave it open after reading it the first time, and then close the window the next day after a quick review.

As for the one-week and one-month review sessions, if I don't use the information within that time period, it probably wasn't worth a third or fourth review anyway. For material in books, I occasionally do "library reviews," where I spend two hours rapidly flipping through as many books in my library as possible within the time limit. This is where the highlighted material and Post-it tabs really pay off.

Audiotapes lend themselves well to the review process. Because they can be listened to in the car, it is much easier to listen to a tape several times than it is to read a book several times. The disadvantage is that there is no way (yet) to highlight an audiotape for selective review.

"The more you know, the easier it becomes to know more."

— *Tony Buzan*

DEVELOPING YOUR VISUALIZATION MUSCLE

Every book and tape program I've found on improving memory has you perform exercises to develop your ability to visualize and manipulate pictures in your mind's eye. They suggest several memory tools based on this skill, such as peg lists and picture stories, which I've found difficult to apply in the fast-paced information blitz of day-to-day work. However, the exercises did mobilize latent memory capacities that seem to spill over into several aspects of my work. By having done the exercises, and by applying them in certain situations, I was doing something in my mind that has improved my ability to remember things in all situations. The following mini-version of the peg list exercise will give you an idea of the principles involved.

Peg lists involve committing a series of number-picture associations to long-term memory, then using them when you need to remember lists of things. For example, here is a list of number-picture associations for the numbers one through five:

1) Space Needle, since it looks like the number one
2) Door, since it has two positions, either opened or closed
3) Stool, since it has three legs
4) Horse, since it has four legs
5) Star, since it has five points

The first step is to memorize this list so completely that when anyone mentions any number, you immediately can think of the picture, and vice-versa. You should be able to walk the list forwards and backwards. This is an excellent chance to try the periodic review strategy discussed in the last section. Try writing them out several times, or calling a friend and describe this weird memory exercise which involves a list of five items, "a Space Needle, a door, etc."

Once this peg list has been transferred to long-term memory, you are ready to use it to remember a list of items. For example, let's say you needed to remember to perform the following five tasks tomorrow and didn't have a pencil to write them in your schedule:

1) Call Joe
2) Meet with Sue Carpenter
3) E-mail Acorn project team
4) Read new "Snowball" strategy report
5) Write bubble sort routine

In your mind you could associate the above tasks to your peg list items as follows:

- Imagine a G.I. Joe army figure climbing the outside of the Space Needle with a giant telephone in one hand while shouting, "Call Me" in Pig Latin.
- Imagine a carpenter working on your office door telling you as you walk in that you are likely to get sued if it doesn't get fixed.
- Imagine your team members standing on a bunch of stools under an oak tree picking acorns and throwing them into a mailbag.
- Imagine riding a horse reading the report as it balances on a snowball plowing down a hill over your competitors.
- Imagine a pen full of star shaped bubbles with numbers on them that float up in sorted order.

The next day when you get to work, you ask, "What was the first thing on my list?" This triggers the memory of the Space Needle, which triggers the memory of G.I. Joe climbing it shouting, "allCay eMay," and so forth. While this probably seems ridiculous, it is a great exercise for strengthening your visualization muscle.

There are some drawbacks to using peg lists in day-to-day work. In addition to taking a fair amount of time to dream up word pictures for each item I want to remember, there is the issue of figuring out how to manage all the different lists. You almost need a peg list to remember your peg lists. Additionally, it is more difficult to apply this technique to a list of concepts than a list of objects.

Another reason I don't fill my mind with ludicrous imagery on a habitual basis is that thoughts are things. Once you develop the skill of being able to create, remember and manipulate visual images deftly in your mind, you must discipline your use of this skill. You must be careful to limit your mind to positive imagery, or at least use negative imagery with extreme caution. Any time you think a thought, you increase the probability that it will come into existence.

MIND MAPS AND INTERACTIVE READING

Creating Mind Maps promotes interactive reading as well as encouraging you to think about the structure of the information being read. When completed, Mind Maps facilitate quick reviews.

Figure 6.3 is a very rough Mind Map I created while studying Dr. Khalsa's book, *Brain Longevity*. It doesn't cover the entire book; just those parts of interest to me. This Mind Map reflects the fact that I was drawing as I went along. I didn't know how many parts of the book I was going to map out or how much detail would accompany each topic. You may want to follow your initial drafts with a second pass. This draft served my purposes adequately. The lesson is this: don't let uncertainty about ideal layout prevent you from Mind Mapping as you read. Why include such a sloppy Mind Map in my book? To encourage you to try doing one. They don't have to be works of art to be useful. Refer to Tony Buzan's book, *Use Both Sides of Your Brain*, to learn how to obtain maximum benefits from using Mind Maps to enhance the reading process.

Oftentimes, the most valuable aspect of drawing a Mind Map is the impact the process has on your understanding and memory of the material. It doesn't matter so much what it looks like on paper as much as what went on in your head while you were drawing it. There are often useful ideas contained in the way the ideas relate to each other that are not apparent when the ideas are viewed sequentially. I find Mind Maps particularly useful as *Gestalt* (i.e., big picture) tools.

"Not everything that can be counted counts, and not everything that counts can be counted."

— *Albert Einstein*

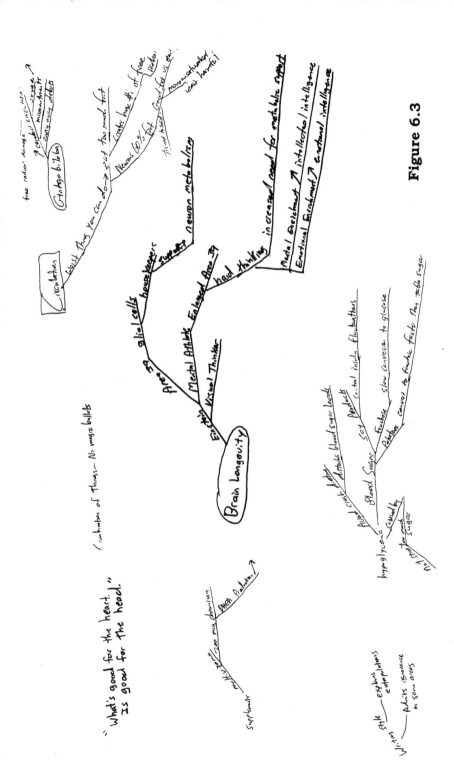

Figure 6.3

USE VISUALIZATION PLUS ARTICULATION

Socrates encouraged students to articulate, thereby drawing forth existing knowledge and sharpening their perception of new material. Articulation also facilitates and deepens your memory of new material.

When you articulate, you are practicing remembering, as opposed to simply re-reading something.

A simple use of this distinction is to discuss useful ideas with a friend during the return trip from a seminar. Another application combines the use of Mind Maps, visualization and review discussed earlier. If you sketch a Mind Map while reading or hearing new material, then during your two to three-minute review sessions, you can take a mental snapshot of the Mind Map, close your eyes, and begin articulating the content of that Mind Map as if you were teaching a class.

As described in *Superlearning 2000*, Win Wenger suggests "asking for an image" before you begin to read. Ask for an image that will help you assimilate the material you are about to read more easily. How did that old saying go? Ask and ye shall _____.

THE MIND LINKS THINGS TOGETHER THAT HAPPEN TOGETHER

When listening to a familiar album, as one song finishes, we often begin hearing the next song in our head before it begins playing. In cases where I need to be fairly precise in my recall of a speech, I use a "rapid talk-through" memorization strategy based on this principle. This involves talking out loud very rapidly, the first sentence of each paragraph or section of the speech. After doing this three times, the sections of the speech are linked together in my mind like songs on an album. In other words, when delivering the speech, as I finish each section, the following section begins to "play" in my mind.

There are two challenges involved in memorizing a speech: one is memorizing the words in each section; the second is remembering which section comes next. This strategy helps with the second problem. Note that when doing a rapid talk-through, I say only key words, and just enough of the first sentence for my mind to "latch on" to the meaning or spirit of the section.

SUMMARY OF OTHER MEMORY DISTINCTIONS

While the four topics above offer the most leverage for improving your memory, there are a few other distinctions that play a role:

- **Emotionalize**: Richly encoded memories, which have many associations, or paths leading to them, are easier to remember. Emotional associations, even minor ones, can generate the neurotransmitters required to "ship the memory" to long-term storage. In *Brain Longevity*, Dr. Khalsa describes how actors use this principle to learn their lines. First they learn the meaning and emotional motivation in the lines, then focus on memorizing the words. The emotion becomes the framework that holds together the left-brain linguistic memories.

- **Primacy and Recency**: We tend to remember the first and last ideas more than the ones in between. This means that many short sessions are better than a single long one, because you will have more firsts and lasts.

- **Synesthesia**: The more sensory experience you incorporate into your memories, the more likely you are to remember them. As Colin Rose describes in his book, *Accelerated Learning*, the Russian psychologist, Professor Luria, spent 30 years studying a man named Shereshevskii (referred to as S.). S consistently exhibited perfect recall over long periods (several years). In addition to having amazing visualization skills, he was also adept in synesthesia, which is the ability to express a memory generated in one sense in terms of another. For example, S described a tone with a pitch of 2,000 cycles per second as looking something like fireworks with a pink-red hue. S continued, "The strip of color feels rough and unpleasant, and it has an ugly taste—rather like that of a briny pickle."

- **Context:** Ideas are easier to remember when they can be associated to a specific context.
- **Unusualness:** Ideas are remembered more easily if they stand out from the ordinary in our minds, which is why Kevin Trudeau's Megamemory course emphasizes the use of outrageous and ludicrous multi-sensory imagery.

DEVELOPING MULTIPLE LEARNING STRATEGIES

Just as it is useful to develop multiple reading strategies that can be applied flexibly, it is also worthwhile to have multiple learning strategies. Peter Senge offers three excellent distinctions about learning:

- All learning occurs over time.
- All learning involves a continual movement between a world of thought and a world of action. No action, no learning.
- Knowledge is distributed throughout the body.

He points out that the Chinese symbol for learning consists of two symbols, one meaning "study" and the other "practice constantly." The Chinese cannot think "learning" without simultaneously thinking "practice constantly." Too often in our culture, the "practice constantly" part is left out to the point where people think they "know" something just because they read about it.

There are as many strategies for learning as there are topics to learn about. Your effectiveness as a learner is impacted by the breadth and depth of your repertoire of learning strategies, and by your ability to switch between them as the learning situation demands. Maslow's statement about all of your problems looking like nails if your only tool is a hammer also applies here. As you expand your awareness of these techniques, you are likely to notice more opportunities to use them. The following material describes a sampling of the more effective strategies I've come across. Sometimes the best strategy is a combination of all of them. I trust that you will use good judgment in selecting learning strategies appropriate for each situation.

"The only kind of understanding that I'm interested in is the kind that allows you to do something."

— *Richard Bandler*

LEARNING BY DOING

The solutions approach is my overall strategy for learning. "Do the thing and you will have the power," wrote Emerson. This strategy seems to work best when the "thing" is solving a real-world problem.

You can read about something until you are blue in the face, but until you are presented with an opportunity to actually apply the material, your "learning" has not even gotten off the ground. Education pioneer John Dewey's motto was "learning by doing." It is my sincere hope that high schools and universities will encourage students to begin taking on projects in their chosen field while still in school. The idea is to get them involved in project teams and an overall process closely aligned with the work they will do when they graduate. This experience would give them a context in which they can understand how the material learned in school is useful.

"The great aim of education is not knowledge but action."

— *Herbert Spencer*

CAPACITY/INFORMATION AWARENESS THEORY

I once read that reading is 90% mental and only 10% eye movement. This makes sense when you consider that we are not just piling a bunch of words into our brains when we read. Words are symbols that are translated into ideas and organized into a useful context. Aldous Huxley touched on this notion when he wrote, "Knowledge is a function of being. When there is a change in the being of the knower, there is a corresponding change in the nature and amount of knowledge."

At the end of Chapter 1, I posed the question: "What can a person do to increase the rate at which they are ready for new learning?" In Chapter 2, I suggested taking on a series of projects of increasing complexity that demand new learning. I believe that our awareness of information expands according to our capacity to use it. Doing something to increase your information handling capacity will tend to expand the amount of information you are aware of. Buying a new bookshelf, a bigger filing cabinet, a larger hard disk, or implementing a new system for managing the flow of ideas in your life can all have this effect. The survival instinct built into our subconscious mind tends to block information from our awareness whose practical use is beyond our ability.

If you buy a bigger hard disk, you can load more software and do more things with your personal computer. If you buy a new bookcase, you can organize your books better and thus reference them more effectively when needed. If you purchase a new time management system where you can log new ideas that pop into your head and review them periodically, you will be more likely to benefit from those ideas, and this will encourage more of them to "arrive." The most useful part of my time management system is the address book I carry around. This has dramatically extended my capacity to interact with my network of contacts. Oftentimes, the information I need exists only in somebody's mind.

My suggestion is that by enhancing your capacity to organize information usefully, you expand the scope of information you can be aware of and still maintain ecology. This takes us back to the solutions approach discussed in Chapter 2. Projects give us problems to solve and provide a framework for making use of vast quantities of information.

COMPOUND LEARNING

If learning seems difficult at first, keep in mind that it will become easier to learn as you begin to climb the compound learning curve. This involves maximizing the amount of related information you transfer to long-term memory so that it can be easily recalled at a conscious level. The memory process is based on linking and association. The fewer items transferred to long-term memory, the less the likelihood that new items will be registered and connected.

If you use the memory-enhancing strategies discussed earlier to transfer new ideas into long-term memory, knowledge will begin to compound, just as interest does in a savings account. With each new learning experience, the percentage of ideas that are new will diminish, and this will allow you to assimilate that material all the more efficiently.

Another reason that learning compounds is that some ideas will actually increase your capacity for new information. For example, if you learn one idea that increases your energy level by 5% and you actually apply the idea, the benefits from this distinction compound daily. If you develop the discipline necessary to use that extra 5% in the pursuit of additional knowledge, it could increase the rate at which you discover additional distinctions. The benefits from these distinctions begin to pile up and can potentially impact your effectiveness by several hundred percent. One percent improvement every day adds up to much more than 365%.

The flip side of the learning equation is that the more you open your mind up to the vastness of potential research material, the more you realize how important it is to specialize in one particular area that suits your particular strengths and talents. You begin to channel an increasing percentage of your research time in refining your distinctions in this specialty area. With each seminar you attend on the topic, the amount of new material presented begins to shrink. At some point, you begin to know more about the topic than most of the attendees and sometimes even the seminar leaders. After maintaining this focus and daily habit of refinement to the point where your knowledge/skill momentum reaches critical mass, you become the one creating the new breakthrough material in your field. You have become a Master.

MASTERY

An individual high on the compound learning curve in a specific area can be a great source of learning. These individuals have maintained prolonged focus and determination to acquire daily distinctions in a specific area to the point where they are not just twice as knowledgeable as the average person in their field, but several times more knowledgeable.

For example, in the computer field, the great programmers are not just two or three times better than most, but dozens or even hundreds of times more effective.

You may recall the story of the power plant that shut down to the point where none of the company workers could get it running again. They ended up calling in a retired engineer who quickly analyzed the situation, walked over to a specific area and tapped on a pipe. The plant immediately came to life. When the company received his bill it was for $1,000.02, broken down as follows: $.02 for tapping the pipe, and $1,000 for knowing where to tap.

"Champions start out to be the best at what they do and then work every day towards the achievement of this goal: To be Number One."

— *Mark McCormack*

Masters know exactly "where to tap" in their particular areas of specialization. I've learned a great deal from several masters of mental effectiveness and you will see references to their work throughout this book. When masters write or speak, it is clear that for every word spoken, they know from ten to a thousand times more material on the subject than they are sharing. They have the luxury of choosing the precise content they feel perfectly matches the spirit of the moment.

To become a master in your field, consider Earl Nightingale's advice in his audiotape series, *The New Lead the Field*. He suggests that by investing one hour a day doing research in your specialty area, you will eventually leave the competition in the dust.

When reading in a new field of study, it is useful to continue doing high level scans of all related material until you feel fairly certain that you have identified the current masters. They are often the ones that are referred to the most by others. In other cases, you will recognize them by the quality of the ideas they present and the work they produce.

MODELING

It seems easier to achieve a goal if I've seen someone else do it, or if I know someone who has done it. For one thing, this changes my beliefs about what is possible. Secondly, it gives me the opportunity to observe their actions and strategies, and to listen to how they think about what they have done. People who accomplish extraordinary things act and think very differently from those who do not. In many cases, the written word does not measure up to the information our senses provide us when an act is observed in person or on video. You must hear the whole song, not just read the individual notes. So it is with useful ideas. Seeing them in action, within the context in which they are applied, can be more valuable than the idea itself.

The potential value of studying highly successful people has been clearly demonstrated: Dr. Georgi Lozanov studied the fastest learners and memorizers; Bandler and Grinder studied effective change agents; Anthony Robbins studied the world's most effective sales people; and Evelyn Wood studied the fastest readers.

Bandler and Grinder have refined this process of observation into a technique they call modeling. Anthony Robbins used these techniques to obtain his black belt in tae kwon do in just eight months by modeling Grand Master Jhoon Rhee. Robbins had the benefit of being a business partner of John Grinder for several months. The best book I've found on NLP (Neuro Linguistic Programming) modeling techniques is *Skills for the Future*[2] by Robert Dilts. In his book, Dilts applies these skills toward modeling the creative thinking processes of Walt Disney.

An excellent article on this topic can be found at **http://www.actwin.com/NLP/random/genius.htm**.

What people do has structure. Modeling is about discovering the structure of an *effective* behavior pattern. The emphasis is on *what* a person does, not *why*. To model someone, ask, "What does this person do inside her head that I can learn to do?" While a modeler can't instantly have the finesse that results from years of experience, you can quickly obtain some highly useful information about the structure of what she does.

Modeling is a substantial topic based on the notion that most of what a person does inside their head has some outward manifestation. Modeling effectiveness is largely achieved by developing the sensory acuity to notice these behavior signals and understanding what internal representations must have triggered them. One source of

---

[2] Available from Meta Publications (408) 464-0254.

such information is eye movement patterns, which are amazingly consistent throughout the human race.

A second major component of an effective modeling strategy is rapport skills. Obviously a person who likes you is more likely to share their secrets. However, modeling rapport is a bit more refined. Our bodies act much like tuning mechanisms. If you use your physiology in the exact same way as another person, they will tend to feel more comfortable around you (i.e., a person with a nasal voice feels more comfortable around other people with nasal voices). Additionally, mirroring someone's physiology sends similar messages to your brain, thereby giving you access to what they are thinking. Anthony Robbins' seminars give you a chance to experience this phenomenon first hand. Discreet observation is an art. When I sense that someone is consciously mirroring me, I sometimes feel uncomfortable.

One of the most powerful ways of doing this is to mirror breathing patterns. Peripheral vision is very effective at detecting movement and can be used to avoid staring at a person's chest during a conversation. Try looking at a computer monitor with your peripheral vision and notice if the screen appears to be flickering.

USING MODELING TO IMPROVE READING SPEED

If you ever catch yourself reading extremely rapidly with high comprehension, take a moment to examine the "structure" of that experience. If you can determine the precise physical, mental, and environmental conditions that support this level of performance, then you may be able to reproduce them more consistently. Ask yourself questions such as:

Physiology:

- What is my energy level? What factors contributed to it being the way it is?
- Am I relaxed, or carrying tension in certain parts of my body?

- How am I breathing?
- How am I sitting? Am I leaning slightly forward? What position are my shoulders in? How am I holding the book?
- Am I tapping my foot or moving my hands across the page in a certain way?

Internal Representations (Mental Focus):

- What am I telling myself will be the benefits from being able to extract information rapidly?
- What beliefs do I have about the quality of the material and what contributed to those beliefs?
- Is there time pressure and where did it come from?
- Am I trying to read the material or just extract information relative to the task at hand?

Environment:

- How is the lighting? Does the room have good air circulation? Is the temperature warm or cold?

If you know someone who consistently reads quickly, you may also want to apply the above questions to them.

WHAT-IF LEARNING

As you will read in the next chapter, "what-if" learning is an important strategy for learning software faster. By investing time up front to identify actions to avoid, and by minimizing the amount of time it takes to do a single experiment, you position yourself to perform a series of quick experiments that will lead you incrementally to a solution. The opposite of this strategy is to sit and wonder what would happen if you did something.

"One test is worth a thousand expert opinions."

— *Bill Nye, the Science Guy*

CHUNK IT DOWN

How do you eat an elephant? One bite at a time. Anytime you are overwhelmed by a task, step back to see if it can be broken into smaller tasks. Creating a one-page list of subtasks to check off is often a big step towards completion.

FOCUS ON RULES

The process of learning a programming language can often be simplified by memorizing syntax rules. This gives you less to remember when you see a complex application of those rules, in part because it can be encoded in terms of things you already know. "This is what math and science is all about," states Richard Bandler in *Using Your Brain*, "—coding the world efficiently and elegantly, so that you have fewer things to remember, leaving your brain free to do other things that are more fun and interesting."

ASK BETTER QUESTIONS

As mentioned previously, questions impact what we focus on. Every learning situation presents a combination of two types of information: interesting and useful. The following questions will help keep you focused on *useful* ideas:

- What am I going to do differently as a result of learning this?
- If I focused all of my efforts on fully implementing just one idea learned today, what one distinction out of all this material would have the greatest long-term impact on my life?
- What has to happen for me to apply what I just learned (e.g., acquire emotional resources, partners, additional knowledge, etc.)?

PLAY THE FOOL

Ralph Waldo Emerson writes in *Compensation*, "A great man is always willing to be little." Sitting on the cushion of advantage can sometimes lull us to sleep. When someone or something jars us by making us aware of a weakness in our character, we have a chance to learn something. Obviously this strategy must be applied selectively. Wisdom is knowing when it is appropriate to question deep prejudices that may be compromising our effectiveness. I must confess spending hours trying to fully understand the wisdom in the following statement by Burke: "No man ever had a point of pride that did not prove injurious to him."

TEACH OTHERS

Emerson believed it was "base" to "receive favors and render none." Creating an opportunity to render favors, such as teaching others who can benefit from the information in some way, may increase your capacity to receive "favors" or new information. We often find ourselves teaching topics that we ourselves need to learn. Reading or listening in any learning situation as if you are going to teach the material to others shifts your paradigm in a way that heightens awareness.

RAPID CONFUSION + INCUBATION

Confusion is an indication that you are on your way to understanding. Can you think of a topic that once utterly confused you, but which you now understand completely and apply regularly? When Peter Senge stated that "All learning occurs over time," I believe he was referring to the process of incubation. When exposed to new ideas, our subconscious mind (the software) begins to "chew" on the information even after we walk away from it. New ideas encourage new dendrites to form in our brain (the hardware). The result is that the next time we get back to the material, it seems less confusing, until gradually it becomes understood and applied.

In his book, *Power Sleep*, Dr. James Maas mentions studies indicating that new dendrite growth occurs during REM sleep. There is also some evidence that random firing of all neuronal pathways occurs during REM sleep, which helps keep memories readily accessible.

Broadening your range of activities is one way to increase the number of new mental "pathways" that form. Another way is to accelerate your confusion rate, at least when it is safe to do so. In other words, once I've decided to learn something, I present my mind with as much of the material as I can as soon as possible. This puts time on my side via the principle of incubation, even if I invest only five minutes a day scanning the new material. There are times when I wished I'd never learned this—times when the feeling of confusion is a bit overwhelming. At least so far, it appears worthwhile to weather the storm.

"The more tracks and pathways you can create and use, the 'clearer,' faster, and more efficient your thinking will become. The boundaries of human intelligence can, in many ways, be related to the brain's ability to create and use such patterns."

— *Tony Buzan*

STRETCH YOUR COMFORT ZONE

We must constantly guard ourselves against the feeling that we have learned something just because we "know" about it. You may have looked at a thousand Mind Maps and memorized every rule regarding their formation, but you haven't learned how to Mind Map until you begin to draw them. Many forms of learning are passive, yet the highest leverage comes from active learning. Will Durant's enjoinder, "Not to think unless we have to" often translates into "Not to learn unless we have to," so give yourself a reason to learn something by taking on a project that forces you to overcome new challenges.

In her insightful book, *Thinking in Future Tense: Leadership Skills for a New Age*, Dr. Jennifer James encourages you to observe the process by which you have changed in the past. She lists several common styles of change to help you do this. As Richard Bandler points out, it is usually easier to change something once you know its structure. Dr. James' discussion of common change strategies helped me understand the structure of my change/learning processes and how to refine them. A great way to tell if you have really learned something is to ask yourself whether or not you have changed your actions as a result.

BREATHING AND LEARNING

Your brain consumes 20% of your total oxygen intake. Anything you can do to increase the quality of the oxygen that gets to your brain will increase your mental effectiveness. Chapter 8 addresses this in depth. However, breathing is discussed here because it plays a particularly important role in the learning process. Consider the words of Ostrander and Schroeder from their book, *Superlearning*: "We seldom give breathing much attention, yet we breathe about 5,000 gallons (35 pounds) of air every day, about six times our food and drink consumption." They point out that when breathing to a regular beat, as opposed to haphazardly, your mind sharpens automatically.

If you retain your breath for a few seconds between breaths, mental activity stabilizes and the mind can focus in on a single point or idea. To varying degrees, the movement of breath is the movement of consciousness.

MUSIC AND LEARNING

In *Superlearning*, Ostrander and Schroeder state that, "a continuous, monotonous rhythm of somewhere around ten seconds seems to open up the mind's ability to remember." Classical music from the baroque period is widely believed the most effective music for this purpose. The precise rhythm of baroque music promotes a sense of well-being and relaxed receptivity.

Music stores often have such huge selections of classical music that the biggest stumbling block for me was figuring out which music to purchase. I've been pleased with a ten CD set I purchased from Costco for $30 called "Baroque Treasuries." This set is distributed by

Delta Music, Inc. (310-826-6151). It contains music by Vivaldi, Bach, Handel, Teleman, Corelli and others. The following movements appear representative of the type of music suggested by the literature. The CD index numbers correspond to the 1990 version of this CD set:

CD	Concerto	Movement	#
Vivaldi: *The Four Seasons*	Concerto No. 4 in E minor, RV 297, "Winter"	Largo	11
Baroque Highlights	Handel: Xerxes	Largo	2
Handel: *Music For The Royal Fireworks*	Concerto grosso in B flat, Op. 3 No. 2	Largo	16

When being exposed to new material, I find it helpful to use these breathing and music techniques to help keep me relaxed and even distract my conscious mind a bit during the initial stages of the learning process. These ideas come from the field of Accelerated Learning. Interested readers are encouraged to read *Accelerated Learning* by Colin Rose for more information.

SUMMARY OF KEY DISTINCTIONS REGARDING INFORMATION MANAGEMENT

- **Clarity.** As the amount of information expands, there is an increasing need for clarification of the exact type of information you are looking for. Your results depend on this clarification. Clarity is power, and it becomes more powerful as available information resources expand. As described in Chapter 2, the "solutions approach" is based on the realization that the subconscious mind is the ultimate information filter. Emerson's statement, "Do the thing and you shall have the power" can be interpreted as, "Do the thing and you will be directed to and made aware of the information you need to do it."

- **Selectivity.** As the amount of information increases in a given area, there is an increasing need to scan that information at a high level and to be very selective of the areas you choose to study in detail.

- **Structure.** As the amount of information we need to deal with increases, there is an increasing need for structure in order to avoid decisional stress. Information tends to expand choices. Careful decisions about the way information will be processed can increase our capacity to handle information. Oftentimes, this means consistency (e.g., putting things in the same place or deciding on rules for handling information flow ahead of time, so you don't have to think about how to organize something every time).

- **Capacity/Awareness Link.** Our awareness of information tends to expand to meet our capacity to use information. Doing something to increase your information handling capacity will tend to expand the amount of information you are aware of. As mentioned earlier, buying a new bookshelf, a bigger filing cabinet, a larger hard disk, or implementing a new system for managing the flow ideas in your life can have this effect. Aldous Huxley's quote sums this up beautifully: "Knowledge is a function of being. When there is a change in the being of the knower, there is a corresponding change in the nature and amount of knowledge."

- **Context.** Our interaction with information is context driven. If you want to expand your awareness and understanding of certain information, give yourself a reason to do so. Take on a project or set a goal that creates a context within which that information can be applied.

- **80/20 Rule.** The Perato principle applies to information interaction, stating that 80% of the value comes from 20% (or less) of the information. Which 20% depends on the specific outcome you are trying to create. When you begin to solve problems associated with creating a particular outcome, questions arise. Those questions direct your attention towards high leverage information.

- **Meta-information.** Meta-information is information about the structure of ideas. Information about the way ideas relate to each other is often highly useful, but seldom easy to extract from text presented in a linear fashion.

- **Compound Knowledge.** Knowledge in a particular field compounds just as interest in the bank. The more you know, the easier it is to acquire new ideas. The more knowledge you transfer into long-term memory, the more effective your subsequent learning efforts will be. When you read the next book on the topic, you can skip over material you already know. This distinction helps me plow through the early stages of the learning cycle where the knowledge compounds at slower rates—I know things will be much different when I get to the steep part of the curve.

- **Masters.** In most fields of inquiry, there are usually individuals or businesses that have reached a level of mastery far beyond average—who are very high on the compound learning curve. The critical mass these masters have built often makes them the premier source for useful distinctions in their area. W. Edwards Deming (total quality management), Milton Erickson (hypnotherapy) and Stephen Covey (self-development) are a few good examples.

- **Profound Knowledge**. One reward for exploring the world of self-improvement is discovering an idea that has a positive impact on many areas of your life. I think this is what Dr. W. Edwards Deming meant by the term, "profound knowledge." For example, an idea that increases the amount of physical and mental energy available to you by 20% not only improves how you feel during the day, but can also increase the rate at which you acquire new information, including additional distinctions about how to increase your energy even more.

- **Ultimate Information Appliance.** As discussed in the next chapter, the computer amplifies our ability to interact with information, just as the phone expands our ability to hear and the car expands our ability to travel.

- **Monetary Value of Information.** "Where there are economic interests, there is often valuable information," teaches Richard Schenkar, a member of the National Speakers Association. In *"The Art of Strategic Planning for Information Technology,"* Bernard Boar writes: "What everyone knows has already happened. What everyone knows is not called wisdom. What the aware individual knows is what has not yet taken shape; what has not yet occurred." The idea is to "see the subtle and notice the hidden so as to seize victory when there is no form." The value of information is often in inverse proportion to the number of people who are aware of it.

- **Current Information.** The most current information is usually in the minds of people who are actually doing the work—solving business problems or conducting the research. When a person takes the time to write their discoveries in language others can understand, it takes away from time they could be using to conduct further experiments. Some things are very easy to do yet difficult to explain in written or linear form. Some information is best transferred intuitively by just being in someone's presence while they are "in the act." On the other hand, some ideas are best mastered through the investment in mental clarity it takes to convey them to others.

- **Information Acquisition Does Not Equal Learning.** Learning has only occurred when you have increased your capacity for effective action in some area. To paraphrase Stephen Covey, attempting to learn by simply acquiring information rather than doing is analogous to furnishing a room by filling it with wood, metal, cotton, cloth, nails, etc. You have all of the components used in dressers, beds, and chairs, but they are not organized in any meaningful or useful way.

- **Active Information vs. Interesting Information.** Richard Bandler was right on target when he said, "The only kind of understanding that I'm interested in is the kind that allows you to do something." So much of what we read is interesting but does nothing to help us decide what to do differently as a result of reading it. Sort information by usefulness. The value of information is based upon its usefulness, which is determined by your current objectives. Peter Drucker tells us, "The greatest wisdom not applied to action and behavior is meaningless data." There is so much information available to us in any given situation that to pay attention to irrelevant information is to risk rendering yourself ineffective. Just as Eskimos have many words for snow, having several words for information may help prevent us from being "snowed under" by infoglut. Below is an attempt to categorize the ways I use information in knowledge work.

  - **Strategic** – Useful in formulating strategic plans—making high-level directional decisions.
  - **Product** – Can be built into a product and thus sold to others. The Japanese have excelled in their emphasis on information that can be built into products and sold to other nations.
  - **Project** – Information that will help you complete whatever project you are working on.
  - **Emotional** – That which inspires you to action you would not have otherwise taken. This type of information is valuable to the extent that it generates action-oriented emotions within you. It

doesn't relate to any one task, it just increases
your motivation to complete the task.

- **Process** – Information that allows you to refine
  the processes you use to perform strategically
  important activities.

- **Systems** – Information about how changes in
  one area impact other aspects of a system.
  Information that helps you identify high leverage
  changes within an overall system.

- **Structural** – Information about the structure of
  information, or in the case of on-line
  information, how to search or filter the
  information. An example of how to think
  structurally is given in the use of Mind Maps as
  a note-taking tool. Mind Maps help you to see
  how ideas in a book relate to each other by
  mapping out the overall structure at a high level.

CONCLUSION

Conscious ⟷ Subconscious
Individual Thought ⟷ Dialogue
Left-Brain Mode ⟷ Right-Brain Mode
Detailed Thought ⟷ High Level Thought

This chapter addressed the fourth major strategy for
employing complementary opposite modes of thinking:
traversing the structure of our thoughts in order to
optimize important mental processes. There are countless
other ways of applying the idea of complementary
opposites, some of which are mentioned in the remaining
chapters. I emphasize these four because they have been
the most useful in my work.

The next chapter will examine methods of applying these
distinctions towards a topic of increasing importance in our
lives: mastering the ultimate information appliance.

CHAPTER 7

MASTERING THE ULTIMATE
INFORMATION APPLIANCE:

STRATEGIES FOR LEARNING SOFTWARE FASTER

"The computer has both created the information explosion and given us the means of managing it."

— *Paul Zane Pilzer*

The computer is to our mind what the car is to our legs, what the phone is to our ears and what the TV is to our eyes—it amplifies our ability to interact with information. Today's personal computer (PC) does far more than "compute." It is the fundamental tool for managing infoglut in the information age.

It is often said that if the auto industry did what the computer industry has done over the past few decades, a Rolls Royce would cost less than $2 and get over 100,000 miles to the gallon. Bill Gates' March 1995 column in the *Wall Street Journal* stated that the price of computing has dropped by more than a factor of 100,000 in the past 20 years. With Intel Corporation highly focused on the Herculean task of doubling the number of circuits on a chip every 18 months, this trend is likely to continue. This means that new software will be easier to use and existing software will run faster. Faster software means that the investment you make today to learn software will reap increasing benefits.

Becoming proficient with PCs involves mastering software. Therefore, the main focus of this chapter is on how the ideas presented thus far in *Brain Dancing* can be applied to the process of learning software faster.

The ideas presented thus far can be applied to a wide variety of topics. Learning software is just one of them. It is the area where I derive the most value from applying these ideas, so you can think of this chapter as one large example. Feel free to skip over any or all of this chapter if you have no interest in learning software. These ideas are not referenced in the remaining two chapters.

Software programs are essentially a collection of highly organized information. There are two basic ways of interacting with this information: as a wandering generality, or in a highly focused manner with a specific project in mind. I use both approaches, but am careful to limit the orientation (wandering generality) phase by setting fixed time limits for this type of learning, and by finding a project to which I can apply the software as soon as possible.

ORIENTATION PHASE

This is the high level scan of the "information lake," using the metaphor established in Chapter 6. Begin this scan by looking at every page of printed documentation at the rate of one page per second. Put Post-it tabs on any page that is obviously highly useful.

As mentioned in the previous chapter, it often helps to be relaxed both mentally and physically while scanning this material. Breathe rhythmically, retaining the breath for a few moments as you scan. If possible, put on some baroque music while orienting yourself to the material.

After installing the software, open up all sample files (documents, spreadsheets, databases, etc.) provided with the product and flip through the screens of text or data as quickly as your hardware allows. Use the sample files to select every menu option and icon to see what they do.

This high-level review helps eliminate the fear of the unknown and gives you an idea where significant functionality can be found. When novice software users get stuck, they are often hesitant to select menu options that they haven't tried before. They sit and wonder what to do rather than just looking around and trying things that seem appropriate. This hesitancy appears to be based on a fear of the unknown and of making mistakes that could cause data loss.

FIGURE OUT WHAT NOT TO DO

Such hesitancy can be minimized by investing time up front figuring out what NOT to do. It is much easier to explore the user interface freely and experiment somewhat haphazardly when you are not working on live data.

Most quality software will give you a warning before letting you do something destructive. So when the software asks you to confirm an action, PAY ATTENTION!

I heard of one case where an individual could have benefited from this advice. Records were mysteriously disappearing from the database. As it turned out, when this individual wanted to print the screen, he would press the "Delete" key. When asked if he was sure he wanted to delete the record, he selected "Yes," thinking, "Yes, I want to print the screen," and the record was deleted.

Be extra cautious with shared data! If your computer is hooked up to a corporate network, then extra caution is warranted. There is a big difference between experimenting with a spreadsheet calculation and trying new queries on your company's accounting database. When in doubt, ask an MIS support person something like: "I want to do some learning experiments. Are there any precautionary measures I should take while using this software?" or, "How can I set up my machine so that I can do some learning experiments without affecting anyone else's work?"

Eliminating hesitancy is discussed further in the "What-if Learning" section later in this chapter.

INFORMATION SOURCE MIND MAP

During the orientation phase, I sometimes create a Mind Map of available information sources such as the following (I've used a few extra words on this Mind Map for clarity to readers. I use minimal words on Mind Maps intended only for my use):

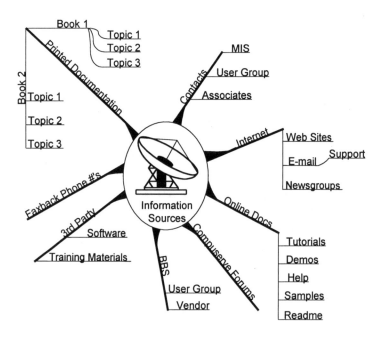

Mind Maps work well for this because it is easy to add new information as it becomes available. I refer to this Mind Map when I'm immersed in the details of solving a problem and get stuck. When working at the detail level, it is sometimes difficult to remember all the places I can turn for assistance. Creating this Mind Map also encourages me to invest time up front identifying all available information sources.

INCUBATION: PUT TIME ON YOUR SIDE

When it looks like I'll be needing to learn a new software package, I invest some time right away orienting myself to the software, even if it is just five minutes. When I get back to the software two weeks or even two months later, my mind has already seen and had time to think about (incubate) the ideas. The more substantial the software, and the more complex the underlying concepts, the more helpful it is to employ the incubation strategy.

Use spaced repetition to give your mind several passes over the material from multiple angles. For example, in one study session, I might scan all printed documentation and go through the tutorial. The next day, week or month, depending upon the situation, I might go through a book that employs a "hands-on" approach that walks me through the construction of a sample application or document. The next learning pass might involve scanning the sample applications or documents provided with the software or obtained from associates. When combined, these various passes round out my understanding from a variety of angles.

CONCEPT AND TERMINOLOGY MIND MAP

My experience suggests that learning software rarely involves memorizing lists of things. Instead, as software is used to solve problems, the information provided on screen becomes enough to jog the memory, one step at a time, towards the desired outcome.

However, most software comes with its own paradigm consisting of unique terminology and concepts. It is helpful to identify these up front and review them periodically to transfer them solidly into long-term memory. This review process can be facilitated by using a yellow highlighter in the manuals or by noting them in an "ongoing" Mind Map. By ongoing, I mean that ideas are added as they come up in both the orientation and project learning phases.

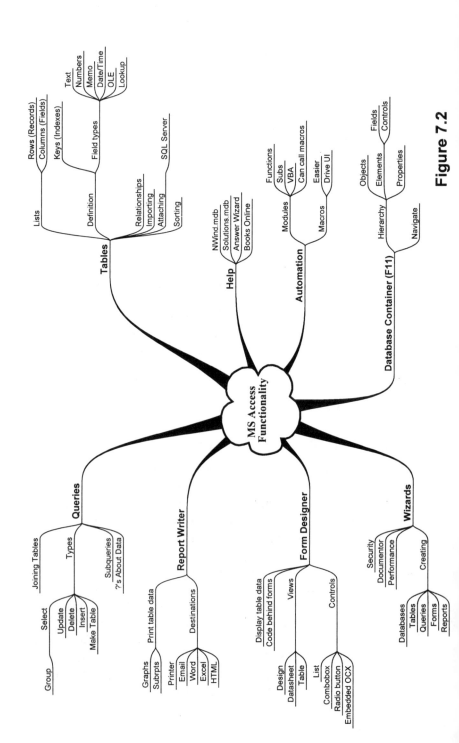

Figure 7.2

As discussed in Chapter 6, review periods of two to five minutes should be completed ten minutes, 24 hours, one week and one month after first learning the material. This Mind Map can be used with the visualization plus articulation strategy discussed in that chapter.

SOFTWARE OVERVIEW MIND MAP

When dealing with software that has substantial functionality and is fairly new to me, I usually create a Mind Map of the overall structure of the software. It delineates the major components and how they relate to each other. Figure 7.2 is an example of what this might look like for the Windows 95 version of Microsoft Access (relational database software). This Mind Map was created using MindJET's MindMan® software. You can download a trial version from: **www.mindman.com.** All other Mind Maps in this book were created using Visio®: **www.visio.com**.

Those of you familiar with Microsoft Access will notice many features have been omitted from this Mind Map. To include them all would require a much larger piece of paper. The benefit comes more from the process of creating the Mind Map rather than the end result. The Mind Map you create will probably more closely reflect your situation (i.e., context). For example, novice computer users would probably emphasize more of the interactive features of Access, while technically inclined users are likely to include more information related to programming.

The process of creating this Mind Map will encourage you to think about the software at "meta" levels. It will help reduce the chance of overlooking a key feature of the software that could save you tons of time (like the Database Wizard).

The figures on the following pages are the actual Mind Maps I used recently to learn how to build data-driven Web sites using Microsoft's ASP (Active Server Pages) and VB (Visual Basic) Script technology. These diagrams don't follow all of the Mind Mapping rules. However, I didn't create them to be published in this book. I created them to help me learn.

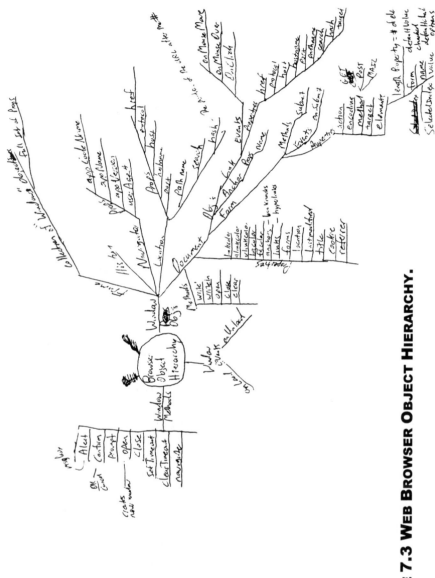

FIGURE 7.3 WEB BROWSER OBJECT HIERARCHY.

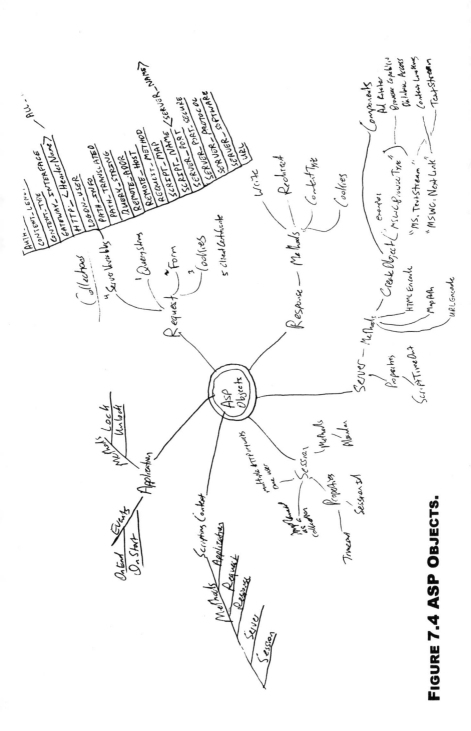

FIGURE 7.4 ASP OBJECTS.

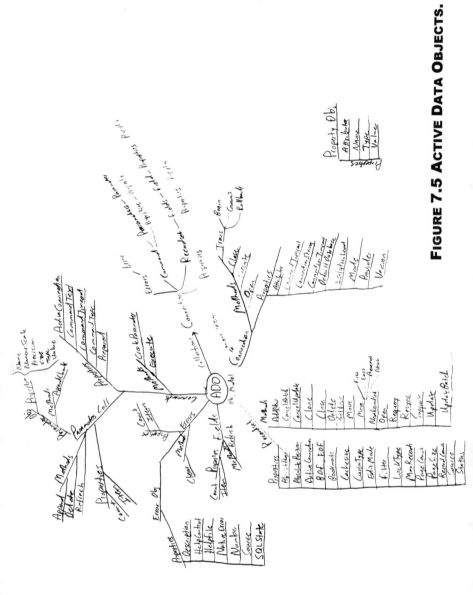

FIGURE 7.5 ACTIVE DATA OBJECTS.

ACTIVE VS. PASSIVE LEARNING

It is one thing to know which keys to press, and quite another to have the ability to create elegant and useful applications or documents with that software. While knowledge can be acquired by dabbling here and there, the development of software skills is best achieved by applying the tool to real world business problems.

After the initial overview, I go back to tutorials and walk-throughs that provide opportunities for active learning (i.e., exercises where *I* do the work). A key objective is to build confidence in my ability to solve problems with the software. This objective is supported when I know every keystroke and mouse click that goes into creating the application or document. When completed, these applications form good starting points for "what-if" learning experiments.

First-hand knowledge is much more effective at building capacity than second-hand knowledge obtained by passively reading articles voicing other peoples' opinions. Both are useful, but time allocations should reflect this distinction.

SETTING UP A LEARNING JOURNAL

After creating all of these Mind Maps, the question arises: Where do you put them? When learning any significant piece of software that I expect to use extensively, I create a three-ring notebook for organizing the information stream with the following sections:

To Do's	Summaries	?'s	Sample Apps	Journal

- **To Do's**: Contains my learning plan. When I have time to study the software, notes that I've made in this section ahead of time allow me to get right to work.

- **Summaries**: This is where the above-mentioned Mind Maps go.
- **?'s**: Recording unanswered questions as they arise frees me to move on to other issues. Many of these potential stumbling blocks get answered as I'm addressing other areas.
- **Sample Apps**: "Post-mortem" type information from applications that I have created. This includes data structure diagrams (discussed later), printouts of key routines (programs) that I used, etc. It may also contain listings of sample applications available from on-line information services and the Internet.
- **Learning Journal**: This "everything else" reference section contains material that I don't expect to use that often organized chronologically.

Any document in this binder that I expect to reference frequently gets its own yellow Post-it note tab. Take about ten 2"x1.5" yellow Post-it notes, cut them in half, and paste them on the back of the original pad. I keep these everywhere I learn and work, and even carry them in my DAY-TIMER. I usually stick a dozen blank tabs on the inside cover of the journal when I set it up. These tabs go along the top of the sheets so they don't block my view of the main tabs along the right border.

This journal is not an excuse to print reams of paper. As much information as possible is stored electronically so that it can be searched more efficiently.

PROJECT PHASE: SKILL VS. KNOWLEDGE

Set an overall time limit for the orientation phase and find an opportunity to apply the software to a real-world problem as soon as you can. This is where the "solutions approach" discussed in Chapter 2 comes in. When applying software to a real-world problem, there are two sets of issues that must be addressed:

- Issues that define what the problem is or what the software must do to effectively solve the problem.
- Information about how the software tool can be applied to meet that need. This is mostly technical details about how the software works.

One of the best ways to simplify the software learning process is to team up with someone (ideally a client who will pay me) who will focus on the "what" side of this equation. I usually refer to this as the "business analyst" role. They don't need to know that much about computers, but they must thoroughly understand the business problem to be addressed. This understanding must include the boundary conditions that must be met in order to increase the business's ability to deliver value to its customers. This team approach also forms the basis for synergistic dialogue, as discussed in Chapter 4.

In situations where a team approach doesn't apply, similar benefits can be obtained by using the software for something you already do manually or already know very well. In this case, the "what" has already been clearly defined.

If this strategy does not apply, then invest time creating a project specification that clearly delineates the "what" side of the equation. Make the first phase very simple, and use idea collection sheets to accumulate ideas for future versions. The specification gives you a clear target to hit and helps build confidence with the new tool. Without such a target, it is easy to get diverted by new possibilities. This increases the likelihood that you will end up with a jumble of features that don't work well, and your self-confidence will not be increased.

Chapter 2 described several strategies for transitioning into new technologies. The most useful is probably the incremental strategy. This involves working on projects involving a combination of existing expertise and the new technology. People you have done work for in the past and who know your work ethic are more likely to trust you in getting the job done with new technology.

The following material elaborates on ideas presented in Chapter 2 as they apply to learning software.

THE 80/20 RULE

Using software for any one application often requires the use of a small percentage of the software's features. Perato's 80/20 rule is applicable here as well—80% of the value comes from 20% of the features. Stated another way, we often spend most of our time working with a small percentage of the features. When learning a new software program, your highest leverage learning time is what you invest in this core 20%. The challenge for most beginners is figuring out what questions to ask—that is, until they start working on a project.

When you start to apply the tool to a real-world business problem, all kinds of questions come up. These questions zero you right in on the core 20% of the software.

METHODOLOGY

Another aspect of developing the capacity for skilled software application has to do with the process used to apply the tool—the methodology. Methodology is about doing the right things in the right sequence: begin with the end in mind, developing the skill of clarifying exactly what the end should be, knowing which pieces of the puzzle to build first, knowing when to stop tinkering, etc.

One of the best ways to learn methodology is to observe or talk to others who've done it before (modeling). This might involve attending user group meetings, hiring a consultant for a couple of hours or just buying a friend lunch. Watching an expert at work can greatly accelerate your software learning, for even the most eloquent words pale in comparison to the information presented to us by our senses.

OTHER IDEAS FOR ACCELERATING SOFTWARE LEARNING

INVEST IN THE BEST

If you place a reasonable value on your time, then you will probably invest far more in learning a software package than the cost to acquire it. Learning time can be reduced when you purchase high quality software engineered for ease of use.

Every software program has its little quirks, shortcuts, etc., that once learned, add up to an ability to produce effective results with that package. The better the software, the less learning time you will have to invest, and the more value you will receive, in terms of capacity, for the time you do invest.

When you purchase software, you are investing in an information stream from the software manufacturer. When making a software decision, ask yourself if the work demonstrates innovation skills likely to result in a stream of high quality state of the art upgrades.

The late Don Estridge, who played a key role in the creation and launch of the original IBM PC in 1981, summed up IBM's research this way: "What we discovered was that the way people responded emotionally to PC's was more important than what the computer actually did." Notice your emotional reaction to the software. Is it enjoyable to work with? Does it inspire ideas for new ways to apply the technology? Great software empowers people to do what heretofore was impractical.

WHAT-IF LEARNING

What-if learners know to experiment when they get stuck. Rather than staring at the screen fearing what might happen if they try something, they know when it is safe to just try it. This knowledge is often based on experimentation done ahead of time. Experienced software users often rely on intuition to guide their experiments. What-if experiments lead to further experiments, which often lead to the solution. They also round out your knowledge of the overall product.

In addition to investing time during the orientation phase figuring out what not to do, here are three ways to make it safer to do what-if learning:

- Learn how to make quick backups: By making a copy of the file you are working on before you do the experiment, you can easily revert back to where things were before doing the experiments. I set up a backup directory called "bu" beneath my working directory, and then periodically copy my files to this directory using a different file name each time. For example, I would copy a file called "chapter5.doc" to "bu\chapter5.211". The "211" tells me it was made on February 11. This allows me to revert back to where I was at several different points along the way. If you are hooked up to a network, periodically copy your files to another computer's hard disk. This way you won't lose all of your work if your computer crashes.

- Just don't save your changes: Some software allows you to make changes in memory and only write them to disk when you tell it to. To use this approach, save your work before you make the change, try the experiment, and if it doesn't work, simply close the file and answer "No" when it asks you if you want to save your changes. Also make sure to disable any auto-save options before relying on this approach. Some Windows software allows you to undo previous changes by pressing "Ctrl-Z" or selecting the "Edit Undo" menu options.

- Single screen experimentation: You can start a new experiment file and copy in the data you need to test your idea. I call this "single screen" experimentation because I try to limit the entire experiment to a single screen of information. This allows me to see everything that is going on when I make a change and encourages me to focus on process, as opposed to content. Keep these small learning applications handy for future reference. When working on a live application, it might help to load your learning application to perform some quick experiments before applying the techniques to live data.

LINE UP A REFERENCE PERSON

When you get to the point where nothing you try produces the outcome you want, the more people you can call on for quick questions, the better. Remember the retired engineer who quickly rectified the situation by tapping the right pipe?

Many times when learning to use a new software program, you get to a point where it's just not obvious what to do. It has nothing to do with intelligence; you are just missing a piece of information that may be fairly unique to your situation. Having quick access to several experts, such as product support lines, user group associates, company support staff or friends, can often save you hours trying to figure out "where to tap."

PROCESS OPTIMIZATION: TYPING & MOUSE MOVEMENT

Typing is where the tire meets the road in using a computer. If you can double or triple your typing speed, it often translates into getting computer-related work done two or three times faster. A simple way to improve your typing skills is to type in the letters of the alphabet five times as fast as you can. Then do it backwards as fast as you can a few times. Do this once or twice a day. Alternatively, you can type the following phrase which contains every letter of the alphabet:

The quick brown fox jumps over the lazy dog.

After doing it a couple of times, you may want to close your eyes and visualize your hands moving across the keyboard as they strike each key.

The Brain Dancing Coach software discussed in Appendix A includes a simple typing tutorial module.

With Microsoft Windows software, the second most frequently performed activity is moving the mouse. One way to optimize this process is to set mouse movement sensitivity to maximum and then get used to it. You want the slightest movement on the mouse pad to translate into the largest movement on the screen. This will result in substantially less hand and wrist movement over time.

With most software, it pays to invest a little time memorizing keyboard shortcuts, which are often faster than using a mouse. If your PC uses the Microsoft Windows operating system, you can set up "shortcut" keys for launching frequently used applications and files. I use these keyboard shortcuts enough to make it worthwhile to set up a help file to keep track of them and created a shortcut to it on my desktop. See **http://BrainDance.com/helpkeys.htm** for more information.

SET UP AN ELECTRONIC KNOWLEDGE BASE

Leaving reference information in electronic form is more efficient to search and saves paper, trees and money. I therefore store as much information in electronic form as possible. There are two types of electronic information I use to complement the on-line documentation and knowledge bases provided by most software vendors: reference text files and sample applications.

A detailed discussion of how to set up and use an electronic knowledge base is beyond the scope of this book. The following discussion provides general guidelines and may require the assistance of someone with at least intermediate computer skills.

REFERENCE TEXT FILES

These knowledge bases are stored in a subdirectory I call "KB," which is placed directly beneath the main software directory. For example, a knowledge base for Corel Draw! would be placed in a directory called "c:\corel\kb." In this directory I store related Internet web pages, excerpts from Internet newsgroups or CompuServe message forums, and e-mail messages from mailing lists. All files in this directory are stored in ASCII text format. This enables me to use a text search utility to quickly scan every file in the directory for specific key words. This functionality is now available in StartGen, a shareware application I developed that you can download from the BrainDance.com Web site for a free trial.

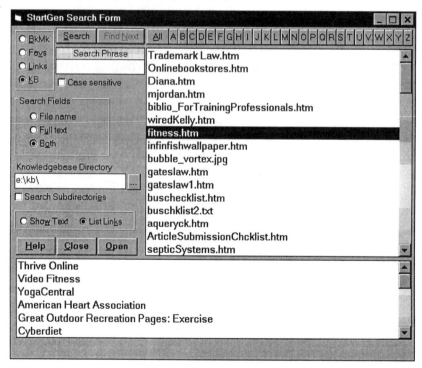

Figure 7.6. StartGen's KBFind feature.

When browsing the Web, I often come across Web pages I want to archive for future reference. You never know when a Web site is going to disappear or when a specific page might be pulled. Consequently, I created a directory called "notes" for archiving key Web pages. I eventually accumulated several dozen files that together form a personalized knowledge base. As shown in the following figure, StartGen's "KBFind" feature makes accessing information in this knowledge base more convenient. StartGen is discussed in more detail later in this chapter.

SAMPLE APPLICATIONS

Sample applications obtained from CompuServe, the Internet, or user group bulletin boards are placed in a directory called "sampapps." Using the above example, the directory would be called "c:\corel\sampapps." Consistently using the same directory names gives me one less thing to decide or remember when learning each new software package.

> **Note**: Electromagnetic radiation (EMR) generated by PC monitors decreases exponentially as you move away from the source. Your monitor should be a minimum of two feet away. While EMR is emitted in all directions, the strongest emissions go out the back and pass through walls. According to Dr. Andrew Weil, the new generation of computer monitors are sufficiently shielded to minimize risk. In any event, when you purchase your next monitor, make sure it is both MPR-II and TCO '92 compliant. Also note that laptops with LCD monitors emit little or no EMR. TCO '95 addresses keyboard and system unit EMR.

SOFTWARE-SPECIFIC SUGGESTIONS

The preceding strategies are fairly generic and can be applied towards learning a variety of software packages. The following discussion narrows the focus a bit by describing specific techniques for getting the most out of the most popular types of software: spreadsheets, word processors, electronic mail, Web browsers and databases.

SPREADSHEETS

- Before thinking about numbers and computation, use block diagrams for depicting the overall layout of the spreadsheet. This is especially helpful when studying a file created by someone else, or when managing an especially large spreadsheet. I use these less often now that tabbed workbooks are available.

Summary
Sales
Expenses

- The best spreadsheets come from the best manual systems. In the early days when I did spreadsheet consulting, I had the good fortune of working with a few companies who had thought out manual spreadsheets to the *nth* degree. They would hand me an 11x17 columnar worksheet crammed with numbers and ask me to create its electronic equivalent. These were the most successful applications I did. Other less organized clients taught me the truth of the adage: "Sometimes when you automate a mess, you just end up doing the wrong things faster."

- Don't make them so complex that you don't understand what's happening with the numbers. When a spreadsheet becomes so complex that management (and some users) view it as a "black box," its usefulness is compromised. Spreadsheet technology gives us so much computational power that it is easy to get carried away in its application.

- Just one number can throw the calculations off significantly. While working on a very large and complex spreadsheet created by someone else, we found an error in a single row that altered the bottom line by over $1 billion. Admittedly, this was a very long-term forecast, but it emphasized the importance of keeping spreadsheets as simple as possible in order to minimize the chances of this happening.

- Forecasts are just forecasts. You still have to make them happen. When I hear stories about forecasts concerning our national debt and deficit, I am reminded that creating a brilliantly architected spreadsheet with every formula perfected is no substitute for brilliant execution. This is especially true with sales numbers, which often have the greatest impact on the bottom line.

WORD PROCESSORS

- Try writing in different fonts or varying the margin widths for overcoming writer's block. For some reason, I do my best writing when working with columns four to five inches wide.

- When writing creatively, it is critical that you minimize mental bandwidth allocated to form as opposed to content. You want to get the content in and organized as fast as possible. Only when this is done do I worry about format. Microsoft Word has a feature called style sheets, which can make revising the appearance of your documents a breeze.

- Integrated outline processors, such as the one provided with Microsoft Word, assist in the process of "going meta." They allow you to quickly switch between a detailed view of your document and a high level outline. On large monitors, an outline view of the same document can be placed alongside your typing window. This helps write individual sections with the overall context in mind.

- Separate the writing and editing phases. One sure way to cure this problem is to write your first draft on paper, and then type it into your word processor for editing. I am often amazed at how I can express ideas better in handwritten form than I can in front of the keyboard. However, the more I practice, the better I'm getting at doing my first draft on the computer as well.

E-MAIL

- In an interview with New Yorker Magazine, Bill Gates indicated that he spends about two hours per day reading and responding to e-mail. With all of the demands placed upon his time, what does that tell you about the potential value of e-mail? According to the article, Gates uses all lowercase and minimizes the use of social niceties for increased efficiency.

- A study done at the MIT Sloan School of Management points out that not only must peoples' mental models appreciate the potential of groupware such as e-mail, but "...where the premises underlying the groupware technology (shared effort, cooperation, collaboration) are counter-cultural to an organization's structural properties (competitive and individualistic culture, rigid hierarchy, etc.), the technology will be unlikely to facilitate collective use and value."[1] If everyone on the team is not committed to checking their e-mail periodically throughout the day and responding promptly, team members are less likely to use e-mail. You have to trust that once sent, the other person will both receive and read the message in a timely manner. The next time you upgrade your computer, consider keeping the old one around as an e-mail machine. This allows you to check e-mail with just a glance, vs. starting the software each time, or tying up memory on your main computer by leaving it running.

- E-mail can increase the information metabolism of a company by minimizing the overhead associated with an information exchange event. The less time it takes to exchange information, the more likely you are to do it, and the more your company can accomplish in less time. It also gives the recipient control over when they read the message. Contrast this with phone calls,

---

[1] Wanda J. Orlikowski, WP #3428-92, CCS TR No. 131, MIT Sloan School of Management, Cambridge, MA.

which immediately interrupt the recipient's concentration. In a recent interview with Seattle television host Barry Mitsman, Intel CEO Andy Grove stated that e-mail was the "life-blood" of his company. He emphasized that e-mail is the primary reason Intel has been able to maintain the responsiveness of a small company in spite of its tremendous growth.

"A lot of companies don't even have electronic mail set up so you can count on everybody reading a message within one working day of when you sent it...Without that basic ability, a company isn't at first base in terms of the information age."

— Bill Gates, Interview in Context Magazine

BROWSING THE INTERNET

As a lifelong learner, I'm always on the lookout for useful information, and this makes the Internet a real test of discipline. It is easy to get carried away when so much information is available, so convenient and for so little cost. The challenge is to incorporate its use into an already busy schedule in a way that complements and enhances choices, rather than reducing them from overuse.

I once asked Anthony Robbins the following question: "How can I silence this voice inside my head which seems to analyze everything I do as I am doing it?" He responded with the thought that rather than eliminate a resource, it is usually much wiser to figure out a way to use it to your advantage. The Internet represents an unprecedented information resource to those who learn how to use it effectively. Doing this requires extreme clarity on exactly what represents useful information, as opposed to merely interesting.

Here are some of the most useful types of information I've found on the Web:

- Information that helps me create and market my Web site
- Information that helps me make new contacts via e-mail
- Information about competitors' products and business models
- Information that expands the scope and nature of the questions I explore

It also helps to remember the two basic strategies discussed in *Brain Dancing* for interacting with any information ocean: with a specific purpose in mind (left-brain) and looking for the unexpected (right-brain). When looking for the unexpected (surfing), it is important to set time limits because the right brain is not aware of linear time, and there is no feedback mechanism for telling you when you are done (when the problem is solved).

With the Internet, it is also necessary to set time limits when operating in left-brain mode. Even with the vast quantity of information currently on the Internet, it still contains only a fraction of our total knowledge. In other words, there is no guarantee that the information you need is even on the Internet.

For example, when I learned that someone I knew had Chrones disease, I logged onto the net and began a left-brain search for everything I could find on the subject. I was amazed how much I learned about the net itself while I conducted the search. In addition to finding a lot of information about Chrones, I also discovered new ways to research any new topic. Doing right-brain orientation surfing had taught me a lot about the net, but the laser beam focus derived from having a specific problem to solve clarified and extended that knowledge significantly.

STARTGEN: THE WEB BROWSER START PAGE GENERATOR

Bookmarks are links to sites you want to revisit. After three years of surfing the Web, I've accumulated over 800 bookmarks. After noticing that I use some bookmarks far more often than others, I decided to organize them into a start page that loaded automatically each time I started my browser. I also noticed that I use search engines quite often and was getting tired of waiting for their opening pages to load (with ads) each time I decided to do a search. So I placed the HTML required to access these engines at the bottom of my start page in order to eliminate this first step. The result ended up looking something like Figure 7.7. I then changed my Netscape and Internet Explorer browsers to bring up this page each time I click the "Home" button on the toolbar.

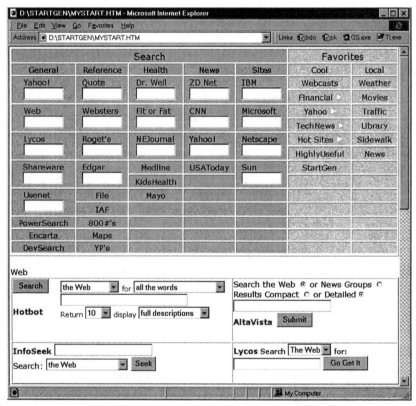

Figure 7.7 Sample Start Page Generated by StartGen.

This turned out to be so useful that I decided to write a software program to help others create their own start page. I did this because the HTML editors I tried kept scrambling the search engine interfaces when I saved the file. The program is called StartGen, and you can download a free copy from the BrainDance.com Web site.

StartGen resulted from the application of the following principles discussed in Chapter 6:

- Any time you do something repetitively, it is worthwhile to occasionally review the processes used for possible refinement.
- As the number of choices expand, there is an increasing need for structure, for habits, for making decisions that last.
- As the amount of information expands, there is an increasing need to scan that information at high level and selectively dive into the details.

Having this file on your local PC allows it to load very quickly. Frequently visited web sites are often just one click away. Maintaining control over the content of this start page reduces the number of decisions you have to make each time you browse the Web. Storing the interfaces to your favorite search engines locally eliminates a step in the search process (i.e., waiting for all of the text and graphics to load from the remote site). And lastly, having quick access to various metadirectories (i.e., top-level directories) increases the chances that you will find what you are looking for.

DATABASES

Do whatever it takes to learn how to read data structure diagrams such as the one shown in Figure 7.8. While they are not that complex, many users seem intimidated by them, or just don't understand their value. These diagrams represent the most useful information available about what and how data is stored in a database on a single page. When this understanding is combined with an ability to use a query engine, such as those included with Borland's Paradox or Microsoft Access, you will be able to ask a vast array of questions about any database with a relatively small amount of effort.

DILBERT reprinted by permission of United Feature Syndicate, Inc.

Here is a brief introduction to data structure diagrams using the "Ledger" application generated by the Microsoft Access 97 Database Wizard.

The data structure diagram in Figure 7.8 shows that this database application contains three tables: Transactions, Accounts and Account Types. The Transactions table is nothing more than an electronic check register. The Accounts table describes how the checks are to be categorized, and the Account Types table describes how Accounts are categorized. As indicated by the arrows, the Transactions and Accounts tables are linked by the AccountID field, and the Accounts and Account Types tables are linked by the AccountTypeID field.

Okay, what do I mean by "linked together" and "field?" As you can see in Figures 7.9 and 7.10, a table consists of rows of information divided into columns. Each column is called a field. These tables are linked based on the "AccountTypeID" field. The "Rental Income" account has been assigned an AccountTypeID of "2".

If you look in the Account Types table, you can see that an AccountTypeID of "2" corresponds to an Account Type of "Revenues." When two tables are "linked" by a field, it means that the data contained in a field in one table corresponds to a row in the other table.

Understanding the above data structure diagram makes it very easy to use a query tool to ask questions such as: "What were my total deposits and withdrawals for each account type or account number?"

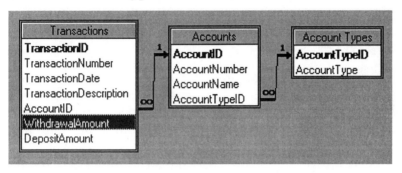

Figure 7.8 Simple Data Structure Diagram.

Accounts : Table			
Account ID	**Account Number**	**Account Name**	**Account Type**
1	610	Meals	1
2	620	Transportation	1
3	630	Lodging	1
4	640	Miscellaneous	1
5	410	Rental Income	2
6	650	Power Bill	1

Figure 7.9 Corresponding "Accounts" Table.

Account Types : Table	
Account Type ID	**Account Type**
1	Expenses
2	Revenues
3	Liabilities
4	Other

Figure 7.10 Corresponding "Account Types" Table.

Even though I've greatly simplified things here, this may take a little more study than most in this book. But keep in mind that this is a powerful set of ideas with broad application in business. It's well worth your effort to learn how to read a data structure diagram. Be aggressive here. Bug a database guru for a little time if you have to. In larger databases, the number of tables and lines will be greater, but these basic ideas are equally applicable.

PERSONAL ECOLOGY

I've met highly successful business people who know very little about PCs. They are great at what they do and have developed systematic strategies for consistently delivering value to their customers. Taking time to flip through computer manuals trying to figure out what keys to press is a diversion from their master strategy. For them, investing the time to learn about computers has been risky to the extent that it required so much time and mental energy that it diverted them from the skillful and consistent implementation of their master plan.

I believe that fear of diversion is a primary reason many people have put off learning to use computers. The key is to set a fixed time limit on the amount of time you will spend each week learning the software, and then stick to that time limit. The sooner you present these issues to your subconscious mind, the sooner it will begin the incubation process. It only takes a few minutes a day to put time on your side.

Thanks to massive economies of scale, the breadth of software applications is continuing its rapid expansion. As PCs become easier to use, more powerful, less expensive, and more interconnected, the ratio of value received per minute invested learning will continue to increase. This will make the PC an even greater means of achieving mental leverage.

EXERCISE

Search the U.S. Patent database to study new inventions by pointing your browser to:

http://www.patents.ibm.com/ibm.html

CHAPTER 8

Optimizing Mental Clarity:

Enhancing Personal Energy Levels

"The secret to effective systems development of any kind, manual or automated, is clear logical thinking and expression—everything else is secondary."

— *Ken Orr*

"More coals!" shouted Anthony Robbins. I was standing barefoot in front of a twelve-foot bed of coals burning between 600 and 2000 degrees Fahrenheit. After I did my first couple of power moves, "Whooossshhh!" "BOOOOOOOOMM!," Robbins asked his assistant to add a little more fuel to the fire.

Two more shovels full of smoldering coals burning bright yellow-orange in the dark night did not sway my determination to walk. I cranked my energy level up another few notches with two more power moves: "Whooossshhh!!" "BOOOOOOOOMM!!"

My energy level exploded past "level ten," and this time Robbins gave me the go-ahead: "You're ready," he said. A few seconds later I was safely across—one of nearly 300 people who walked that night in 1988 at the Museum of History and Industry in Seattle.

Before continuing, I want to make it very clear that I am in no way recommending that you do a firewalk. If, however, you ever find yourself considering a firewalk,

make sure you do it with the guidance of a professional trainer with a proven track record. Improperly performed firewalks can be extremely dangerous!

My feet tingle as I write, several years later, just as they have every time I've ever shared this story with others. Crazy, you say? Well, that's what I would have thought before that night. In fact, I wasn't planning on walking. After studying the cutting edge material in Robbins' *Unlimited Power* book and audiotapes, I knew I could learn plenty just by listening.

That night, Robbins gave an absolutely incredible presentation. He also made the risks of walking very clear to the audience. This was not brainwashing; it was an opportunity for personal growth for those willing to stretch. When the group headed for the coals, I went along and even got in line at the coals for a brief moment. I remember thinking that this could really put a damper on my upcoming snow skiing plans—that was all the reason I needed to get out of there.

Always in "constant learn mode," I realized that this was a great opportunity to study the others who were walking. So I walked around and stood two feet from the side of the coals as others walked across. Person after person walked successfully, including a 70-year-old man, and with some special assistance, an 11-year-old boy.

Robbins' words began to replay in my head: "If you can't, then you must! And if you must, then you can!" In other words, if you know you can safely do something, and if you were to do it, it would help you reach farther towards your true potential. If you don't follow through, you are living a life of limitation, cheating yourself and everyone around you. Something inside told me that there was an important lesson I could learn by walking. Yes, it was risky, and I'd just seen over 200 people walk successfully, including a friend I'd known for almost 20 years. This was no illusion. If I followed the guidelines prescribed, this was something I could safely perform. So back in line I went, and I'm extremely glad that I did. I feel a deep sense of gratitude to Anthony Robbins for creating this learning opportunity.

In addition to learning how to break through limiting fears and take action, one of the most important lessons wrapped up in this experience was this: your energy level is not something that just happens to you—that would make us all puppets. Energy is something you can create within yourself on demand if you know the "levers."

Energy is required to understand and apply every technique presented in this book. This chapter is about the metaskill of being able to cultivate high levels of personal energy. I call it "Optimizing Mental Clarity" to emphasize a significant side benefit I experience while doing things that increase my natural energy level: The quality of my thinking improves and I have more mental energy to apply to each moment of my life. I am able to work longer hours without getting tired and I get more done during the time I work. When I spend time with my family, this energy allows me to give more of myself in these moments as well.

Contrast your thinking at peak mental alertness with the experience of doing thought intensive work after a large heavy lunch. When the mind is clear, ideas come more easily, thoughts are formulated faster with greater precision, and communication with others is more effective. Within three months of completing Robbins' seminar, my income doubled to over $8,000 per month. One year after that I "imploded," and that's why Chapter 9 is about personal ecology.

The emphasis of this book has been to point you in directions most likely to yield the highest leverage—the most benefit per minute of time invested. With this in mind, I've devoted the first half of this chapter to the topic of juicing. This is followed by an overview of several other key distinctions for maximizing personal energy that you may want to explore.

Time you invest now to learn new distinctions for cultivating personal energy will benefit you for the rest of your life, to the extent that you apply them wisely. This topic, more than any other, has the potential to impact every aspect of your life. More energy means more energy for learning, and because learning compounds over a lifetime, it can accelerate your journey along any compound learning curve.

JUICING: THE ULTIMATE SUPPLEMENT

We are constantly participating in a "dance of life," which involves continual give and take throughout nature. Try taking a breath with the realization that you are inhaling oxygen produced by vegetation somewhere on the planet. You are nourishing your cells with their exhalation of oxygen, and when you exhale, you give back to the environment nutrients plants use to sustain their existence. We owe our lives to plants not only for the oxygen they create, but also for the nutrients they extract from the soil and store in their roots, leaves and fruit.

Juicing is the process of using a juice extractor to separate the juice of fruits and vegetables from the fiber. You drink the juice and discard the fiber. Chewing, swallowing, digesting, assimilating—this entire process is aimed at one end—extracting nutrients from food in a way that your body can assimilate them into your blood stream, and thus circulate them throughout the body to nourish your cells. The human body is a juice extractor! Juicing removes the burden of the first three steps from your body. This frees up energy that can be used for other things.

Juicing does not replace the need to eat! It can reduce the amount you need to eat since your body doesn't have to filter through as much "bulk" in order to sift out the essential nutrients it needs. This is why I refer to juicing as the ultimate supplement. It amplifies your intake of high quality nutrients directly from the source—Mother Nature.

From myself and other "juicers" I've observed, new activities began to blossom in our lives. For example, I know a restaurant owner who feels that juicing gave him the boost he needed to dust off his magic act. As a result, hundreds of people now fill high school gymnasiums to enjoy this magical entertainment that has been dormant for years.

As with any significant change in your dietary patterns, you are advised to seek advice from appropriate medical and nutritional authorities before beginning to juice. This is especially important if you have any history of blood sugar disorders such as diabetes or hypoglycemia.

If I handed you a pile of food and asked you to turn it into a rock or a board, you'd laugh thinking that it would take a miracle. Yet every day your body does something even more miraculous by transforming such food into arms, legs, brains, heart, all of which work together to dance, think and love.

WHICH CHEMIST DO YOU TRUST?

The two primary purposes of eating are:

1) To provide the necessary nutrients to our cells, and
2) To consume enough fiber to cleanse our intestinal tract.

People consume supplements because they believe that the quality of the material they consume will impact the quality of their health and energy. In the energy portion of my seminars, I hold up a plate of uncooked vegetables (carrots, kale, green bell pepper, etc.) in one hand, and rattle a bottle of vitamin pills in the other. I then ask the audience, "Which chemist do you trust more: the one who made these (referring to the plate of veggies), or the one who made these (rattling the bottle of pills)?"

Most people get the point. The problem is that most of us don't have the time, energy or the teeth to chew and assimilate this much produce once or twice a day. The answer is not to eat them but to drink them!

As the "Juiceman" Jay Kordach says, "Every fiber of our being is made from Earth, yet we cannot just reach down, take a handful of soil and consume it. We are totally dependent upon the plants to lower their roots into the soil, extract certain combinations of nutrients, and convert them into substances we can consume." Kordach encourages people to go directly to the source for nutrients as much as possible.

In his book, *Smart Eating,* Covert Bailey points out that muscles not used tend to atrophy and that this may also apply to our digestive system. The basic idea is that supplements make it so easy for the body to assimilate nutrients, that over time, the digestive system could become "lazy." There may be some truth to this. It is all the more reason not to go overboard with juicing or vitamins. This may explain why I've developed the habit of nibbling on the produce as I prepare it for juicing.

One of the best ways I know to give my digestive system a healthy workout is to eat the following once a week:

1. Take a cup of organic short grain brown rice (you can buy this in bulk from the health food store), some olive oil, chop up a large carrot, some parsley, celery, mushrooms (use sparingly and only if needed for flavor) and a few cloves of garlic.
2. Put it all in a stir fry pan and pour in enough water to cover everything plus about a half inch.
3. Let it simmer for about twenty minutes, turn off the burner and let it sit for another ten minutes.

Most of the water should be soaked up by the rice and it should be fairly tender. I sometimes add a little sea salt and unsalted butter for added flavor. This makes two servings for less than $2.

Juicing is an experiment and the last word on this topic has not yet been written. The benefits I've received over the past ten years have been significant, but I must again encourage you to proceed with caution.

ENZYMES

While enzymes are a fascinating subject, precise and consistent information on their role in digestion has been hard to come by. From what I've been able to learn so far, the enzyme theory goes something like this: raw food is alive and contains enzymes that assist the body in digesting and assimilating the food and nutrients therein. Cooking food diminishes the vitamin and mineral content and destroys the enzymes. This places the burden of generating digestive enzymes on the pancreas. Not only does this require nerve energy, but over time, it also begins to take its toll on the pancreas. I have no idea how difficult it is to "generate enzymes" at the molecular level, but it seems to make sense to give my pancreas all the help I can.

MAKING JUICING PRACTICAL

With full acknowledgment that everyone is different in their nourishment needs, I will share with you the results of my eight years of experimentation with juicing. The eleven guidelines for making juicing practical are:

1) avoid synthetic vitamin A and E,
2) trust your taste buds,
3) apply the ten minute rule,
4) juice once or twice a day consistently,
5) use a carrot/apple base,
6) emphasize vegetable juice,
7) variety is key, so vary the remaining 25%,
8) use organic produce as much as possible,
9) drink juice immediately,
10) juice on an empty stomach, and
11) feed your mind while you juice.

AVOID SYNTHETIC VITAMIN A AND E

Vitamins A and E are fat soluble, which makes it difficult for your body to dispose of unused portions. I take a natural vitamin E supplement occasionally because it is difficult to obtain from food. Make sure your vitamin E is natural rather than synthetic: d-alpha tocopheryl succinate is natural, dl-alpha tocopheryl acetate is synthetic.

If your body is getting all of the vitamin A it needs from natural sources, taking synthetic vitamin A (or synthetic beta-carotene) significantly increases the likelihood of toxic buildup in the body. People have been known to die from such overdoses!

A friend of mine started juicing regularly while continuing to take a multi-vitamin containing synthetic vitamin A. On the positive side, juicing eliminated his need to take colitis medication. On the negative side, he soon began getting headaches, which his doctor told him was one symptom of vitamin A overdose.

This symptom can be misleading. Have you ever gotten so busy at work that you let your house cleaning go for a while? Things start piling up. The same thing happens to your body when you eat in a way that causes it to work overtime. When a person begins to juice, nerve energy is freed up to do house cleaning that had been neglected due to other needs. This sometimes results in headaches and mucus discharge (e.g., runny nose) until the cleansing is complete. I don't know how to tell the difference between a cleansing headache and one caused by a vitamin A overdose. All I can say is consult a physician if you get headaches after beginning to juice, and avoid synthetic vitamins A and E just to be safe.

As far as I can tell, you cannot overdose on natural sources of beta-carotene. Nevertheless, the adage "moderation in all things" seems prudent here as well. Carrots contain no vitamin A, only beta-carotene, which the body converts to vitamin A as needed. I've read or heard of people consuming one gallon of carrot juice per day for extended periods of time with no ill effects.

However, common sense tells me to be careful here. "All excesses are ultimately their own undoing," to quote Paul Harvey. Our bodies have built-in warning systems which help us minimize the chances of consuming too much fresh juice, which leads us to guideline number two.

TRUST YOUR TASTE BUDS

I trust my taste buds' "judgment" to know if my body needs the nutrients in the juice. If the juice tastes bad, I dump it out. I use a mental scale of one to ten, where one is lousy, five is neutral and ten is great. I dump any juice that registers below four.

There is a larger issue involved here—that intelligence is distributed throughout the body. I'll bet most people have had the experience where even the thought of eating a certain food turned their stomach. Or maybe the food didn't pass the "smell test." What I didn't learn until recently, however, was that our ability to "tune-in" to this bodily intelligence is increased as we detoxify our body with healthy eating habits.

Sometimes carrot juice doesn't sound good to me. Even the thought of carrot juice makes my stomach turn. Rather than generalize that I must not like carrot juice any more, I simply switch my dietary pattern for a day or four. Any time the first sip of a juice makes my stomach turn, I trust that my taste buds are telling me either that I do not need the nutrients in the juice, or that perhaps one of the ingredients was spoiled. In either case, I do not hesitate to dump this juice down the drain, regardless of the cost or time invested to make it.

When in doubt, dump it out.

This "taste bud test" is the key means of compensating for the fact that everyone is different in their nutritional needs. Specifically, our ancestral dietary patterns have impacted our capacity to assimilate nutrients from various sources. For example, some people are better equipped to handle the coarse proteins in dairy products (my research indicates that cow's milk causes far more problems than it solves). In addition to hereditary differences, our body chemistry fluctuates with the seasons. Our taste buds seem to know what season it is internally and which food will provide the nutrients we need.

The taste bud principle is only meant to be applied to foods that our understanding and wisdom tell us are healthy to consume. For example, chocolate might taste good even though common sense tells us its use should be minimized.

Naturopathic physician Peter D'Adamo has written a controversial book called *Eat Right for Your Type*, in which he describes how each of the four major blood types differ in their ability to assimilate the nutrients in food. While this approach is not endorsed by some highly respected authors I've consulted, there appears to be a large number of people who have benefited from it. The discussion groups at Dr. D'Adamo's Web site are quite active (**www.dadamo.com**).

Dr. D'Adamo's book appears to be a sincere effort based on scientific observation, so I was surprised to hear that respected medical and naturopathic physicians questioned the scientific basis for the approach. So many people are benefiting from Dr. D'Adamo's work that I feel there must be at least some truth to it.

If you agree with Dr. D'Adamo's approach, you may want to refine this "taste bud" test based on your blood type. According to Dr. D'Adamo's research, the suggestions made in this chapter are compatible with all blood types except where noted.

This informal agreement with my taste buds allows me to juice on a consistent basis, while others seem to lose interest in juicing after a month or two. Another key reason people lose interest in juicing is the time it takes, which leads us to the first of several strategies I have for minimizing the impact juicing has on my schedule.

APPLY THE TEN MINUTE RULE

The longer it takes to juice, the greater the likelihood that I won't do it consistently. Consequently, I do the following two things to keep the time it takes—from preparation to consumption and cleanup—to under ten minutes:

- use a juicer that can be assembled and cleaned quickly
- systematize the process to minimize the number of decisions required each juicing session.

Selecting a Juicer

The most important criteria are:

- effective nutrient extraction
- low temperature buildup (doesn't heat up juice and thus destroy life-enhancing nutrients)
- quick cleanup
- durable and reliable
- large quantity of juice before jamming
- price

My favorite juicer is the Champion, which I used for six years before switching to a Juiceman II as an experiment. I've used the Juiceman II (**www.juiceman.com**) for four years now and it has held up well, although the screen is quite clogged and needs replacing. It takes a little more time to clean up than the Champion but seems to extract more juice with less pulp and less temperature build-up. For intuitive reasons, I've decided to switch back to the Champion.

Since juice made by the Champion contains a little pulp, it is wise to "chew the juice" before swallowing. This mixes saliva with the juice which starts the digestive processes required to digest the pulp. "Thicker juice" may take longer to assimilate and thus slow the rate at which blood sugar rises.

Champion juicers, available from most health food stores, are made by Plastiket (209-369-2154) and are known to last a long time. I have had two wear out after about two years of heavy usage. In both cases the seal wore out, which cost about $55 plus shipping for Plastiket to repair. I've also noted that the screen clogs up over time and should be replaced about once a year (under $4). They make great tasting juice and can be assembled and cleaned quickly.

If a juicer heats up substantially when being used, it can reduce the nutrients and enzymes in the juice. The Champion does pretty well here except with stringy vegetables such as celery and parsley. Slicing them into chunks before juicing can solve this problem.

Surprisingly, both the Juiceman II and Champion do a reasonable job with wheat grass, which is one of the most important juices to consume. Wheat grass contains high levels of chlorophyll and a wide variety of trace nutrients. It is highly concentrated, so I dilute it with lots of carrot/apple juice.

Systematizing the Juicing Process

The following are techniques I use to minimize the number of steps and decisions I have to make each time I juice. This reduces the time and effort required.

- I leave my juicer on the counter at all times. A portion of kitchen counter space next to the sink is designated as my "juicing area."

- I set aside shelf space right above the juicer as the drying area. When I'm done juicing, I place the rinsed components on a paper towel for them to dry. This saves me from having to dry them by hand.

- I use the same bowl (to catch the juice) and holding dish (to set the washed produce on before juicing) all week. They are just rinsed off after each use. I have a designated place for each of these. The holding dish goes right behind the sink so the water actually drains into the sink. The rinsing bowl is placed on the edge of the sink but could just as easily be placed in the drying area cupboard with the other juicing parts.

- I've designated certain areas in my refrigerator for juicing supplies to minimize the amount of time I spend looking for things.
- When using the Champion juicer, I use plastic produce bags to catch the pulp and a wire twist to hold the bag in place. With the Juiceman II, I put plastic bags in the pulp bucket so it doesn't have to be cleaned.
- I organize my shopping list around juicing basics and rotationals. The items listed in the following figure are the basics I try to juice each week. You could add "organic if available and affordable" after every item except the carrots and celery, which I insist on being organic.

Food	Quantity
Organic carrots	5 pounds
Apples	5 pounds
Parsley	1 bunch
Organic celery (no brownish patches)	1 small bunch
Garlic	½ of a bulb
Ginger	2 inches of root
Beets and/or beet leaves	1 (golf ball size)
Kale	1 bundle
Wheat grass	1 small 4"x4" tray
Spinach	1 bundle

JUICE ONCE A DAY (EXCEPT SUNDAY) CONSISTENTLY

My current objective is to juice once a day on a consistent basis. Consistency is more important than periodic bingeing. When I first started, some days I juiced three times a day. After a month or two, I reduced my frequency to once or twice a day to make it more practical, and stayed at this pace for several years. My current pace is about five times per week.

USE A CARROT/APPLE BASE

I use a base of 75% organic carrot/apple juice and then add the intense vegetables (parsley, kale, spinach, etc.) to that. Note the following key issues:

- In his book, *Brain Longevity*, Dr. Dharma Singh Khalsa writes that carrots are converted to glucose (blood sugar) much faster than table sugar. Apples help compensate for this because they are high in fructose, which converts to glucose much slower. Refer to Dr. Khalsa's book for specific recommendations on how to manage blood sugar levels for optimum brain health, and just how important it is that you do so.

- Apple is the only fruit that can be combined with vegetable juice.

- Dr. D'Adamo encourages people with blood type O to avoid apple juice, but lists apples themselves as neutral for type O. I suspect by "juice" he is referring primarily to bottled apple juice and cider, as opposed to juice that is freshly made.

- Dark green juice is too concentrated to be taken straight and is thus hard on the liver if consumed without dilution.

- Beet juice is especially concentrated and deserves special caution. About one half the size of a golf ball is the most I will juice at a time just to stay on the safe side.

- Dark green juice usually tastes bad by itself. The carrot/apple base makes consuming the other vegetable juices more palatable.

- Organic carrot juice is the single most important juice you can drink.

- I don't juice apple seeds, just in case there's some truth to the rumors that they contain small amounts of strychnine. This issue isn't addressed in any juicing book I've read.

- Tart apples are best, as recommended by healing pioneer Dr. Max Gerson. I prefer Granny Smith.

Since you will be drinking a fair amount of carrot juice, it is essential that you locate a reliable source of organic carrots. Carrot and celery are the only ingredients that I insist be organic. Dr. Andrew Weil also cautions against eating non-organic apples and recommends avoiding celery with brownish patches. High quality organic kale, spinach and parsley have also been easy to find at a reasonable price.

Whenever I've used non-organic carrots, I seemed to gradually lose interest in juicing.

How much to drink per session depends on your individual circumstances. What sounds good to you? When I started, I drank over 25 ounces per session. For the last couple years, 10-16 ounces has felt about right.

In actual practice, 75% is probably the minimum carrot/apple base, since many of the intense vegetables don't put out much juice. I just grab two or three carrots, an apple and add whatever amounts of dark leafy greens feel appropriate. With kale, that is either one large leaf or three small ones. With spinach, I add as much as I feel like washing (up to the 25% limit). Parsley is the second most nutritious vegetable (alfalfa is #1) so I include it whenever possible. As mentioned previously, beets should be used with caution.

EMPHASIZE VEGETABLE JUICES

If I only have time to juice once a day on a regular basis, I want to get the most bang for my nutritional buck, so I drink primarily vegetable juices. In general, vegetables contain more nutrients than fruit. I also like to eat fruit far more than I like to eat vegetables. Thirdly, common sense tells me it is far easier for my body to extract nutrients from fruit than woody, fibrous vegetables.

There are times when I make exceptions to this rule. Some mornings, the carrot/apple/greens juice just doesn't sound good to me. Other mornings, the prospect of a fresh fruit drink sounds just too good to pass up. Cantaloupe, honeydew and watermelon are the highest nutrient content fruits. Most of the nutrients are in the rind, which is inedible. When the rind is juiced along with the rest of the melon, the result is a taste I really enjoy. I usually cut away any gray or questionable spots on the rind, especially with cantaloupe. When in doubt, cut it off and throw it away. I use organic melons whenever possible for juicing. Juicing non-organic melons seems no different than juicing non-organic apples; I just wash them as thoroughly as possible and always use a scrub brush on cantaloupe. There are also pesticide removal sprays available for the extra cautious. It is especially important to drink melon juice on an empty stomach. Dr. D'Adamo suggests that you avoid cantaloupe and honeydew melon if your blood type is O or A.

In the wintertime when melons are not available, I occasionally drink freshly made pineapple juice, which tastes nothing like what you get in the cans and bottles. You can juice pineapple rind. However, I usually throw most of it away because my understanding is that tropical fruits often come from places where pesticide usage laws are less stringent. (Many fruits are now labeled with their country of origin.) Plus, all those nooks and crannies makes it very difficult to wash thoroughly.

Apple lemonade is another favorite substitute (three to four apples plus ¼ or ½ a lemon WITH the rind). **Do not juice orange peels!**

I usually give my body one day a week where I do not drink vegetable juices. On this day, I emphasize fruit juices, rest, and minimal amounts of food in general. This frees up nerve energy for cleansing and gives my digestive organs a rest.

You are not what you eat. You are what your body is able to assimilate.

VARIETY IS KEY, SO VARY THE REMAINING 25%

Scientists have labeled certain types of nutrients with letters: A, B, C, D, E, K, etc. Yet plants know nothing of our vitamin coding system, and the nutrients plants concoct are based on formulas provided by nature. The nutrients are balanced to form a synergistic whole, and the components and proportions may not be fully understood or classified. Rather than wait for scientists to catch up with nature's formulations, I like to go right to the source: plants. Since different plants emphasize different elements, I try to vary that remaining 25% (what I add to the 75% carrot/apple base) as much as possible throughout each week, month and year. The idea is to provide my body with access to as many of the trace elements it needs to fully nourish my cells, thus relieving my organs of the burden of having to generate the missing nutrients internally. In truth, it is probably not possible to fully achieve this, but the basic approach I use seems to have a good chance of providing a sufficient base of material to generate that which is lacking.

I complement the nutrient variety this strategy provides with supplements that are **100% pure food grown**. One source of food-based supplements is the Living Source Food-Grown Nutrient Systems made by Rainbow Light Nutritional Systems. Their address is 207 McPherson Street, Santa Cruz, CA 95060. I take one of their "Complete Nutritional System" supplements daily along with my morning juice. Each tablet costs about twenty cents and contains the following nutrients in addition to a wide variety of traditional vitamins and minerals from natural sources:

Superfoods: Spirulina, Chlorella, Bee Pollen, Wheat Grass, Barley Grass, Chlorella, Rice Bran, Kelp, Dulse, Chlorophyll, and Alfalfa Concentrate. **Plant Source Enzymes:** Protease, Amylase, Lipase, Cellulase, and Papain. **Custom Herbal Blend**: Siberian Ginseng [root], Schisandra [fruit], Fo-Ti [root], Fennel [seed], Ginger [root], Nettle [tops] and Licorice [root].

These tablets are a shotgun approach to filling in the trace mineral gaps in my nutrient intake. I may be wrong, but my taste buds seem to agree here—they actually taste okay. I've also started taking a couple alfalfa tablets as well. The list of trace nutrients and minerals in alfalfa is too long to list. According to Dr. D'Adamo, people with blood type O should avoid alfalfa.

However, I never take any supplements when I've included wheat grass in my juice. My taste buds give me a very strong "NO" signal in this matter. This may be due to the fact that wheat grass is so nutrient-dense.

USE ORGANIC PRODUCE WHENEVER POSSIBLE

Organic produce is higher in nutrient content and usually tastes better than non-organic. It is grown without the use of pesticides and should therefore contain virtually no chemical residue.

A side benefit from buying organic is that you help support farmers who are attempting to be gentler on the environment. A primary reason that the American Bald Eagle was placed on the endangered species list was the impact DDT buildup was having on their reproductive efforts. We don't know what impact massive pesticide use will have on the environment long term. The technology to grow organic has always been available, and we should support the farmers going the extra mile to apply it.

For many years, organic produce gained a reputation as not looking too good (i.e., usually covered with spots, smaller than the non-organic produce, and somewhat shriveled up). I have been buying organic produce now for over six years and can tell you that if the organic produce looks like this in your store, you need to find another store. The organic produce I buy looks better and healthier than non-organic! I don't mind paying up to 25% more for organic produce given all of these factors.

Transitional Produce

To qualify as organic, fields in which produce is grown must go at least two years without the use of pesticides.

Produce grown on the fields during this two year period is referred to as transitional. It's not technically organic even though no pesticides are used. I want to support the farmers making the transition, so I buy this produce whenever I can fit it into my budget.

Pesticides/Chemicals

While I try to buy as much organic produce as possible, I do not let the possibility that the non-organic produce may contain pesticides deter me from juicing once or twice per day. Unless the bag of potato chips, box, bag or can of food you buy says "made from organically grown..." on it, chances are pretty good it has an equal amount of pesticides.

Here's a list of produce sources in preferred order:

- Grow as much of your own as you have the time and inclination for. A great book on this is *How to Grow More Vegetables Than You Ever Thought Possible on Less Land Than You Can Imagine* by John Jeavons.
- Organically grown or transitional.
- Locally grown.
- Produce marked as free of pesticide residue. Fred Meyer stores have pioneered an effort to do this.
- Buy from a produce department supplied by a conscientious produce buyer—one who shops for nutrient quality. Remember that you vote with your dollars. If you accept less, that's what farmers will produce and stores will stock.

Where to Buy Organic Produce

The best organic produce I have found is grown by Cal-Organic Farms (805 845-3758), which apparently is also the largest organic produce farm in the United States. To locate their produce in your area, I would first call the local health food stores listed in the Health Food Products—Retail section of your yellow pages.

DRINK IMMEDIATELY AFTER JUICING

I drink juice immediately after making it. Fruits and vegetables are alive! When juiced, the nutrients and life force start to dissipate. In some cases, such as cabbage, this occurs quite rapidly. According to a study quoted by Jay Kordach in his juicing tapes, 80% of the vitamin C is gone within 1 minute! The nutrients in green cabbage known to help heal stomach ulcers also dissipate extremely fast.

The second reason to drink juice immediately is enzymes, as discussed earlier in this chapter. They are the life force in the food.

JUICE ON AN EMPTY STOMACH

The objective is to get the nutrients into your bloodstream as quickly as possible so they can nourish your trillions of cells. To get into the bloodstream, the nutrients must first pass through the stomach, into the intestines, and finally through the intestinal villa. Drinking the juices on an empty stomach facilitates this process. My energy level seems higher if the juices are taken on an empty stomach.

This is also consistent with the principle of natural hygiene: *Don't drink liquids with your meals, as it tends to dilute the digestive fluids and thus slow the process of digestion and assimilation of your meals.* Slowing digestion has two drawbacks: it takes more energy to digest and assimilate the nutrients, and secondly, the nutritional value may be compromised if food spoils in the stomach. For more information on this read *Fit For Life,* by Harvey and Marilyn Diamond. Better yet, experiment for yourself. Try eating the same meal two days in a row. Drink liquids with one meal and skip them the next—see if you notice a difference.

"Do, or do not. There is no 'try'."

— *Yoda,* from *The Empire Strikes Back*

FEED YOUR MIND WHILE YOU JUICE

I keep a cassette tape player near my juicing area so I can listen to educational tapes, which feed my mind with fresh ideas while I am feeding my body. You can listen to audiotapes while you are doing other things. It is easier to listen multiple times than to read a book multiple times. Reading requires your full attention. Given that reviewing helps the compound learning process, audiotapes allow you to retain a higher percentage of the material covered. Additionally, this added educational benefit helps make it personally ecological to juice.

Here are some suggestions on where to find educational audiocassette material:

- Educational cassettes can be checked out from your local library. Electronic search tools may allow you to search by medium.
- Nightingale-Conant (800 525-9000) carries the most comprehensive catalog of educational/self-development audiotapes that I am aware of.
- Audio-Tech Business Book Summaries (800 776-1910). For $135, this service will send you 34 audio book reviews of top business books over the course of a year. Each review is 30 minutes in length and begins with a five-minute synopsis of the key ideas presented in the book.
- Books on Tape (800 626-3333) makes a good case for having the world's largest selection of unabridged audio books, including over 2,500 best sellers. This is a great source for biographies in addition to carrying several self-development titles.
- Bookstores and video stores. The more people that ask for them, the more they will supply.

VARIOUS JUICING ISSUES

Here is a discussion of some issues frequently raised that were not covered above:

"*Don't I need the fiber?*"

Fiber is essential for maintaining a healthy digestive system. The juicing strategy I'm suggesting is designed primarily to supplement your existing meals.

"*But I enjoy eating*"

Let me ask you a question: If you drink soda pop, does that prevent you from eating your meals? Just think of juicing as creating your own can of soda pop. However, rather than "shooting blanks" at six trillion cells, you are loading your body up with powerful nutrients it needs to cleanse and build a strong healthy body at the same time you are quenching your thirst. A side benefit to juicing for some is that by providing their body with more of the nutrients it needs, the fewer hunger pangs it sends off, and thus the less they have to eat during and between meals.

"*I don't have time for juicing*"

There is a time management principle called Quadrant II described by Stephen Covey in his book, *The 7 Habits of Highly Effective People*. Covey suggests concentrating your efforts on *important* tasks before they become *urgent*, thereby gaining maximum leverage from your time investments. Juicing is Quadrant II time at its best. I believe it is far easier to keep myself healthy than it would be to cure myself once ill. Juicing helps keep me healthy by nourishing my trillions of cells with the finest nutrients nature has to offer. Juicing is not something that is urgent, but it is most definitely important.

Knowledge work deals in intangibles. Subtle shifts in energy levels and mental clarity can literally make the difference between something taking hours to complete vs. just a few minutes. When creating a software application, hundreds of decisions must be made each day. One wrong decision can lead me down a path that costs hours. Juicing supports my efforts to operate in a peak state a high percentage of the time.

IRRADIATED FOOD CAUTION

Irradiation is a technique used to prolong shelf life of fresh produce by exposing it to certain types of radiation. The thought of this doesn't exactly thrill me. Common sense tells me to avoid food that has been irradiated.

THE PESTICIDE ISSUE

Non-organic produce contains pesticide and herbicide residues and should therefore be washed thoroughly if organic produce is not available. There are vegetable washes available which can help remove pesticides. I don't use them in the interest of time, which may turn out to be a mistake. As stated earlier, I use organic whenever possible, especially carrots, which covers the majority of the produce I'm consuming. The remaining produce is washed thoroughly. Keep in mind that processed food is no less immune to these chemical residues than fresh produce. You have to be careful of anything you consume in large quantities.

ECOLOGY

If you are concerned about consuming excessive resources by juicing, try to compensate by cutting back in other areas. According to John Robbins, author of the landmark book, *Diet for a New America*, you can save more water by not eating one hamburger than you can save by not showering for six months.

COMPOST YOUR PULP

Since most of the nutrients have been removed from the juice, I don't recommend using the pulp for baking or salads. The best use seems to be to place it in a compost pile and thus recycle the material into the soil. The carrot pulp tastes like sawdust.

NIBBLING AND CHEWING YOUR JUICE

I nibble on the produce while preparing the juice. While this is probably not recommended by the "experts," I do it because I enjoy the taste of the food and it gets my digestive system revved up. If you don't nibble, then you should "chew your juice"—at least the first couple drinks, by sloshing them around in your mouth. One doctor encouraged me to mix a little of the pulp back in with the juice to prevent my blood sugar level from rising too fast. As mentioned earlier, juicing an apple along with the carrots also helps. According to Dr. Khalsa, carrots rate very high on the glycemic index (i.e., they convert to blood sugar very quickly). Until more definitive evidence is available, I'll continue to monitor the results of my own experiments, paying close attention to messages from my taste buds. Blood tests taken during a recent physical were encouraging.

JUICING SUMMARY

Since everyone is unique, juicing may benefit some more than others. I am absolutely convinced that juicing has significantly enriched the quality of my daily life. If you are new to juicing, I hope the above guidelines prove useful as you take the leap of faith required to experiment. If you have already tried juicing, I hope this discussion will renew your enthusiasm that juicing can be practical for time-conscious knowledge workers.

If you want to give juicing a try, the smartest money would be to order a copy of the Juiceman audiotape series (888 889-0899). Note that they sometimes make special offers on juicers that include this six-tape set. There is something about the way Jay Kordach presents ideas about juicing that inspires people to do it. These tapes also contain important information for couples planning to have children.

OTHER MENTAL CLARITY DISTINCTIONS

OPTIMIZING NUTRIENT INTAKE

Juicing is a great source of nutrients, but it doesn't eliminate the need or desire to eat. Here are a few topics in the area of optimizing nutrient intake that have proven helpful. These issues are covered more thoroughly in the book *Fit for Life,* by Harvey and Marilyn Diamond and Chapter 11 of Anthony Robbins' book, *Unlimited Power.* Some people have had problems with some of the suggestions in these books so it would be wise, as always, to coordinate any changes to dietary patterns with your medical or naturopathic physician.

I also admire the teachings of Dr. Andrew Weil whose excellent Web site (**www.drweil.com**) contains a searchable database of nutritional issues. Dr. John McDougall's Web site is worth a look as well (**www.rightfoods.com**).

FOOD COMBINING

Some foods should not be eaten with others. Proteins are digested by acid-based fluids while starchy carbohydrates are digested by alkaline-based fluids. If you eat meat and potatoes at the same meal, it will take much longer to digest because the digestive fluids will neutralize each other. This causes foods to remain in the stomach longer, spoil and require more digestive energy to process. Robbins' book mentioned above includes a food-combining chart with specific guidelines. You can begin to follow this rule by eating only one concentrated food (i.e., tofu, meat, pasta, potato, bread, etc.) at each meal, and by eating it with a salad or lightly steamed vegetables.

> *"The ability to transform energy and even create it within you is one of the profound secrets of life. Like a tree, you are one of the great power-stations of nature."*
>
> — *Master Lam Kam Chuen*

Optimizing Nutrient Intake

* Food combining
* Controlled consumption
* High water content foods
* Effective fruit consumption
* Eating mostly vegetarian
* Distilled water
* Eat right for your blood type

Stretching

* Static hold
* Multiple passes
* Alternate between stretch & complete relaxation
* Slow graceful motion
* Improve balance
* Focus thoughts

Optimizing Oxygen Intake & Utilization

Refine breathing habits

* Complete breath
* Alternate nostril breathing

Do daily aerobic exercise

* Steady, nonstop
* Comfortable pace
* 12 minute minimum
* Use muscles of lower body

Optimize environmental oxygen

* Sleep w/ window open
* Filter air
* Fight dust
* Plants
* Negative ions

Figure 8.1 Overview of Other Mental Clarity Distinctions.

CONTROLLED CONSUMPTION

Eating a huge meal will wipe out the benefits received from every other guideline in this chapter. To quote the Diamonds, "Even the finest, most nutritious food available will spoil in your system if it is overeaten." Robbins' teaches that the best way to eat a lot is to eat a little. "That way, you'll be around long enough to eat a lot."

"You cannot be a man of action if you overeat and under-exercise."

— *Napoleon Hill*

Uncooked High Water Content Foods

For several years I've followed the practice of eating as many uncooked vegetables as possible at mealtime. It is often said that cooking reduces vitamin and mineral availability. Cooking also kills enzymes that can help digestive processes in some cases. My latest research indicates that this rule must be applied selectively. Here are a few things to consider on this issue:

- Overcooking vegetables such as broccoli and asparagus to the point where they are mushy is clearly "overkill."
- According to Dr. Weil, some of the nutrients in some foods are more bioavailable when cooked. While this may be true, other nutrients in those same foods are diminished or destroyed when cooked. While great strides have been made classifying and understanding various nutrients in foods, there is a good chance the other nutrients have yet to be discovered.
- Some foods in their raw state contain harmful toxins. Foods Dr. Weil would never eat uncooked are peas, beans, alfalfa sprouts and mushrooms.
- Cooking food usually kills unfriendly bacteria (Cryptosporidium and Cyclospora) and parasites. If you have any doubts about the safety of the uncooked produce you consume, consider using a non-toxic vegetable wash solution.

Effective Fruit Consumption

Anyone who thinks fruit gives them intestinal gas should try eating that fruit on an empty stomach. If you do this and only eat one type of fruit at a time, it will quickly move into the intestines and be digested in less than fifteen minutes. If the stomach isn't empty, the fruit gets held up in the stomach and that's where the gas comes in. For many people, fresh organic fruit eaten on an empty stomach is a great way to energize and cleanse your system.

EATING MOSTLY VEGETARIAN

What do the following people have in common: George Bernard Shaw, Benjamin Franklin, Thomas Edison, Gandhi, Albert Einstein, Leonardo da Vinci, Voltaire, Sir Isaac Newton, Henry David Thoreau, Dr. Albert Schweitzer, Aristotle, Tolstoy, Pythagoras, Plato and Socrates? According to Anthony Robbins, they were all vegetarians. Coincidence?

In September 1992, Paul Harvey News reported the following results from research conducted by Elder George Vandeman in Thousand Oaks, California:

- Middle-aged males who regularly eat meat suffer from fatal coronary disease three times more often than vegetarian men of the same age.
- A meat-based diet has been linked to a disproportionate incidence of breast and colon cancer, high cholesterol, high blood pressure, angina pectoris, osteoporosis, kidney stones, urinary stones, and rheumatoid arthritis.

According to Paul Harvey, several related studies have demonstrated that such health problems can be reversed with a vegetarian diet.

Dave Scott—six-time winner of the grueling Ironman Triathlon—has been a vegetarian for the last fifteen years. He gets his protein from meals that include soy and the soy derivative, tofu. Cindy New of Montreal, winner of the 1995 Montreal Marathon, has been a vegetarian for the last twelve years. She was quoted as saying that most world-class runners experimenting with high-energy foods have become vegetarians.

Dr. D'Adamo's research indicates that people with blood type A do best on a vegetarian diet, while type O's are better suited to meat-based diets. Type B's and AB's can handle a mixed diet, but type B's should avoid chicken. If you do eat meat, one approach is to emphasize fish such as salmon. Another is to find a source that is range-fed without hormones or antibiotics. Dr. D'Adamo suggests that people with blood type B avoid tofu, while other soy-based products are apparently okay for type B.

There have been times when I've gone for months without eating meat of any kind, and must say that there have been moments when I felt nutritionally out of balance. This probably would have been avoided had I learned about Brenda Davis several years ago.

Brenda Davis, co-author of *Becoming Vegetarian*, is an amazing resource for nutritional information, whether or not you eat vegetarian. Here are some key points she made at a recent seminar that apply to anyone, but are especially relevant to vegetarians (note that these remarks have **not** been qualified based on Dr. D'Adamo's blood type research):

- **Zinc**: Zinc deficiency can stunt growth, impair taste and appetite and compromise one's immune system. It can be tough to meet recommended intakes from natural sources and even tougher to absorb sufficient amounts from the diet, so it is important to consume whole grains (refined grains have less than a third of the zinc provided by whole grains), legumes (including tofu and/or tempeh), nuts, and seeds. Soaking legumes, sprouting grains, roasting nuts and seeds, and raising breads with yeast will increase zinc absorption. If you take a multivitamin/mineral supplement make sure it contains zinc (about 5 mg/day for children and 5-10 for adults), in addition to selenium and magnesium.

- **Calcium**: Calcium is necessary for the maintenance of optimal bone health. However, calcium intake accounts for only about 11% of calcium balance. The most important factor in calcium balance is calcium excretion which is most adversely affected by protein and sodium. The more protein and sodium you consume, the more calcium you need. Thus, people living in countries consuming a high protein, processed food diet (i.e., typical North American diet) require more calcium than those living in countries with a cereal-based food economy. Great plant sources of calcium include fortified soy milk, dark greens (broccoli, kale, collards, Chinese greens and other low-oxalate greens are best—oxalates found in spinach, Swiss chard, rhubarb and beet greens bind with the calcium in these foods making it unavailable for absorption), raw almonds, sesame seed paste, legumes, figs, and blackstrap molasses. Davis also mentioned that 50-70% of the calcium from most low oxalate vegetables is absorbable as compared to 32% in cow's milk.

- **Protein**: Davis cites the World Health Organization's recommendation that 10-15% of your calories come from protein. In her book, *Becoming Vegetarian*, Davis gives specific recommendations for both vegetarians and non-vegetarians. When sufficient calories are provided from nutritious plant foods, total protein intake is generally adequate.
- **Amino Acids**: If protein intake is questionable, lysine is most commonly the limiting amino acid. If you focus on getting enough of this one, the others tend to take care of themselves. Including legumes (i.e., beans, lentils, tofu) on a daily basis is the simplest way to do this. Davis states that soy provides an excellent balance of all essential amino acids and is the most versatile of all legumes.
- **Iron**: Black tea and oriental green tea contain tannins, which when combined with iron, form an insoluble compound. Try to avoid drinking them during meals. Milk and cheese are low in iron and can decrease the iron availability from accompanying foods by up to 50%. It is thus important not to replace meat and poultry with cheese and other dairy products when switching to a vegetarian diet—meat and poultry are best replaced by legumes. Cooking in a cast iron skillet can increase the iron content in foods by two to sixteen times. Vitamin C increases iron absorption from other foods two to

three times. Blackstrap molasses is a good source of iron, potassium, magnesium, and vitamin B6. I use it to sweeten my Pero instant natural beverage, a caffeine free coffee substitute. I like Pero, but dislike the taste of coffee. Although spinach contains a lot of iron, it also contains oxalic acid, which binds to the iron making it unavailable for absorption. Spinach is still a good source of other nutrients, however.

- **Oils**: The three oils Davis uses are flax seed, canola, and extra virgin olive. She recommends Omega Nutrition organic flax seed oil (or other organic, fresh pressed flax oil), but cautions that it spoils very quickly and must be kept in the refrigerator or freezer. One teaspoon a day is all most people need, although more may be beneficial for some people. I take 1 tablespoon to make sure that I finish the bottle before it spoils (you may wish to freeze half if you prefer to use less). Flax seeds are our best plant source of omega-3 fatty acids, which tend to be lacking in most diets (omnivores get much of their omega-3's from fish). Omega-3 fatty acids are precursors to hormone-like substances called eicosanoids which help regulate numerous body systems. They are necessary for the proper development of healthy cell membranes, including those of the brain and eye. Most people get insufficient omega-3's in their diet and are well advised to reduce their use of omega-6 rich oils (corn, sunflower, safflower, etc.) and increase their use of omega-3 rich oils such as flax and canola oil (flax is far more concentrated in omega-3's). Other good sources of omega-3 fatty acids include dark greens, tofu and other soy products, walnuts, and wheat germ. Don't cook with flax seed oil. Take vitamin E with it to help counteract any free radical reactions that may occur due to its unstable nature.
- **Vitamin D**: In addition to calcium and weight-bearing exercise, vitamin D is also an important

factor in bone health. Light skinned people need 10-15 minutes of warm sunshine to the hands and face per day to get their daily requirement of vitamin D, while dark skinned people need ½ hour or more. Both dark skin and sunscreens reduce vitamin D formation. Some foods are fortified with vitamin D and are particularly useful for insuring sufficient amounts during cold months where vitamin D production from sunshine may be limited or non-existent.

- **Riboflavin and B12**: Vitamin B12 is found primarily in animal foods, so if you are consuming a plant-based diet, you need to have a reliable source of this nutrient. Seaweed, while often assumed to be an excellent source of vitamin B12, contains a mixture of vitamin B12 and B12 look-alikes (analogues that do not function like true B12 but attach to B12 receptors, thereby potentially contributing to a B12 deficiency). Claims have been made that blue-green algae may be an exception, but further research is needed to verify this. A great source of B12 and riboflavin is fortified nutritional yeast. This is not the kind of yeast you use to make bread (nutritional yeast does not leaven bread). Davis recommends Red Star T-6635+ vegetarian support formula (most other brands are not fortified with vitamin B12, thus are not sources of this nutrient—read the label).

- **Wheat bran**: Wheat bran is an excellent source of insoluble fiber making it a reasonable addition to the diets of those who consume low fiber, animal-centered diets. However, vegetarians who use plenty of whole grains, legumes, vegetables and fruits generally get plenty of fiber, and daily use of wheat bran may reduce mineral absorption and/or make the diet too bulky for small children. Apparently, this does not apply to oat bran (which provides soluble fiber), and is still considered effective at reducing cholesterol (according to the latest clinical studies).

I'm still experimenting to find an optimum nutritional plan, and occasionally eat meat for variety or in social situations. I also eat **organic** soy-based products such as tofu several times per week (EdenSoy Original is a great milk substitute for cereal). One thing seems clear: we have been conditioned to consume far more meat than we need.

DISTILLED WATER

Most people have caught on to the fact that our tap water quality has deteriorated over the years. I've been using distilled water as recommended by Anthony Robbins and the Diamonds, and find it agreeable. Distilled water tastes so neutral that I can drink it at room temperature without adding any flavorings. For variety, I occasionally add a couple drops of stevia leaves water extract by Nature's Way Products.

OPTIMIZING OXYGEN INTAKE AND UTILIZATION

Oxygen is the most important nutrient we consume. We can go for months without food, days without water, but only minutes without oxygen.

In their *Mentally Tough* audiotape, Dr. James Loehr and Peter McLaughlin describe the strategy Bobby Fischer used to defeat Boris Spassky for the 1972 chess title. Fischer hired a physiology specialist to study videotapes of Spassky's matches to determine why his performance declined towards the end of long matches. The specialist concluded that it was due to the slumped posture Spassky used throughout the match. This posture diminished the oxygen flow to his brain, which eventually got the best of him. As a result, Fischer altered his training to boost oxygen flow to his brain. He started swimming underwater for as long as possible in order to build lung capacity, and this, among other things, helped him win.

The brain consumes over 20% of the oxygen we take in even though it makes up only 3% of our total body weight. Given that oxygen is one of the brain's primary fuels, it

makes sense to consider ways of optimizing the flow of
this nutrient to the brain. Three main strategies for acting
on this distinction are:

- refine your breathing habits,
- optimize environmental oxygen, and
- develop a strong cardiovascular system by doing
  aerobic exercise consistently three to five times
  each week.

REFINE YOUR BREATHING HABITS

Your breathing pattern can significantly influence your
energy level. The increase can be so profound that yoga
teachers recommend mastering *asanas* (stretches to
discipline the body) before doing *pranayamas* (breathing
exercises). If you don't have the discipline to direct the
increased energy levels resulting from *pranayamas*, it can
be harmful.

Not all breaths are created equal. It is often helpful to
walk outside in the fresh, unprocessed, non-dried out air
and take a few "complete breaths" as taught by yoga
instructor Richard Hittleman. Use common sense while
doing this exercise and pay attention to any signals from
your body indicating that you may be overdoing it. There
should be no straining during any part of this breathing
exercise. A complete breath involves the following steps:

1) Empty your lungs by exhaling completely. First
   empty your chest and then contract your abdomen
   to empty the lower lungs.
2) As soon as you've completely exhaled, begin to fill
   your lower lungs with air by expanding the abdomen.
   You're doing it right if your stomach sticks out and
   your chest doesn't move.
3) When your lower lungs are filled with air, begin
   filling the upper lungs by expanding the chest area.
4) When you think you have inhaled as much as you
   can, try raising the shoulders a bit and see if you can
   inhale a little more.

5) Hold this breath for five to ten seconds or until your body tells you it would be wise to begin exhaling.

6) Completely exhale and repeat these steps.

Both inhaling and exhaling should be done through the nose in a controlled manner. According to Harvey and Marilyn Diamond in *Fit for Life II*, we should emphasize abdominal breathing, since the lower part of the lungs absorbs 80% of the oxygen.

This next exercise sounded weird to me when I first heard of it. However, when I finally got around to trying it, I found it to be useful. I try to remember that usefulness overrides weirdness in many cases. Alternate nostril breathing quiets the mind. I find this especially useful after getting all pumped up to deliver a speech or presentation at a meeting. "By understanding that each nostril connects to the opposite side of the brain and using this information in a breathing exercise, you can actually balance the two sides of the brain, and the result is an amazing sense of equilibrium," according to the Diamonds. The steps are as follows:

1) Block one nostril with your thumb and the other with your ring finger. Your index and middle finger go on your forehead.

2) Breath in through the right nostril, hold for five to ten seconds, then block the right nostril and exhale through the left.

3) Inhale through the left nostril, hold for five to ten seconds, then block the left nostril and exhale through the right.

The Diamonds recommend repeating this six times to achieve the desired effect. When doing this, they recommend that you hold your breath for about half as long as it takes you to inhale or exhale. In his book, *What a Great Idea*, Charles Thompson cites research indicating that when breathing, we tend to favor one nostril for about 90 minutes and then switch to the other. He points out that when breathing out of the left nostril, the right brain is dominant, and vice versa. Refer to his book for details on how to use this distinction for optimum creativity and how it can help you get to sleep at night.

One of the quickest ways to quiet your mind and increase your ability to concentrate is to change the way you are breathing.

OPTIMIZE ENVIRONMENTAL OXYGEN

Many of the particles floating around in the air are smaller than the eye can see. One way to test your home's air purity is by setting a glass of distilled water on the dresser or living room coffee table before going to sleep. In the morning, take a drink. The dirtier the air, the worse it will taste. Here are a few suggestions for optimizing the quality of oxygen in your environment:

- Sleep with the window open, at least where it is safe to do so.
- Try an Allergy Free air filter as recommended by Paul Harvey (800-ALLERGY).
- Give your home an occasional air bath as Ben Franklin used to do. This involves leaving all windows and doors wide open for a few minutes, especially when it is very windy out.
- Fight dust in every way you can.
- Keep plants in your environment, especially in an office where the air is highly processed.
- Soak up negative ions by spending time in the outdoors as often as possible, especially in the mountains or near water. If you really want to go for it, look in the yellow pages for an Alpine Industries dealer near you. Ask them if they will let you try one of their negative ion generators for a couple days before deciding to buy. If you do try one, start with low levels of generated ozone, and increase it very slowly over a period of several weeks if at all. When I tried one, my sleeping improved and my energy level

soared. However, I also experienced trouble breathing one morning while taking a shower. Athletic individuals sometimes experience this reaction to increases in ozone, especially in humid environments. Despite this experience, the technology showed much promise. My energy level remained noticeably higher for three weeks following my day and a half trial.

AEROBIC EXERCISE

Covert Bailey has made significant contributions to the fields of exercise, nutrition and health. His Web site (**www.covertbailey.com**) has a searchable database of health information. In his book, *The New Fit or Fat*, he teaches what I consider to be the most important principle of weight control:

Consistent aerobic exercise can change your metabolism so that you burn more fat, even when you are not exercising.

The number of calories you burn when you exercise is not as important as exercising in a way that changes your cell metabolism. Cells contain enzymes designed to burn fat. Their efficiency can be enhanced via aerobic exercise. This is why fat people gain weight even when eating less than skinny people—their fat burning enzymes have atrophied. The way to improve your cell metabolism is to exercise aerobically four to six times per week, for twelve to thirty minutes each workout. Bailey teaches that you need to get your heart rate up to certain levels and keep it there for the duration of the workout. An important point is that you should be able to carry on a normal conversation while doing this exercise. Otherwise you are working too hard. Bailey points out that some people have small hearts that like to beat fast while others have large hearts that beat slower. For this reason, standard heart rate charts based only on age may not apply to you.

BODY CLOCKS

Our bodies are governed by a series of internal clocks that operate on daily, weekly, monthly, yearly, and lifetime cycles. Carol Orlock's book, *Know Your Body Clock*, will help you understand these cycles and coordinate your schedule accordingly. Research in the field of chronobiology has shown that we are geared for different types of activities at different times of the day. Here are some of the ways I use these distinctions to keep my schedule in synch with these rhythms:

6AM-1PM: This is usually when the mind is best geared for mental activities and communicating. This is when I schedule my most thought-intensive activities and make important decisions. Mental alertness and efficiency peaks between 9 and 11AM.

1PM-4PM: Mental abilities wane and physical abilities improve. This is when I workout and do low bandwidth administrative tasks.

6:30PM: A good time to manage personal finances, since our ability to add and subtract numbers improves around this time.

7PM: Piano practice, since early evening is the best time to learn a musical instrument.

This schedule corresponds to best times for most people, but not necessarily for all. Peak performance times usually correspond to the time when your body temperature peaks. For myself, this occurs in the morning.

Orlock also helped me regain control over my sleeping schedule. We sleep in 90 minute cycles. If an alarm clock wakes us up in the middle of one of these cycles, it can throw a wrench in our whole day. If I need to cut my sleep short, I do it in 90 minute increments.

The time at which light first hits our eyes plays an important role in setting our sleeping clocks. If I want to shift my body clock forward, I advance the time at which light first hits my eyes in the morning.

Melatonin is the hormone our body produces to make us sleepy. The darker it is, the more melatonin we produce. This explains why covering your eyes is important when doing a power nap, as described in Chapter 5. Not getting enough natural light during the day can cause your melatonin levels to lose their pronounced amplitude near bedtime. Before reading this, I worked in a fairly dim office. This was encouraging melatonin production throughout the day, making it more difficult to get to sleep at night. *Power Sleep*, by Dr. James Maas, is another book on this subject worth a look.

"Exercise is the greatest medicine ever invented."

— *Covert Bailey*

The heart is a muscle as well, but we cannot exercise it directly. It gets exercised when we mobilize the large muscles in the body and thus force the heart to pump more blood to them. Aerobic exercise, in summary:

- is steady, nonstop,
- lasts a minimum of twelve minutes,
- has a comfortable pace, and
- uses the muscles of the lower body.

In his book, *Brain Longevity*, Dr. Khalsa writes that in addition to increasing blood flow to the brain, aerobic exercise spurs growth of new brain cell branches, protects the body against the stress response and burns off harmful stress hormones.

He writes that exercise causes the release of various neurological and endocrinological secretions, including norepinephrine, the stimulating brain chemical that serves as one of the most important neurotransmitters involved in the laying down of new memories and moving memories from short-term to long-term storage. To quote Dr. Khalsa, "What's good for the heart is good for the head."

Dr. Khalsa writes that the body secretes cortisol in response to stress. When produced in excess, day after day, as a result of unrelenting stress, cortisol kills and injures brain cells by the billions. Dr. Khalsa believes this to be the primary cause of brain degeneration during the aging process. He believes that learning how to manifest the "relaxation response" (the exact opposite of the adrenal-driven "stress response") is a critical survival skill. Any technique that can decrease your stress is a valuable tool in a brain longevity program.

The key challenge is fitting exercise into a busy schedule. I view exercise as a "pay me now or pay me later" issue. It is far easier to stay healthy through exercise than to heal from a major illness.

While there is no guarantee that exercise will save me a trip to the hospital sometime in the future, the increase in vibrant health and energy I feel each day as a result is real and definite. Applying the lessons taught in Chapter 3, I don't think about avoiding the hospital (remember that the mind cannot focus on the opposite of an idea). Instead, each time I see the door to the gym, I recall a picture of myself experiencing vibrant health and energy as a result of the exercise I'm about to perform. "See your future, be your future," to quote a friend of mine.

One way to make exercise more practical is to systematize—to develop what I call exercise engrams. You know you have an exercise engram when you only have to make one decision to perform the exercise. Virtually everything else is done on automatic pilot. I have a gym bag in my car at all times and have committed my weight workout to memory. All I have to do is get to the gym and my body pretty much takes over from there. I know exactly how long it will take and am careful to avoid distractions so my workouts won't interfere with other responsibilities (the personal ecology issue again).

To develop an engram, you set time limits and obey them strictly. Design a workout that makes sense for you and then commit all of the steps to memory. This happens automatically for me after I do the workout a few times. The basic idea is to organize yourself so as to minimize the number of decisions that must be made once you've decided to work out. In truth, decisions will have to be made, but you will have defined the context so clearly that making them takes very little effort.

When things get tough during a workout, it sometimes helps me to focus on how many steps are left. It helps to have some certainty that doing the last step means that I will be done. For example, when doing my eighteen minute warm-up on the stationary bike prior to lifting weights, if I have biked for twelve minutes and twenty seconds, I picture the number "6" in my mind and think to myself, "just six more minutes." When things get tough while lifting weights, it may help to look at a card showing exactly how many steps you have left before being done.

If going to the gym isn't an option for you, consider purchasing a mini-trampoline for $30 at a variety store. I'm on about my seventh one. The alternating G forces help mobilize fluids in the lymphatic system, which is responsible for removing toxins from the body. The book *Fit for Life II* offers suggestions on mini-trampoline workout techniques. I just alternate between jumping jacks and running in place with my arms over my head, my objective being to use as many muscles as possible in the workout.

STRETCHING

In addition to encouraging people to eat the right foods, Dr. NakaMats emphasizes participating in the "right athletics." As discussed in Charles Thompson's book, *What a Great Idea*, he does not feel that jogging, tennis, and golf are conducive to generating creative brain waves. You may get ideas while doing these things, but NakaMats feels they probably won't be your best ideas. Personally, I get my best ideas when doing activities that require a lot of discipline such as stretching. This section gives you an overview of material available for refining your stretching habits.

> *"Getting old is not a matter of age; it's a lack of movement."*
>
> — *Anthony Robbins*

Stretching, by Bob Anderson, is a great book on this topic. In it, Anderson explains the rules for stretching, which stretches to avoid, and gives specific routines for each sport.

Other excellent sources of stretching information are books and tapes by Callan Pinckney. Her "Callanetics" routines are a synthesis of exercises she learned while traveling around the world. She teaches the Pelvic Curl and other exercises which emphasize strengthening muscles that support a healthy posture, but which aren't exercised in most workouts. Among other things, I like her concept of doing things in triple slow motion.

The stretching information with the most impact I've ever found has been an introductory yoga video by Richard Hittleman. Little did I know when I rented that $3 video from Blockbuster Video that it would have such a profound and positive impact on my life. He shattered my preconceptions about yoga being something only for hippies. I was surprised to learn, from other sources, that Kareem Abdul-Jabbar credits yoga with allowing him to play as long as he did without injury. Supermodel Kim Alexis strongly endorsed yoga on a recent Larry King show. She mentioned that Jane Fonda now does yoga more than any other exercise. Yoga is recommended by the Diamonds in *Fit for Life II*, in recent books by Harvard Professor Andrew Weil, and by healing pioneer Dr. Dean Ornish.

Yoga has three main components: stretches (*asanas*), breathing exercises (*pranayamas*) and some philosophical underpinnings. You do not need to understand the philosophies in order to benefit from the stretching and breathing exercises. There are as many levels in yoga as there are in the game of tennis. Just because you're not ready for Wimbledon doesn't mean that you can't participate and enjoy the benefits from the activity.

If you would like to begin by attending a class, I encourage you to attend one based on the teachings of B.K.S. Iyengar **(www.iyoga.com)**.

"Any technique that can decrease [your] stress is a valuable tool in a brain longevity program."

— *Dharma Singh Khalsa, M.D.*

A good place to start is with Richard Hittleman's books and videos which can be ordered from: Clear Lake Productions, P.O. Box 3007, Santa Cruz, CA 95063.

The following stretching guidelines were synthesized from all of the above sources:

- Use a static hold. Do not bounce. You want to move to a position of moderate stretch and then hold it without movement. Avoid straining or forcing. Breathe in a relaxed manner while holding the position.
- Use a multiple-pass approach. Hittleman has you do each stretch three times and rest momentarily between each attempt. This allows the body to work its way up to a more complete stretch in a less stressful manner.
- Alternate between stretch and complete relaxation. After each stretching exercise, you are encouraged to relax completely, without movement, for a few moments. This allows the body to equalize itself after energy flow has been increased by the release of tension.
- Use slow, graceful, controlled motion. Personally, this is the part that requires the most discipline. Since my normal energy usage pattern is to do things as quickly and efficiently as possible, slow and graceful is a synergistic oscillation.
- Balance. Several of the stretches in yoga are designed to improve your balance and to balance the sides.
- Think about the area being stretched. You might even try visualizing the area being stretched as surrounded by white light. Imagine the color going out with your breath when you exhale. If you do it right, the tension gets washed away as the white light is exhaled.

Some stretches require caution. For example, I've injured my neck twice doing the Plough. Both injuries occurred as a result of not being adequately warmed up, and I may have been doing it improperly as well. I'd also wait a while before trying a headstand. Here are a few guidelines for stretching:

- stretch before meals or 90 minutes afterwards,
- do it in a place where you have plenty of fresh air,

- do it in a quiet place where there will be minimal distractions,
- use a towel or mat, and
- dress in comfortable clothing.

According to Richard Hittleman, the spine must have continual and methodical exercise. In his book, *Be Young With Yoga*, Mr. Hittleman writes that unless it receives the proper care, the spine gradually becomes compressed, stiff and actually constricts. This causes a person to become less active, which stiffens the spine even more. Hittleman believes that this vicious circle can be broken when a person begins to manipulate their spine through the careful practice of yoga. He believes this is true regardless of age.

CONCLUSION

A key distinction many people overlook is that healthy eating, breathing, stretching and regular exercise are not just about extending your life span or reducing your lifetime medical bills (although they will probably do these things as well). The key benefit to these activities is the improvement in the quality of every moment you are alive. Adopting these habits can improve the quality of life you experience at each moment, whether that moment involves knowledge work or sharing yourself with family and friends.

Vince Lombardi stated that "Fatigue makes cowards of us all." Similarly, an infusion of personal energy can inspire us to set our sights on more challenging horizons. While acquiring specialized knowledge and skill can increase capacity, this won't do you much good if you don't have the energy to apply it. The more energy you cultivate, the more discipline it takes to direct that energy into productive channels. You must also maintain a balance between cycles of exertion and cycles of recovery, which leads us to the issue of personal ecology.

CHAPTER 9

PERSONAL ECOLOGY:

GUIDELINES FOR MAINTAINING BALANCE

Simplifying my life has been one of the most complicated things I've ever attempted.

Some people are using less than 10% of their brain because they are using less than 10% of their heart.

You can become the fastest reader or the most creative genius, build teams of extremely bright people for conducting synergistic dialogue, become a fast learner, establish highly organized information management systems, develop high levels of personal energy, and take on projects that give you an opportunity to employ huge levels of untapped brainpower; but if you consistently violate the rules of personal ecology, you risk wiping out all the gains you have achieved in these other areas.

Each life is maintained by a complex series of relationships. When something happens in one area that throws the overall system out of balance, a series of forces are mobilized to correct the situation. I use the term personal ecology to describe the ongoing process of keeping your life in balance. When engaging in an activity that threatens this balance, I say that it is not "personally ecological." Personal ecology is governed mostly by subconscious mental processes designed to help keep you alive. If you do something that is not personally ecological, these subconscious mental processes usually figure out some way to distract you from doing that activity.

Figure 9.1

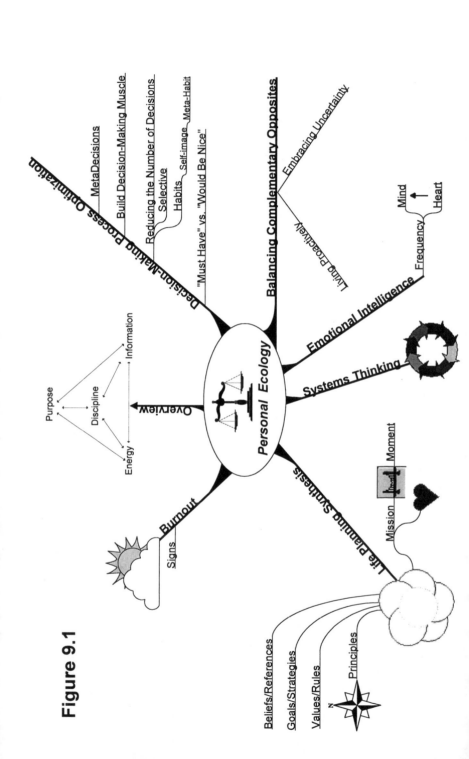

Personal Ecology

Overview
- Purpose
- Discipline
- Information
- Energy

Decision-Making Process Optimization
- MetaDecisions
- Build Decision-Making Muscle
- Reducing the Number of Decisions
  - Selective
  - Habits
    - Self-image
    - Meta-Habit
- "Must Have" vs. "Would Be Nice"

Balancing Complementary Opposites
- Embracing Uncertainty
- Living Proactively

Emotional Intelligence
- Frequency
  - Mind
  - Heart

Systems Thinking

Burnout
- Signs

Life Planning Synthesis
- Mission
  - Heart
  - Moment
- Beliefs/References
- Goals/Strategies
- Values/Rules
- Principles

For example, it takes discipline to have a strong work ethic. It also takes discipline to balance this mental activity with adequate emphasis on the other dimensions of life: physical, spiritual and social/emotional. If your work ethic is not disciplined and these other dimensions are consequently neglected, eventually the subconscious mental processes responsible for maintaining personal ecology will figure out a way to divert you from work. For myself, this often meant getting sick, which forced me to stop working, at least until I figured out how to eat and exercise in a way that diminished my susceptibility to flu viruses. Eventually, my back started bothering me from long hours of sitting or I'd do something stupid which would throw my back out and make it almost impossible to sit in front of a computer. By not disciplining my work ethic, I was throwing myself out of balance and bringing into play a series of forces that eventually diminished my ability to work.

While in my twenties, I owned a plant that looked something like Figure 9.2. One day it dawned on me that the more this plant grew, the more likely it was to fall over from its own weight. In many ways, the same was true for me.

During this time I was single, spent very little time with family and friends, was running my own business without any employees due to inadequate financing, and went

Figure 9.2

for years without taking a week off. My work week often ended at twelve midnight on Saturday evening, since Sunday was my day off. My idea of a healthy meal was natural peanut butter and strawberry jam on the cheapest brown bread ($.33/loaf) I could find, and this was usually eaten while I continued working or while driving. I was not attending church regularly and did not connect regularly with my support network.

Now, such a pace might work for a week or two—for example, when coming down the home stretch on a major project—but as a predominant way of life for several years, I was asking for trouble. These tendencies eventually caught up with me and I made some bad decisions that forced lifestyle changes. The above ideas are presented so you will understand that it was a combination of things that contributed to the imbalance.

When Esther Dyson said, "People who succeed in the computer industry tend to accumulate more and more power until they implode," this was something I could relate to. The more I succeeded as a computer consultant, the greater the demands placed on my time by circumstances and other people. Eventually, the weaknesses in my life management systems were exposed, and I crashed and burned. I could relate to Forrest Gump running clear out of the stadium after scoring a touchdown: he didn't know when to stop either.

PRINCIPLES

"Happiness is the full use of your power along lines of excellence."

— John F. Kennedy

My mission with *Brain Dancing* is to help you mobilize untapped intellectual resources within the context of a balanced lifestyle.

There is an abundance of information available that you can use to improve your life. How fast can you climb and still maintain balance? That depends on your ability to direct your energy into applying information towards a specific purpose in a consistent and disciplined manner. This last sentence is summarized in Figure 9.3.

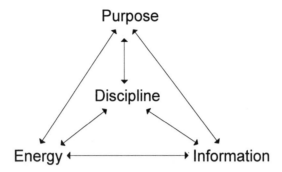

Figure 9.3

The fundamental truths that govern our lives are not written in English or any other natural language. Any attempt to describe them in their entirety is analogous to the parable of the six blind men and the elephant. Each man touched the elephant in a different place, and each came away with a different impression of what an elephant looked like. When it comes to fundamental truths, we are not unlike these blind men. Each person "touches" the fundamental truth elephant in a different way depending upon the context they have defined for their lives. The above diagram doesn't apply to everyone or every situation. However, it is useful in understanding the idea of personal ecology as I have described it throughout this book.

This diagram was inspired by Peter Senge's systems theory as discussed in *The Fifth Discipline*. Systems theory addresses the relationships between elements in a system. Leverage is attained by identifying the limiting factor that if changed, would have a favorable impact on the overall system. Discipline is the leverage point in self-development. We will have as much energy and be aware of as much information as we can apply towards a worthwhile purpose in a disciplined manner.

Your capacity is enhanced when there is an increase in any one of the above dimensions. Personal ecology is at risk any time you expand your purpose, energy or information awareness without a corresponding increase in discipline. The following discussion elaborates on the interplay between these four elements of personal capacity. It is my attempt to answer the following questions:

- Why do some people die soon after retirement?
- Why do so many people fear public speaking to such a degree?
- Why do people often put off reading a book when they know it would be highly applicable to their current situation?
- Why do teachers seem to come into our lives when we are ready for the guidance they have to offer?

ENERGY RIVER THEORY

Have you ever wondered why some people die soon after retirement? The project-oriented nature of my career has given me the opportunity to experience several "mini-retirements." The problem that arises for me is what to do with all of the energy I was directing towards the project. It feels analogous to having a river blocked so that the water backs up and spills out into other areas not accustomed to the excess energy. This process of redirecting large amounts of energy has been fairly stressful at times. It may be the anticipation of this energy redirection that makes some projects so difficult to complete.

Hans Selye touched on this when he wrote, "I think we have to begin by clearly realizing that work is a biological necessity. Just as our muscles become flabby and degenerate if not used, so our brain slips into chaos and confusion unless we constantly use it for some work that seems worthwhile to us."

Public speaking is another situation requiring the disciplined use of energy. Isn't it amazing that people often fear public speaking even more than death? One of the reasons for this is that standing up before an audience often results in a massive surge in energy. This is due in part to having lots of people focusing their attention on you. You can label this extra energy fear or excitement, but the bottom line is that you must learn to direct this energy in healthy ways or public speaking may actually be life threatening. One of the simplest ways to do this is to free up your hands so that you can gesture freely and expressively. Use that energy to move your body energetically.

In an earlier chapter, I mentioned Anthony Robbins' skill as a public speaker. He speaks with more energy than anyone I've ever seen. On more than one occasion, I've noticed that he was actually drenched with sweat an hour or two after beginning to speak. By using public speaking energy on stage with intensity and power, he almost turns it into an athletic event.

In Chapter 4, I mentioned that visually oriented people talk faster and that this allows for higher bandwidth conversations. Anybody can develop the ability, or flexibility, to switch into visual mode for such a conversation. However, such conversations may be harmful to individuals who have difficulty turning off the adrenaline flow after the conversation. For some people, discipline is the price for making fast-paced conversation "ecological" for them. Others seem adept at such conversations without using adrenaline energy. It takes very little effort for them to go at a rapid pace.

As mentioned in Chapter 8, yoga students are encouraged to master *asanas* (body postures and stretches) before they begin refining their skills with *pranayamas* (breathing exercises). *Asanas* help you manage existing energy flows in the body, whereas *pranayamas* cause an increase the flow of energy. Yoga teachers warn that violating this principle can result in significant damage to your brain and nervous system. This energy redirection aspect of yoga can make it difficult at times. It is also a primary reason why yoga has been one of the most valuable disciplines I've ever pursued.

Chapter 5 pointed out that when doing right-brain mode activities, it is easy to lose track of time. Setting time limits and adhering to them is the discipline that opens the doors to mobilizing right-brain mental processes. I also pointed out that it takes an act of discipline to override this tendency to habitually prefer one mode (right or left-brain). This is because doing this often requires you to establish a new "energy river" in your mind. The process is similar to walking along a trail in a forest. At some point you notice that the trail doesn't lead directly to where you want to go, so you veer off the trail and plow through tall grass and brush to get there. The first time down this trail is the toughest, but gradually you wear a new path and it gets easier with each journey. This is how you form a new habit of thought—a new energy river.

Personally, I'm in a constant battle with discipline when it comes to eating. This may be due to the fact that I've worked long hours for several years and could use about a month off to fully regain my balance. During this time, I've been directing as much of my personal energy through my mental batteries as possible. Writing this book hasn't been the most relaxing diversion from brain intensive work at Microsoft. One of the ways I give myself a break is by eating. This redirects energy into my stomach and gives my brain a break.

On mornings when I'm feeling weary from long work hours, it is tempting to swing by the cafeteria for a mind-numbing bagel or plate of hash browns loaded with ketchup. But, as often as possible, I resist the temptation and settle for an Odwalla fresh vegetable juice. My experience has proven time and again the truth of Emerson's words when he wrote in *Compensation*, "...we gain the strength of the temptation we resist." When such a temptation is resisted, it strengthens the muscle within that allows us to redirect energy into activities we deem important, in spite of the direction of current emotional winds.

We must become disciplined energy processors. Even if your goals are written out to the *nth* degree, and you do everything you've learned to increase your energy level, all is for naught if you don't have the discipline required to direct that energy towards achieving your goals with consistent action and disciplined thinking. Jim Rohn was right on the mark when he said, "For every disciplined effort, there are multiple rewards." This is true because it increases your fundamental capacity for effective action.

DISCIPLINED INFORMATION USE

Information shapes our lives in countless ways, as does a lack of information. As mentioned in Chapter 1, we are in fact, in-formation. We learn that a new food lowers cholesterol, so we eat more of it. We learn that a certain type of exercise reduces risk of heart disease, so we do more of that, etc.

What about that book sitting on your desk? The one you know you should read to help you get over some current stumbling blocks? The one you somehow never get around to reading? With the information comes a responsibility to use it wisely. Doing this requires discipline to direct energy into new pathways, and some people would rather go through life with ignorance as their scapegoat.

The truth is, you may not be ready for that information. There may be a situation in your life that demands more of your attention. It may be that the information in the book, if applied, would change your life in more ways than you are ready for. It may increase your capacity in ways that you may not be ready to handle. As the amount of information we are aware of expands, so does the number of possible choices. Sometimes, we may not yet have the strength of character required to make such new choices wisely. The section on "decision-making" later in this chapter addresses this notion further.

Developing your visualization muscle is a powerful mental skill. The information presented in Chapter 3 on how to develop visualization skills should only be applied to the extent that you can use this new capacity in a disciplined manner. Thinking in pictures allows you to think both positive and negative thoughts more efficiently.

Therefore, you must simultaneously develop the discipline required to maintain control of your thoughts, to prevent your imagination from "running wild."

If, for example, someone begins discussing negative situations in your presence, you must turn off your visualization skills momentarily to prevent the corresponding images from appearing in your mind. Thoughts are things; they are first cause. If a person is avoiding the development of this skill, I believe it is due in large part to them not being ready to exercise the mental discipline that would make it ecological for them to proceed. Personally, my skills in this area have been increasing steadily over several years, as opposed to all at once.

PURPOSE

As the amount of information we are aware of expands, there is an increasing need to clarify our objectives in order to narrow the band of relevant information. We must then exercise the discipline to direct most of our attention towards information relevant to that outcome. It often amazes me how many "interesting" distractions pop up as I attempt to narrow my focus. *Useful* information must come before *interesting*.

Clarifying or enriching our sense of purpose can also open doors to new information. Continuing the book avoidance example above, if you decide that you are ready for advancing your personal development, then ask yourself what context would make it necessary for you to read and apply the ideas in the book. It may be that you only need to look at your current situation from a different angle (see the discussion of metaphors in Chapter 3 for related ideas). In other cases, you may need to create a new context or purpose altogether.

One way to enrich context is through visualization. Truly effective visualization generates creative tension. It takes discipline to direct this tension, or energy, into the actions that will make your dream a reality. Sometimes it takes discipline to not act until you are ready. "Creative tension" is the term Peter Senge uses to describe what goes on in your mind when you acknowledge the gap between the way things are now and the way you would like them to be.

Shopping provides us with a microcosm of the creative tension experience. Consider a situation where you are shopping and see something that you really want but can't quite afford. You could buy it right then and there by putting it on a credit card, so you definitely believe it is a reality that can be manifested. However, if you don't act on the impulse to buy immediately, then to the extent that you care about owning that item, you will experience creative tension. As the energy of creative tension begins to flow in the core of your being, ideas will present themselves to you as to how this tension can be released. Creative tension will begin to present alternatives to your awareness like cutting back a little here, working a few extra hours there, taking on additional projects, selling something, etc.

Some of these options may be quite tempting, especially as you continue to hold on to the awareness of the gap between current reality and how things could be. To the extent that you can allow creative tension to run its course until the right moment (with no compromise of basic principles), you have increased your capacity for effective action by the disciplined use of purpose.

Chapter 3 referred to Alan Kay's statement that, "It's not what the vision is, it's what the vision does." Effective visualization generates creative tension: a force driving you towards new levels of creativity and action. Discipline comes in when you have to decide whether or not to act. Ask yourself if you can truly afford the time, energy and money this choice will require, or if you need to wait until you're better prepared. Ask yourself if this alternative is consistent with your values (i.e., the boundary conditions you've established up front).

"If you have a lot of energy and don't know what you want, you're what we call dangerous... You're like fuel spilled all over the place, and wherever someone drops a match, kaBoom! That's where you go."[1]

— *Anthony Robbins*

Creative tension results from both a candid acknowledgment of where you are and a belief that you are capable of manifesting the vision. Shopping for your dreams *as if* you are ready to decide is one way to step into the future and create the required feeling of certainty. The lesson for knowledge workers is this: do whatever it takes to step into the future and experience your goal as if it is about to come true. Use that experience to solidify your belief that it will come true. Then step back and allow the energy of creative tension to flow through your life and work its wonders.

DISCIPLINE

The above discussion explained the interplay between the four fundamental aspects of personal capacity: energy, purpose, information and discipline. Rarely do we make a change in one of these dimensions without a corresponding change occurring in the other areas. As you exercise the discipline to develop your ability for directing energy into productive channels, you are increasing your capacity for managing success. This discipline develops the character supporting the process of making sound decisions, and makes it more likely that you can maintain balance as you begin to succeed. In many cases, this discipline involves making sound judgments in the face of expanding options due to your success. The more information you ask your conscious mind to process, the more important it is to develop the discipline required to quiet your mind, to clear

---

[1] From Anthony Robbins' Personal Power video, *The Keys to Your Unlimited Success.*

it of thought and give it a rest—which is what meditating is all about.

"Almost everyone can handle adversity. But, to test a person's true character, give him power."[2]

— *Abraham Lincoln*

OPTIMIZING THE DECISION-MAKING PROCESS

I began Chapter 1 by stating that decisions represent the fulcrum of mental effectiveness. In the spirit of "going meta," this section discusses ways of optimizing the decision-making process.

Richard Bandler believes that some people get by with lousy decision-making skills because they aren't motivated to do much. By making sure his clients have an effective decision-making strategy before teaching them a powerful new motivation strategy, Bandler increases the chances that they will use the increased motivation wisely.

What are the elements of a good decision-making strategy? Effective decision-making is an art, and having a great strategy is no guarantee that it will be applied intelligently. We make hundreds, if not thousands, of decisions each day at various levels of consciousness. To apply a conscious process to every decision would quickly overwhelm us with what Alvin Toffler called "decision stress."

The decision-making process should begin with one or more metadecisions that classify the relative importance of decisions and identify which elements of your decision-making strategy should be applied. J. Edward Russo and Paul Schoemaker use the term "metadecision" to describe choices about the decision process itself—choices that are likely to determine the character of the whole effort. The following metadecisions were adapted from their book,

---

[2] As quoted in *Beyond Success*, by Brian Biro.

Decision Traps: The Ten Barriers to Brilliant Decision-Making and How to Overcome Them:

- Is there a larger issue "upstream" that is driving the need for this decision?
- What type of decision-making process should be used to make this type of decision?
- How long do decisions of this nature usually take?
- Must this decision be made at all? Now?
- When should the decision be made? Are the deadlines arbitrary?
- Can this decision be made by proceeding sequentially through the decision-making process, or will it require a more iterative approach?
- Where should I concentrate my time, energy and attention?

Refer to *Decision Traps* for their complete list of metadecisions. After addressing issues raised during the metadecision process, effective decision-making involves the following steps to varying degrees:

- Clarify the decision to be made. What is the central issue being decided and why? Examine the chain of events that led to the need for this decision. Russo and Schoemaker recommend that you invest time optimizing the frame of mind in which the decision will be made. They write, "The way people frame a problem greatly influences the solution they will ultimately choose."
- Establish boundary conditions for evaluating options. How will you know that you made a good decision? What factors must be present for you to proceed?
- Generate options and evaluate. Gather intelligence. Whenever possible, base decisions on facts rather than hunches. Intuition can be tapped into for possible options to be evaluated and in cases where a decision must be made without complete information. In those cases, intuition may be best thing you have to go on.

- Identify and assess risks. Those with high downside risks require more time and energy.
- Perform an ecology check. Under what conditions would you not want to carry out this decision? Whom and what else could it effect?
- Learn from feedback.

Chapter 6 described a layered reading strategy that helps you become highly selective in the material you read at slower speeds. As discussed in Chapter 1, Peter Drucker writes that effective executives reduce the number of decisions required of them by focusing their energies on strategic decisions at "the highest level of conceptual understanding." These high-level decisions then provide a framework within which other people can make decisions more easily. Effective executives I've had the chance to study, aggressively pursue the information that will help them make important decisions. Better information means better decisions, and the fewer decisions they have to make, the more energy they can invest in making them well. This also applies to knowledge workers desiring to manage their time more effectively. The next section of this chapter on organizing your life at the highest level is a direct application of this idea.

Another key technique for minimizing the number of decisions you have to make is to use habits and engrams. "Time teaches all things to he who lives forever but I have not the luxury of eternity," writes Og Mandino in his classic, *The Greatest Salesman in the World*. The first law he teaches is to "form good habits and become their slaves."

In his breakthrough book, *Psycho-Cybernetics*, Maxwell Maltz observes that it takes about 21 days to form a habit. He also points out that the ultimate habit, the "meta habit," which tends to influence the formation of all the rest, is that of our self-image. For a complete discussion of effective habit formation, you are also encouraged to read Benjamin Franklin's autobiography and Stephen Covey's book, *The 7 Habits of Highly Effective People*. Each time I refer back to Franklin's thirteen virtues, I seem to understand them better and increase my appreciation of the staggering wisdom upon which they are based. A key distinction Franklin applied was to only focus on one new habit each week[3]. I adapted his system to come up with the following Excel spreadsheet for tracking habit development:

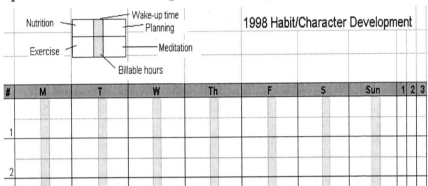

At the end of each day, I fill in codes in the designated boxes to track progress on key habits. The codes in the upper left summarize the nutritional supplements taken that day (I am tracking these in detail because I'm still refining my nutritional habits). The "CY" in the exercise quadrant indicate that I did my standard cardiovascular workout (ten minutes on the mini-tramp followed by twenty minutes on the Cardio-Glide) and one of my two standard Yoga routines.

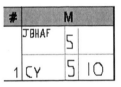

The three columns on the right are for summarizing the results for the week on my top three habits for the quarter. The goal is not to know exactly how many I did of each, but rather to monitor the trend as I move from week to week.

---

[3] You can obtain a copy of this spreadsheet by visiting **http://BrainDance.com/habits.htm**.

As the number of choices in our lives increases, there is an increasing need for structure and habits: for making decisions that last. Chapter 8 described how I use juicing and exercise engrams to reduce the number of decisions I need to perform these activities. When I juice or exercise, I pretty much just make one decision—to begin—and my body takes over from there. Granted, I started out by carefully designing and continually refining both of these activities. The key benefit is that by reducing the number of decisions involved, I've removed a barrier to doing them. It is the same process we use to learn to drive. Use it to reduce the number of decisions required to carry out frequently performed tasks.

Napoleon Hill observed that successful people make decisions quickly and change their minds slowly if ever. The clearer you are about your goals and values, the easier it is to recognize an opportunity consistent with them and to quickly reject all others. When anticipating an important decision, I've found it helpful to create a one-page summary that separates essential criteria from the "would be nice" issues. For example, when shopping for a house, I created a sheet that listed my top five criteria as follows:

Must Have	Bad ← Rating → Excellent				
1. Quiet neighborhood	1	2	3	4	5
2. Convenient location	1	2	3	4	5
etc.	1	2	3	4	5

This was followed by additional criteria that I considered pluses, but didn't consider essential.

Would be nice	Bad ← Rating → Excellent				
1. Hot tub	1	2	3	4	5
2. All appliances included	1	2	3	4	5
etc.	1	2	3	4	5

When a potential house showed up on my radar screen, this sheet allowed me to quickly reject a great many houses that otherwise would have eaten up my time. When a strong candidate showed up, I could more easily afford to thoroughly research the decision.

Decision-making is a skill developed by making decisions. Work your way up to big decisions. In his *Personal Power* audiotape series, Anthony Robbins emphasizes that our decision-making muscles must be strengthened daily by making decisions and following through with action.

You may also want to try Ben Franklin's decision-making technique. He took a blank sheet of paper and drew a line down the middle. After writing the pros on one side and the cons on the other, he crossed them off as they balanced each other out. For example, a single pro item might offset two or three cons.

With this perspective on the decision-making process, I will now discuss the ultimate form of "going meta"—organizing your life at the highest level. This involves making a series of decisions about how you will run your life. For myself, learning how to work hard has been the easy part. Learning how to organize myself so as to perform that work within the context of a balanced lifestyle has been a different story. To quote Ross Perot: "The principles of management and leadership are simple. The hard part is doing them, living up to them day after day, not making lots of excuses for ourselves." Mr. Perot feels that complex management theories are often just an excuse for not facing up to how hard it is to live by some very basic principles.

ORGANIZE YOUR LIFE AT THE HIGHEST LEVEL

Have you ever noticed how life sometimes wraps up valuable lessons in the simplest of moments? This happened to me once back in college when all I did was sit down in my car seat. Up came this cloud of dust, and the sun shining through my windshield made sure that I noticed. I brushed it away with my right hand and most of the dust went to the left. I noticed one speck, however, that started to the left and then veered up and to the right.

Upon closer examination, I could see that this was not dust at all but rather a tiny little bug. Perhaps because this bug was so small, it made me stop and wonder what was in this speck that made it so different from all the rest.

Life!

This little speck contained the stuff of life and was thus blessed with the ability to choose its own path, regardless of which way the wind was blowing.

I once asked Norman Cousins, author of *Anatomy of an Illness*, if there was any one event in his life that got him started on the path of such amazing accomplishments. "Yes, as a matter of fact there was," he responded. After a pause that seemed like minutes, he continued, "I was born!"

Each of us has been blessed with the miracle of life, and thus the ability to choose our own path, regardless of which way the wind happens to be blowing in our life at any given moment.

There are three basic strategies for running your life: going with the flow (totally right-brain), schedule everything you do and do everything you schedule (left-brain), or some combination of both. Chapter 5 encouraged you to use the synergy of opposites to enhance creativity, and I believe we can also find synergy in the opposites of willpower and going with the flow. Sometimes there is wisdom in the wind!

Not long after "imploding" from overwork and underplay, I was dribbling the ball at a soccer clinic. Two defenders stood between me and the goal and I was working hard to get by them. Suddenly the clinic director blew her whistle and declared: "Okay, now we're going to play without goals."

The goal markers were removed and play resumed. I just stood there. One minute I was working aggressively to dribble past the defenders towards the goal, and the next, I didn't know which way to go. The defenders resumed their attack, and I dribbled away from them. Suddenly we were playing "keep away."

Reflecting on this event afterwards, the lesson was clear: I was dribbling through life without goals! Rather than working proactively to create a life I had chosen, to a large extent, I was simply reacting to whatever challenges life tossed my way.

You may be wondering where the synergy of opposites lies. Yes, this experience encouraged me to exercise willpower by directing my life proactively. However, I did not plan on learning this lesson that afternoon! Learning a life lesson was not on the schedule. I was just there to play soccer. In *The Celestine Prophecy*, James Redfield does a masterful job of explaining how to embrace such coincidences.

Deepak Chopra, in his book, *The Seven Spiritual Laws of Success*, addresses the issue of balancing the laws of intent and desire with the laws of least effort and detachment. With these laws, Chopra presents these seemingly opposite notions: "Inherent in every intention and desire is the mechanics for its fulfillment." And, "In detachment lies the wisdom of uncertainty...in the wisdom of uncertainty lies the freedom from our past, from the known, which is the prison of past conditioning. And in our willingness to step into the unknown, the field of all possibilities, we surrender ourselves to the creative mind that orchestrates the dance of the universe."

Balancing the application of these two opposites is where the rubber meets the road in self-development. The rest of this chapter focuses on the willpower side of the equation.

One of the excuses I had frequently used to avoid an intensive goal-setting session was that I wanted to be in an absolute peak state of mind and body. I viewed goal setting more as an event than an ongoing process, so I wanted to be darned sure that I wrote down the "right" things.

Well, this "dribbling through life without goals" metaphor really lit a fire under me. I reasoned that if all I did was wait for the next gust of wind to blow before using my ability to choose my own way, then the wind would still be in control! So I set a date and began exercising and eating as healthy as I knew how.

My goal-setting day finally arrived and after four hours of brow-knitting and thought-intensive writing, I had several pages of goals. The excitement from having accomplished this soon clashed with reality when Monday morning arrived, and all of the urgencies of my ongoing responsibilities kicked in. I felt a lot like a steamship captain who must look far in the distance to chart his course because he knows that his ship will continue in the same direction long after he has turned the wheel.

Gradually (and with Stephen Covey's help), life has taught me that developing a personal mission statement and goals is more of an ongoing process than something you can wrap up in a single day. To paraphrase Dr. Covey, "These are things you have to 'detect' more than invent."

The next time the winds of circumstance begin to blow in your life, think of that little speck of dust that chose its own way, and then get on with the *process* of 'detecting' your way. The following material demonstrates how to apply the three-step Mind Mapping process presented in Chapter 5 to help you accomplish this. The better the tools, the better the end result is likely to be.

> *"When we talk about time management, it seems ridiculous to worry about speed before direction, about saving minutes when we may be wasting years.[4]"*
>
> — *Stephen R. Covey*

LIFE PLANNING SYNTHESIS FOLDER

Organizing your life at the highest level is the ultimate form of "going meta." The life planning

---

[4] For a complimentary four-week sample of the Seven Habits Organizer, call 1-800-680-6839. This is an excellent introduction to Covey's principles.

synthesis folder is a simple manila folder containing the following five sections:

- **Mission Statement:** The special contribution you would like to make—how you want to be remembered. In Peter Senge's words, "First and foremost, the bedrock of what draws us into action is that we deeply care." What is it that you truly want to create in your life—what do you deeply care about? Listen to the song, "Climb Every Mountain" from *The Sound of Music*. You know you have found your mission when you have found a dream you can give all the love you can give every day you're alive. Find a dream that "juices" you— a dream towards which you can apply the very essence of who you are. In his classic book, *Man's Search for Meaning*, Viktor Frankl encourages people to find a meaning that is unique and specific, in that it must be fulfilled by you alone.

"Within each of us lies the chance for greatness in some area. Identify that gift which is unique to you, and in your pursuit of developing that gift, let no one deter you in your task."

— from the movie *Chariots of Fire*

- **Principles:** This section is a one-page Mind Map of the fundamental principles that govern our lives. This is something that evolves through time to reflect your best understanding to date of what these principles are. When you learn a great idea, this sheet will allow you to evaluate its importance as it relates to other valuable lessons you've learned. Figure 9.4 is an example of this type of Mind Map. Remember the fundamental truth elephant—create your own from scratch based on your own perspective on fundamental principles.

- **Values and Rules:** What is most important to you, expressed in terms of the states you would like to experience daily, and those you would like to avoid. Next to each value, place the rules you use to determine the extent to which you are living these values. A primary benefit of clarifying values is optimizing your decision-making process. Values are often the fundamental criteria used to accept or reject an option. Refer to *Awaken the Giant Within* by Anthony Robbins for details on this topic.
- **Goals/Strategies:** What are your top goals in each of the four main areas of life (physical, mental, spiritual, and emotional/social)? Work-related goals are expressed in terms of the skills you would like to develop and problems you would like to be able to solve (i.e., capacities). Include here evidence procedures for recognizing when a goal is achieved and symbolic representations of key strategies.
- **Beliefs/References:** What beliefs will you need to support the achievement of these goals? When you realize that your beliefs are a choice, the next logical step is to select beliefs in alignment with your mission, values, etc. What reference experiences do you have (or need to create) to support these beliefs at a gut level?

I try to keep the number of pages in this folder to a minimum. Each of these sections is developed using an extended version of the three-step Mind Mapping process discussed in Chapter 5. The process goes something like this:

- Get five unlined sheets of 11"x17" paper and start an idea collection sheet for each of the above categories. By "start" I mean just write the purpose of the sheet (example: "Mission") in the middle of the page. I seem to have better luck with these if I turn the sheets sideways.

- Place these sheets in a 9"x12" manila file folder and label it "Life Planning Synthesis." Don't fold these large sheets until you absolutely have to. I find that having the crease in the middle of the page disrupts the flow of ideas. I only fold them after I have placed a substantial number of ideas on the page.
- Periodically schedule 30-minute sessions to brainstorm one or more of these topics. The 30 minutes are divided up something like this:
  - Set a timer for five or ten minutes and write as many ideas on the sheet as quickly as you can.
  - Take a five-minute break to bounce on a mini-trampoline, go for a quick walk or stretch out.
  - Spend the remaining 15-20 minutes adding any additional ideas that come to mind. During this time, feel free to consult reference texts such as those by Anthony Robbins or Stephen Covey.
- Set the sheets aside for a day or two. In the mean time, place a stack of Post-it notes in your purse, wallet or time management system if you carry it with you. Anytime an idea comes to you regarding one of these sheets over the next few days, write it on one of these notes. If your time management system has room, try writing the ideas there.
- The next time one of your 30-minute life planning sessions rolls around, these notes can be reviewed during the second half of the brainstorming process. Add the useful ideas to the appropriate idea collection sheet.
- Repeat the above process until you feel like you have accumulated a critical mass of ideas about each section. Now it's not so intimidating to plan that 4-hour session because you are ready for it!
- Plan a day when you will have about four hours of uninterrupted time. If possible, go to a hotel near water. Prepare yourself for this day by taking especially good care of your health. Make a special effort to exercise and eat as healthily as possible.

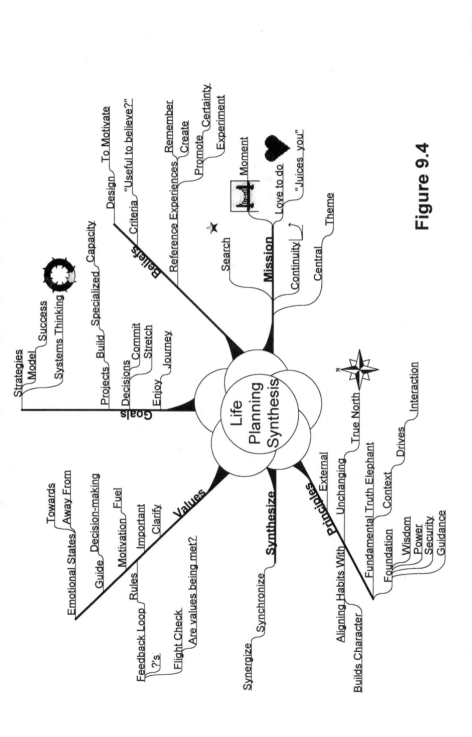

Figure 9.4

- When the day arrives, use a similar process of oscillating between intense brainstorming and right-brain stimulating breaks. The desired outcome from this event is either highly organized Mind Maps or written statements for things like your mission statement or strategies. Use symbols and reference favorite metaphors as much as possible. Being able to traverse the various ideas as rapidly as possible helps you view each individual idea within the context of others.

This folder is a tool for centralizing all high level life-management documents. Before doing this, I had goal sheets stored in several places. This was a result of doing exercises in books and at seminars. If someone asked what my goals were, I had to stop and think which ones I should refer to. The folder system also gives you a convenient reference tool when doing your weekly planning.

"You know I thought I had mono once for an entire year—turned out I was just really bored."

— From the movie, Wayne's World

This exercise has also allowed me to align multiple activities synergistically. It's not unusual for a single activity to contribute simultaneously to two or three goals. For example, each time I gave a speech at Toastmasters club, I used it as an opportunity to refine the material in this book. Everything in this book also applies to the process of writing, giving speeches and developing computer software. As I applied this material to speaking and my work, I was able to further refine my understanding of what ideas were truly useful, and thus should be included in this book.

Synthesize, synchronize, and synergize.

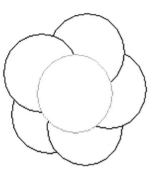

This folder helped me synthesize what is important, and then synchronize my efforts for maximum synergy. In this way, the overall results of my actions became greater than the sum of the individual efforts. Visually, this concept looks like a series of overlapping circles. Each activity overlaps my core mission to at least some degree so that all activities are more likely to benefit from success in any one area.

How do you know if you did a great job on these documents? To paraphrase the words of Alan Kay again, it's not what the documents are, it's what they do for you. Neat and pretty is irrelevant unless what you end up with is a set of ideas that consistently inspire you to action.

"First you have to have fun. Second, you have to put your love where your labor is. Third, you have to go in the opposite direction to everyone else."

— Anita Roddick

For many years I was careful to avoid participating in multi-level marketing companies. Then along came Fund America. This company had made deals with major companies such as Citibank and MCI, and was being endorsed by several people I had great respect for. I pulled out my electronic spreadsheet to analyze the opportunity, and my excitement went through the roof! All of a sudden, I was launched. I was leaping out of bed in the morning, bounding with newly found energy and getting more excited about this opportunity all the time. After careful thought, I decided that it would distract me from my main area of focus. As much as it hurt, I let this one go (Fund America folded not long after this).

But what a lesson this experience taught me! Where did all of this energy and excitement come from? It came from within. It was there all along waiting to be tapped by the right combination of circumstances. I believe this same level of energy and excitement exists within each individual, and that you aren't done with your life synthesis folder until those sheets of paper unleash these resources. Two quotations from Anthony Robbins sum up this notion: "People aren't lazy, they just have impotent goals," and "Giant goals produce giant motivation."

What was unique about the Fund America opportunity that made such an impact? I could clearly relate to the substantial benefits, and I believed it was possible for me to achieve them. Emotionally, I had stepped into the future and felt the gap between where I could be and where I was. I had discovered creative tension.

So how do you translate the above words into the true experience of creative tension? Seeing is believing. Do something as if you are ready to realize one of your dreams. Visualizing your dream helps, but you can aid your visualization efforts with a variety of activities. You can go shopping, interview someone who has already done what you want to do, or visit a company or department that has done something similar. These activities can substantially boost your visualization efforts by providing the raw material (sights, sounds, and emotions) for more effective visualization. Getting to know someone who has already done something significantly impacts my beliefs about what I can accomplish.

The subconscious mind is the seat of action. Ultimately, the purpose of this work is to communicate a concise message to your subconscious in a way that ignites your action-oriented engines. The effectiveness of any communication is not what is said, but rather the meaning that is effectively transferred.

You can use things in your environment: sights, sounds, smells, temperatures, seasons, etc., to remind you of key components of your life planning synthesis. I often use symbols of the powerful forces in nature (snow-capped mountains, crashing waves, the stars at night, etc.) to remind me of what nature is capable of. Since I'm a part of nature, I must have access to at least some of these resources to the extent that I am able to direct them towards a worthwhile cause.

"People often overestimate what they can do in a year, and underestimate what they can do in a decade."
— *Anthony Robbins*

BRIDGING THE MISSION WITH THE MOMENT

I've found it helpful to associate daily activities to my highest values and mission statement. My Toastmasters club once had a visitor promoting leadership by participating in community activities. She talked about her work with the Campfire Girls organization and why it inspired her to participate. She had linked up in her mind that she was touching the future of our country by making this special effort to nurture our future leaders. Given the passion with which she spoke about this topic, these were not just fancy sounding words: they were words she lived and breathed every moment she participated in that organization.

I can give you two examples of how I applied this strategy in writing this book. On April 27, 1994, I read an article about someone donating twelve million dollars to the Federal Government to help pay off the national debt. The article pointed out what a trivial impact this donation would have since the debt, as of April 24, 1994, totaled $4,558,348,698,138.33. It reminded me of a television show I'd seen where Japanese bond traders decided to emphasize the contribution they were making to our bond market. One day, they boycotted the U.S. market, and it went to its knees. American traders were just wandering around with nothing to do until about one in the afternoon, when the Japanese decided they had made their point. In my mind, the lesson was that we have actually compromised our fundamental freedom as a nation by running up such a huge debt. I care deeply about my country. I keep an American flag next to my desk to remind me that the toughest day at the office pales in comparison to the average day on the front line. Given what I knew about the link between capacity and desire, I could see that such a financial burden would absolutely shape the destiny of our nation.

If giving twelve million dollars to the Government won't help, then I wondered what an individual could do to make a difference in this situation. My answer was to try to mobilize the untapped intellectual resources of America's knowledge workers. If it is true that most people are using less than 10% of their mental capacity, then if I could figure out a way to unleash even an additional 10% of a large number of people over an extended time period, this might compound and actually have an impact. I concluded that this was our nation's greatest underutilized resource!

As if this wasn't enough to inspire me to write, I learned from a Paul Harvey news broadcast that the comet Tuttle was expected to pass fairly close to our planet in the summer of 1994. There was some speculation that this comet could actually strike Earth on its next pass in the year 2130. This inspired me to write a speech entitled "The Dance of Life," describing that day in the future when all nations on Earth pool their resources to create and launch a rocket to blast this comet out of the sky before it slams into our planet. Birds have the gift of wings, horses the gift of great running speed, and flowers great beauty. Only humans are blessed with the gift of intellect capable of saving "Team Earth" from this catastrophe.

If such a day should arrive, would it come down to the abilities of a few engineers working several all-nighters with lightning-fast reading speeds and amazing creative skills? Probably not. Our chances seem much better if a significant number of people begin using even 10% more of their intellectual capacity on a consistent basis over the decades preceding this event. The benefits from this activity would compound to increase the capacity of our planet and give our scientists and engineers a fighting chance.

These may seem like crazy ideas, but that's all they are—ideas. The important thing to note is that they did inspire me to invest hundreds of hours into this book. Their value stemmed from their emotional impact. What ideas will it take to inspire you to act on your dreams?

"Deep within each heart,
there lies a magic spark,
that lights the fire of our imagination."

— *from the song, The Power of the Dream,*
by David Foster, Linda Thompson and Babyface

SYSTEMS THINKING

Peter Senge's book, *The Fifth Discipline,* is an excellent overview of the vast and rich set of distinctions referred to as "Systems Thinking." He writes that when some people rise above the trees and see the forest, all they see is a bunch of trees. Senge's ideas have profoundly impacted every chapter in this book.

This entire chapter is an application of Systems Thinking to the overall process of mobilizing untapped intellectual resources. The idea is to see through complexity in order to identify the underlying structures generating change. This involves identifying the balancing processes built into the system that are currently limiting growth. If these balancing processes are not identified, working harder may just cause these balancing processes to kick in more.

When applied in the context of personal ecology, make sure you understand the benefit you are receiving from such limiting factors before reducing their influence in your life. The best example I can think of is the way some people sabotage their financial success because they are not ready for decisions resulting from the increased flexibility.

MIT professor Marvin Minsky's book, *Society of Mind*, provides an excellent metaphor for understanding the structure of our subconscious mind. It is a collection of parts, subsystems, or subroutines all working together to help ensure survival. While some of our behaviors may not make sense at first blush, there is sometimes a hidden benefit motivating the subconscious part to continue the behavior. Once the targeted benefit is being achieved in other ways, the subconscious part will loose at least some of its motivation to continue the behavior.

Ever been "carried away" with a project—gotten so involved that you lost track of other responsibilities while you were off on some tangent? The subconscious parts driving motivation notice these things, especially if you overdo it. In response, the subconscious will create limiting factors that reduce the probability that you will get "carried away" in the future. From the personal ecology viewpoint, you can expand the scope of projects you are likely to begin by developing habits, systems of behavior, social relationships and support systems, that promote a reasonable amount of balance when immersed in a project. When the subconscious awareness/motivation parts believe it will be personally ecological to open the valves, they are more likely to do so. For myself, solid habits in the areas of exercise, nutrition, yoga and meditation have been cornerstones to a systemic infrastructure conducive to personal growth.

Senge explains that there will always be more limiting processes as you grow. As each source of limitation is overcome, growth returns until you bump into a new source of limitation. My words can hardly do justice to the ideas Senge conveys in *The Fifth Discipline*. I recommend the "Limits to Growth" exercise in Chapter 6 of Senge's book.

BURNOUT WARNING SIGNALS

If you ever find yourself out of balance, remember that it is probably due to a combination of factors and will probably require a combination of changes to return to balance. How do you know when you are out of balance? If there are problems in your life, it may mean that the universe is trying to get your attention. To quote Shakti Gawain, "If you don't pay attention, the problems will intensify, until you finally get the message and start to listen more carefully to your inner guidance."

Here are some other indicators that I watch out for:

- Having difficulty saying "no" to unexpected demands on my time.
- The quality of my relationships with others is a great measure of emotional stability. People often serve as mirrors. Every person is in my life for a reason.
- I'm having trouble making eye contact with others.
- I am having trouble forgiving someone. To quote Joseph Murphy, "If I should tell you something wonderful about someone who has wronged you, cheated you, or defrauded you, and you sizzle at hearing the good news about this person, the roots of hatred would still be in your subconscious mind, playing havoc with you." It's usually easier to deal with such situations when I haven't depleted my life energies with overwork for extended periods.
- Tendency to notice mistakes others are making, which, upon closer examination, are really projections of mistakes I'm making.
- Actions inconsistent with feelings.
- Having difficulty being honest with myself or identifying true feelings, making it somewhat challenging to be honest with others. A good test for this one is to go for a long drive and notice if any ideas seem to nag at my consciousness.
- Not getting at least five hugs a day.
- Prolonged periods without cardiovascular exercise.

- Difficulty getting to sleep at night.
- I'm not dealing with time pressures well. I'm rushing around with high levels of anxiety, not concentrating on being fully present each moment.
- Noticing that I haven't been laughing much lately.
- Having difficulty concentrating, often getting distracted by random worries.
- Frequent bingeing, especially on sweets, is usually not a good sign.
- Lack of a support group or not meeting with them to compare notes occasionally.
- Not taking at least one day off per week. This one can mess me up in a hurry.
- If I can't remember the last time I scheduled a vacation or opportunity for mental rest.
- If I am not looking forward to work on Monday.

Our consciousness is not designed to notice slow gradual changes to our well-being. There have been several times when I had no idea how badly I needed a vacation until I was 100 miles down the road.

In *Think and Grow Rich*, Napoleon Hill writes that proper character development will increase your ability to identify opportunities in time to capitalize on them, and to notice "impending dangers" in time to avoid them. Pay attention to the messages life is sending you, whatever the source and whatever the form. Sometimes they may indicate a need to give yourself a break. But remember Sigmund Freud's words, "Sometimes a cigar is just a cigar"—not every random event carries a lesson. How do you tell the difference? Meditate in order to develop your ability to listen accurately to intuitive guidance. The more I meditate, the more I believe it is an essential practice for maintaining balance while striving to mobilize untapped brainpower.

Unexpected messages are also a great opportunity to revisit your values, goals and purpose. If the activity is still in alignment with your highest clarity in these areas, then perseverance is probably in order.

KEEP BRAIN DANCING IN PERSPECTIVE

There are four main dimensions to life: spiritual, social/emotional, mental and physical. You can live a life while neglecting one of these dimensions no more than you can drive a car after removing a wheel. *Brain Dancing* is primarily a book about mental tools, with one chapter on the physical issues of nutrition and exercise. I purposely avoided spiritual issues as much as possible, because I believe these ideas can be useful to people of all religions.

Regarding the social/emotional dimension, I highly recommend Daniel Goleman's book, *Emotional Intelligence*. One key distinction Goleman mentions is how a section of the brain called the amygdala directs our emotional responses. When information is taken in through the senses, a small portion of it is sent directly to the amygdala. This allows a faster, though less precise response to occur in cases of possible danger. The emotional response starts to occur before the sensory information is fully registered and processed by the neocortex (conscious mind). "This bypass," writes Goleman, "seems to allow the amygdala to be a repository for emotional impressions and memories that we have never known about in full awareness."

"Emotional aptitude is a meta-ability, determining how well we can use whatever other skills we have, including raw intellect."

— *Daniel Goleman*

I believe this distinction explains the basis for phobias and for NLP (Neuro Linguistic Programming) anchors discussed in Chapter 3. The reason anchors and phobias trigger an automatic response without conscious effort is because the reaction is driven by a strong impression stored in the amygdala's emotional memory banks.

Emotions are often beyond words, and trying to analyze them mentally sometimes sends my mind into a free-fall, whirling through issues and scenarios over and over. Emotions don't compute! Another way to deal with them is taught by Sara Paddison in her book, *The Hidden Power of the Heart*. The other way is to use heart intelligence. This involves changing the frequency at which you are thinking to one based on the higher frequencies of the heart, such as love.

This is why the last line in the thought spectrum chart included in Chapter 1 was as follows:

Frequency Center: *Heart* ←————————→ *Mind*

Learning to direct your mind with positive thoughts from the heart is an essential survival skill. Paddison shares specific exercises for self-activating the frequency of love in your heart and keeping it going. Her book is based on research conducted at the Institute of HeartMath® in Boulder Creek, California. Measurements with electrocardiograph machines have proven that these exercises can literally change how our hearts beat[5].

> *"While struggling for more efficiency, the majority of people overlook the possibility that deeper caring is one of the most efficient energy expenditures a person or organization can make."*

> — *Doc Lew Childre, president, HeartMath LLC*

In addition to using heart frequencies to quiet mental chatter, I have also found them useful while developing software. While pushing myself to complete a project

---

[5] Call (800) 450-9111 for more information or visit: **http://www.heartmath.org/Articles/nathel/2.html.**

ASAP, sometimes it helps to step back and remember how much I love creating software that others find useful. I think about how grateful I am for the chance to create structured thought that can be easily transferred to millions of computers around the world as electronic bits. This love and gratitude quickly reorganizes my entire mind-set in a way that boosts both my motivation level and effectiveness.

Dr. Candace Pert has invested the last twenty years studying the movement of amino acid chains in the human body—the chemistry of emotion and memory. Refer to the following link to read an interview with Dr. Pert describing her theory of emotion:

http://www.net-connect.net/~jspeyrer/pert.htm

In reading this article, it occurred to me that one reason the multiple-pass approach to learning works is because it gives certain cells time to replenish the neurotransmitters needed to lay down new memories.

"Love and intimacy are at the root of what makes us sick and what makes us well. I am not aware of any other factor in medicine—not diet, not smoking, not exercise—that has a greater impact."

— *Dean Ornish, M.D.*

CONCLUSION

If you want to get more out of this book, give yourself a reason to do so. Decide to help a student study more effectively, or find someone who needs help and agree to find information that will help them. Then pick up this book with the intention of locating information that will help you do so. You'll see ideas you didn't notice before which directly relate to this new problem. In addition, your peripheral awareness will make note of several other ideas in a way that you can come back to them or use them in other situations. Giving yourself a context with which to interact with the information lake called *Brain Dancing* provides your mind with a framework for a useful understanding of the material.

As it is with this book, so it is with life on a larger scale. We are surrounded by an infinite sea of intelligence and information. Our vast subconscious mental processes are continuously scanning this infoscape for ideas that relate to the directions we have told our subconscious we want to go. The more precise the direction, the more selective it can be, and the more useful the information it will reveal to you.

The scale of knowledge worker productivity is exponential. The key to maintaining balance is to operate at peak performance levels as much as possible throughout each day. This will allow you to get so much done during work hours that taking time off for personal activities justifies itself as a means of maintaining high productivity. In

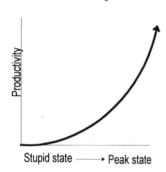

knowledge work, peak performance is accomplished by building specialized capacity via a succession of projects of increasing complexity, cultivating high levels of personal energy, and then directing this skill, knowledge and energy towards a purpose you care about, with all the focused discipline you can muster.

"You are guaranteed to miss 100% of the shots you don't take."

— *Wayne Gretzky*

APPENDIX A

BrainDance.com Web Site

Seminars: To be informed of upcoming Brain Dancing events in your area, send an email message to **events@BrainDance.com**. Include your mailing address and phone number.

Links: The following page contains updated links to all of the Web sites mentioned throughout this book:

http://BrainDance.com/refdoc.htm

Newsletter: To subscribe to our free online newsletter, send an email to **pk@BrainDance.com** with the word "subscribe" on the subject line. You can read back issues by visiting:

http://BrainDance.com/pk.htm

StartGen: You can download a fully functional version of StartGen free of charge or learn more about it from the following Web page. There is no "timeout," just a reminder message after 30 days. Registration is $29.

http://BrainDance.com/sgen.htm

Brain Dancing Coach: There are two versions of this software: a free trial version and a retail version priced at $39 plus shipping. The fully functional trial version contains a subset of the modules available in the retail version. You can download the trial version or learn more about it from the following Web page:

http://BrainDance.com/bdc.htm

T-shirt: T-shirts are available featuring the dancing brain on the front of this book for $17.95 plus shipping. Available in medium (©as shown in the pictures on the following page), large or XL. Visit the following Web page for more information:

http://BrainDance.com/tshirt.htm

Audiotape: A 90 minute overview of *Brain Dancing* recorded by the author is available for $14.95 plus shipping.

Special Offer: Call **(800) 718-8901** to order any of the above products or additional books. Mention the "book offer" and you will receive a 10% discount. You may also order online at:

http://BrainDance.com/order.htm

Front

Back

Visit **http://BrainDance.com/tshirt.htm** to see high-resolution color versions of these pictures.

BIBLIOGRAPHY

The online version of this bibliography at **http://BrainDance.com/biblio.htm** contains links to each author's Web site where available.

Aguayo, Rafael. *Dr. Deming: The American Who Taught the Japanese About Quality.* New York: Fireside Books, 1990. ISBN: 0-671746-21-9.

Anderson, Bob. *Stretching.* Illustrated by Jean Anderson. Bolinas, CA: Shelter Publications; New York: distributed in the US by Random House, 1980. ISBN: 0-936070-01-3.

Bailey, Covert, and Gates, Ronda. *Smart Eating: Choosing Wisely, Living Lean.* Boston: Houghton Mifflin, 1996. ISBN: 0-395752-83-3.

Bailey, Covert. *The New Fit or Fat.* Boston: Houghton Mifflin, 1991. ISBN: 0-395605-33-4.

Bandler, Richard, and Grinder, John. *Frogs into Princes: Neuro Linguistic Programming.* Edited by John O. Stevens. Moab, UT: Real People Press, 1979. ISBN: 0-911226-18-4.

—. *Reframing: Neuro-Linguistic Programming™ and the Transformation of Meaning.* Edited by Steve and Connirae Andreas. Moab, UT: Real People Press, 1982. ISBN: 0-911226-24-9.

Bandler, Richard. *Using your Brain--for a Change* [sound recording]. Boulder, CO: NLP Comprehensive, 1989.

—. *Using your Brain--for a Change.* Moab, UT: Real People Press, 1985. ISBN: 0-911226-26-5.

Biro, Brian. *Beyond Success: the 15 Secrets of a Winning Life!* Hamilton, MT: Pygmalion Press, 1995. ISBN: 0-964745-30-5.

Boar, Bernard. *The Art of Strategic Planning for Information Technology: Crafting Strategy for the 90's.* New York: John Wiley & Sons, 1993. ISBN: 0-471599-18-2.

Buzan, Tony and Barry. *The Mind Map Book: How to Use Radiant Thinking to Maximize your Brain's Untapped Potential.* New York: E.P. Dutton, 1994. ISBN: 0-525939-04-0.

Buzan, Tony. *Speed Reading.* New York: E.P. Dutton, 1984. ISBN: 0-525480-76-5.

—. *Use Both Sides of Your Brain.* New York: Dutton, 1983. ISBN: 0-525480-11-0.

Calbom, Cherie and Keane, Maureen. *Juicing For Life.* Garden City Park, NY: Avery Pub. Group, 1992. ISBN: 0-895295-12-1.

Chopra, Deepak. *Quantum Healing Workshop* [sound recording]. New York: Mystic Fire Audio, 1990.

—. *The Seven Spiritual Laws of Success: A Practical Guide to the Fulfillment of your Dreams.* San Rafael, CA: Amber-Allen Pub. Distributed by Publishers Group West, 1994. ISBN: 1-878424-11-4.

Chuen, Master Lam Kam. *The Way of Energy: Mastering the Chinese Art of Internal Strength With Chi Kung Exercise*. New York: Fireside Books, 1991. ISBN: 0-671736-45-0.

Context Magazine, Diamond Technology Partners, Premier Internet issue, http://www.contextmag.com.

Covey, Stephen. *First Things First: to Live, to Love, to Learn, to Leave a Legacy*. New York: Simon & Schuster, 1994. ISBN: 0-671864-41-6.

—. *Principle Centered Leadership*. New York: Fireside Book, 1992. ISBN: 0-671792-80-6.

—. *The 7 Habits of Highly Effective People* [sound recording] (8 cassette version). Provo, UT: Covey Leadership Center Inc., 1993.

—. *The 7 Habits of Highly Effective People: Restoring the Character Ethic*. New York: Simon and Schuster, 1989. ISBN: 0-671708-63-5.

Cusumano, Michael, and Selby, Richard. *Microsoft Secrets: How the World's Most Powerful Software Company Creates Technology, Shapes Markets, and Manages People*. New York: Free Press, 1995. ISBN: 0-028740-48-3.

D'Adamo, Dr. Peter J. *Eat Right For Your Type: The Individualized Diet Solution to Staynig Healthy, Living Longer & Achieving Your Ideal Weight*. New York: C. P. Putnam's Sons, 1996. ISBN: 0-399-14255-X.

de Bono, Edward. *Six Thinking Hats*. Toronto: Key Porter Books, 1985. ISBN: 0-919493-73-4.

Diamond, Harvey and Marilyn. *Fit for Life II: Living Health*. New York: Warner Books, 1988, 1987. ISBN: 0-446346-60-8.

—. *Fit for Life*. New York: Warner Books, 1985. ISBN: 0-446513-22-9.

Dilts, Robert, and Bonissone, Gino. *Skills for the Future: Managing Creativity and Innovation*. Cupertino, CA: Meta Publications, 1993. ISBN: 0-916990-27-3.

Drucker, Peter. *The Effective Executive*. London: Pan Books, 1970, 1967. ISBN: 0-330025-07-4.

Durant, Will. *Our Oriental Heritage: Being a History of Civilization in Egypt and the Near East to the Death of Alexander, and in India, China and Japan from the beginning to our own day: with an Introduction on the Nature and Foundations of Civilization*. New York: Simon & Schuster, 1935, 1954, 1963.

Easwaran, Eknath. *Meditation: Commonsense Directions for an Uncommon Life*. 2nd Edition, Petaluma, CA: Nilgiri Press, 1978. ISBN: 091513215X.

Edwards, Betty. *Drawing on the Right Side of the Brain: a Course in Enhancing Creativity and Artistic Confidence*. Los Angeles: J. P. Tarcher; New York. Distributed by St. Martin's Press, 1979. ISBN: 0-874770-87-4.

Emerson, Ralph Waldo. "Compensation" and "Self-Reliance." Essays available in several editions.

Ferguson, Marilyn. *The Aquarian Conspiracy: Personal and Social Transformation in the 1980's*. Los Angeles: J. P. Tarcher. Distributed by St. Martin's Press, 1980. ISBN: 0-312904-18-5.

—. *The Brain Revolution: The Frontiers of Mind Research*. New York: Taplinger, 1973. ISBN: 0-800809-61-0.

Frank, Stanley D. *Remember Everything You Read: The Evelyn Wood Seven-Day Speed Reading and Learning Program.* New York: Times Books, 1990. ISBN: 0-812917-73-1.

Franklin, Benjamin. *Benjamin Franklin: Writings.* New York: Library of America, 1987. ISBN: 0-940450-29-1.

Gawain, Shakti. *Creative Visualization.* Berkeley, CA: Whatever Pub., 1978. ISBN: 0-931432-02-2.

Goldberg, Phillip. *The Intuitive Edge: Understanding and Developing Intuition.* First Edition. Los Angeles: J.P. Tarcher. Distributed by Houghton Mifflin, 1983. ISBN: 0-874772-32-X.

Goleman, Daniel. *Emotional Intelligence.* New York: Bantam Books, 1995. ISBN: 0-553095-03-X.

Harvey, Paul. Syndicated news broadcasts.

Hill, Napoleon. *The Law of Success.* 4th Ed. Chicago: Success Unlimited, 1979.

—. *Think and Grow Rich.* Rev. Ed. Greenwich, CN: Fawcett Pubs., 1990. ISBN: 0-449214-92-3.

Hittleman, Richard. Be Young with Yoga. New York: Warner Books, 1980. ISBN: 0-446916-06-4.

—. Yoga Video Course I (Elementary). [video recording]. Currently available only from Steve Mark Harris Productions, PO Box 3007, Santa Cruz, CA 95063.

Jeavons, John. *Grow More Vegetables Than You Ever Thought Possible on Less Land Than You Can Imagine: a Primer on the Life-giving Biodynamic/French Intensive Method of Organic Horticulture.* Berkeley, CA: Ten Speed Press, 1979. ISBN: 0-913668-98-2.

James, Ph.D., Jennifer. *Thinking in Future Tense: Leadership Skills for a New Age.* New York: Simon & Schuster, Inc., 1996. ISBN: 0-684-81098-0.

Kirschner, M.D., Harry Edward. *Live Food Juices.* Monrovia, CA: H. E. Kirschner Publications, 1957.

Kordich, Jay. *The Juiceman* [sound recording]. Seattle, WA: JM Marketing, 1989.

—. *The Juiceman's Power of Juicing.* New York: Morrow, 1992. ISBN: 0-688114-43-1.

Lakoff, George, and Johnson, Mark. *Metaphors We Live By.* Chicago: The University of Chicago Press, 1981. ISBN:0-226-46801-1.

Loehr, Dr. James E., and McLaughlin, Peter J. *Mental Toughness Training* [sound recording]. Chicago: Nightingale-Conant, 1990.

—. *Mentally Tough: the Principles of Winning at Sports Applied to Winning in Business.* With Ed Quillen. New York: M. Evans and Co., 1986. ISBN: 0-871314-93-2.

Maas, James B., and Wherry, Megan. *Power Sleep: The Revolutionary Program That Prepares Your Mind for Peak Performance.* New York: Villard Books, 1998. ISBN: 0-375500-95-2.

MacKay, Harvey. *Swim with The Sharks Without Being Eaten Alive* [sound recording]. Chicago: Nightingale-Conant, 1988.

Maltz, Maxwell. *Psycho-Cybernetics: A New Way to Get More Living out of Life.* Englewood Cliffs, NJ, Prentice-Hall, 1960.

Mandino, Og. *The Greatest Salesman in the World.* Toronto; New York: Bantam Books, 1985. ISBN: 0-553234-72-2.

McCarthy, Michael J. *Mastering the Information Age: A Course in Working Smarter, Thinking Better, and Learning Faster.* Los Angeles: J.P. Tarcher. Distributed by St. Martin's Press, 1991. ISBN: 0-874775-37-X.

McCormack, Mark. *What They Don't Teach You at Harvard Business School.* Toronto; New York: Bantam Books, 1984. ISBN: 0-553050-61-3.

Meyer, Christopher. *Fast Cycle Time: How to Align Purpose, Strategy, and Structure for Speed.* New York: Free Press; Toronto: Maxwell Macmillan Canada; New York: Maxwell Macmillan International, 1993. ISBN: 0-029211-81-6.

Microsoft Corporation. *Building Client/Server Applications with Visual Basic 4.0.* Redmond, WA: Microsoft Corporation, 1995.

Minsky, Marvin. *Society of Mind.* New York: Simon & Schuster, Inc., 1988. ISBN: 0-671-65713-5.

Moyers, Bill D. *Healing and the Mind.* [video recording]. New York : Ambrose Video Pub., Inc., 1993.

Murphy, Dr. Joseph. *The Power of Your Subconscious Mind.* Englewood Cliffs, NJ: Prentice-Hall, 1963.

Newsweek Magazine, New York: Newsweek, March 16, 1998. p50, *Healer of Hearts*, an article on Dean Ornish, M.D.

Nightingale, Earl. *The New Lead the Field* [sound recording]. Chicago: Nightingale-Conant Corp., 1986.

O'Hanlon, William. *Taproots: Underlying Principles of Milton Erickson's Therapy and Hypnosis.* New York: Norton, 1987. ISBN: 0-393700-31-3.

Orlikowski, Wanda J. *WP #3428-92, CCS TR No. 131* [research paper]. Cambridge, MA: MIT Sloan School of Management.

Orlock, Carol. *Know Your Body Clock: Discover Your Body's Inner Cycles and Rhythms and Learn the Best Times for Creativity, Exercise, Sex, Sleep, and More.* New York: Citadel Press, 1995. ISBN: 0-806517-03-4.

Ornish, Dr. Dean. *Love & Survivial: The Scientific Basis for the Healing Power of Intimacy.* New York: Harpercollins, 1998. ISBN: 0-060172-13-4.

Ornstein, Robert. *The Psychology of Consciousness.* New York: Viking, 1972.

Orr, Ken. *Structured Systems Development.* New York: YOURDON Press, 1977. ISBN: 0-917072-06-5.

Ostrander, Sheila, et al. *Superlearning 2000.* New York: Delacorte Press, 1994. ISBN: 0-385312-74-1.

—. *Superlearning.* New York: Dell Pub. Co., 1979. ISBN: 0-440580-99-4.

Paddison, Sara. *The Hidden Power of the Heart.* Boulder Creek, CA: Planetary Publications, 1992. ISBN: 1-879052-17-2. (800) 372-3100.

Peck, M. Scott. *The Road Less Traveled* [sound recording]. Chicago: Nightingale-Conant Corp., 1986.

Peters, Tom. *Liberation Management: Necessary Disorganization for the Nanosecond Nineties.* New York: A. A. Knopf, 1992. ISBN: 0-394559-99-1.

Pilzer, Paul Zane. *Interview with Anthony Robbins* [sound recording]. Available by calling (800) 445-8183.

—. *Unlimited Wealth: the Theory and Practice of Economic Alchemy.* New York: Crown Publishers, 1991. ISBN: 0-517582-11-2.

Pinckney, Callan, and Meyer, Barbara Friedlander. *Callanetics for Your Back.* New York: Morrow, 1992. ISBN: 0-517075-34-2.

Pinckney, Callan. *Callanetics* [video recording]. Universal City, CA: MCA Home Video, 1986.

Redfield, James. *The Celestine Prophecy: An Adventure.* New York: Warner Books, 1994. ISBN: 0-446518-62-X.

Robbins, Anthony, and McLendon, Joseph. *Unlimited Power: A Black Choice.* New York: Simon & Schuster, 1997. ISBN: 0-684824-36-1.

Robbins, Anthony. *Awaken the Giant Within: How to Take Immediate Control of Your Mental, Emotional, Physical & Financial Destiny.* New York: Summit Books, 1991. ISBN: 0-671727-34-6.

—. *The Five Keys to Wealth and Happiness.* San Diego: Robbins Research Institute, Inc. 1987.

—. *Personal Power!* [sound recording]. San Diego: Robbins Research International, 1993. (800) 898-8669.

—. *Personal Power: The Keys to Your Unlimited Success* [video recording]. Irwindale, CA: Guthy-Renker Corporation, 1989.

—. *Powertalk! Strategies for Lifelong Success,* [sound recording], Vol. 20. San Diego: Robbins Research Institute, 1992.

—. *Unleash the Power Within: An Owner's Manual to the Brain* [video recording]. La Jolla, CA: Robbins Research Institute, Inc., 1987.

—. *Unlimited Power* [sound recording]. Chicago: Nightingale-Conant Corp., 1986.

Robbins, John. *Diet for a New America.* Walpole, NH: Stillpoint, 1987. ISBN: 0-913299-55-3.

Roddenbery, Gene. *A&E Biography* [video recording]. Los Angeles, CA: Weller, Grossman Products in association with A&E Television, 1994.

Roddick, Anita. *Body and Soul: Profits with Principles, The Amazing Success Story of Anita Roddick & the Body Shop.* New York: Crown, 1991. ISBN: 0-517585-42-1.

Rose, Colin. *Accelerated Learning for the 21st Century: The Six-Step Plan to Unlock your MASTER-mind.* New York: Delacorte Press, 1997. ISBN: 0-385317-03-4.

Russell, Peter. *The Brain Book.* New York: Hawthorn Books, 1979. ISBN: 0-801508-86-X.

Russo, J. Edward, and Schoemaker, Paul. *Decision Traps: The Ten Barriers to Brilliant Decision-Making and How to Overcome Them.* New York: Doubleday/Currency, 1989. ISBN: 0-385248-35-0.

Sagan, Carl. *Cosmos.* New York: Random House, 1980. ISBN: 0-517-12355-X.

Schuller, Dr. Robert H. *Tough Times Never Last But Tough People Do Tape* [sound recording]. Chicago: Nightengale-Conant Corporation.

Selye, Hans. *Stress Without Distress.* New York: New American Library, 1975, 1974. ISBN: 0-451078-34-9.

Senge, Peter. *The Fifth Discipline: The Art & Practice of the Learning Organization.* New York: Doubleday, 1990. ISBN: 0-385260-94-6.

—. *The Fifth Discipline: The Art & Practice of the Learning Organization* [sound recording]. New York: Bantam Doubleday Dell Audio Publishing, 1994.

Silva, José. *The Silva Mind Control Method*. New York: Pocket Books, 1978, 1977.

Singh Khalsa, Dharma, M.D. *Brain Longevity: The Breakthrough Medical Program that Improves your Mind and Memory*. New York: Warner Books, 1997. ISBN: 0-446520-67-5.

Thompson, Charles. *What a Great Idea! The Key Steps Creative People Take*. New York: Harper Perennial, 1992. ISBN: 0-060553-17-0.

Toffler, Alvin. *Future Shock*. New York: Bantam Books, 1970.

Trudeau, Kevin. *Mega Memory Tape* [sound recording]. New York: American Memory Institute, 1989.

Twain, Mark. *Life on the Mississippi*. New York: Modern Library, 1994. ISBN: 0-679600-95-7.

Untermeyer, Louis. *The Makers of the Modern World: The Lives of Ninety-two Writers, Artists, Scientists, Statesmen, Inventors, Philosophers, Composers, and other Creators who Formed the Pattern of our Century*. New York: Simon and Schuster, 1955. pp. 287-293.

Vilas, Donna and Sandy. *Power Networking: 55 Secrets for Personal & Professional Success*. Austin, TX: MountainHarbour Publications, 1992. ISBN: 0-962782-50-5.

von Oech, Roger. *A Kick in the Seat of the Pants: Using Your Explorer, Artist, Judge, & Warrior to be more Creative*. New York: Perennial Library, 1986. ISBN: 0-060155-28-0.

—. *A Whack on the Side of the Head: How You Can Be More Creative*. New York: Warner Books, Inc., 1990. ISBN: 0-446-39158-1.

Walker, Norman. *Fresh Vegetable and Fruit Juices: What's Missing in your Body*. Prescott, AZ: Norwalk Press, 1978.

Wing, R. L. *The TAO of Power: A Translation of the Tao Te Ching by Lao Tzu*. Garden City, NY: Doubleday, 1986. ISBN: 0-385196-37-7.

Wordsworth, Chloe. *Introductory Talk & Demostration On Holographic Repatterning*. (520) 204-9960.

INDEX

Vitamin T: Thought for Food

by Patrick Magee

Quote

The reason clarity is power; the reason you should start with the end in mind; is that having a clear idea about where you want to end up forms the basis for communicating direction to your subconscious mind, which is the seat of action and the ultimate information filter.

Question

What beliefs will accelerate my balanced progress towards the achievement of my goals? What can I do to increase the extent to which my mind "resonates" with these beliefs?

Metaphor

Imagine a large heavy steel ball on a hard flat surface. Your task is to get it rolling. Initially, it barely even budges. With continued effort, it gradually begins to pick up momentum. Once the ball is rolling, it takes quite a bit of force to stop or change its direction. So it is with goals we set for ourselves and strive for. Choose your directions wisely.

Affirmation

I resonate with love, gratitude and success.

Laugh

Seattle rain joke: A visitor asks a young boy when the last sunny day was in Seattle. "I don't know," he replied, "I'm only 6."

Health Distinction

"*All excesses are ultimately their own undoing.*" — Paul Harvey

---

This is a sample of Patrick Magee's newspaper column. Have your local newspaper email **vitamint@BrainDance.com** for publishing information.